HARVARD HISTORICAL STUDIES

THE CIVIL SERVICE AND
THE PATRONAGE

THE CIVIL SERVICE AND THE PATRONAGE

BY

CARL RUSSELL FISH, Ph.D.

NEW YORK
RUSSELL & RUSSELL · INC
1963

FIRST PUBLISHED IN 1904
REISSUED, 1963, BY RUSSELL & RUSSELL, INC.
L. C. CATALOG CARD NO: 63—12563

PRINTED IN THE UNITED STATES OF AMERICA

PREFACE.

THIS work is the outgrowth of a statistical study of removals from office begun in the Seminary of American History and Institutions at Harvard University. The results of this preliminary study were published in the *Annual Report* of the American Historical Association for 1899. The interest thus aroused led to a broader investigation, which has been continued for about five years. From materials accumulated not strictly pertinent to the subject of this volume, an article on "Lincoln and the Patronage" was contributed to the *American Historical Review* for October, 1902.

The subject which this book attempts to treat defies concise definition; and as the boundaries have perhaps not been drawn so as to satisfy all who will be led by its title to refer to it, a few words are necessary to guide those who use it. The leading words of the title limit each other; it is a history of the civil service from the standpoint of the patronage, and of the patronage with regard solely to the public offices. The aim has been to give fully the development of policy and practice as to the relation of these two elements of our public life, from the foundation of the government to the present day. In addition, it has been thought wise to outline the distinguishing policy of each successive administration, though in some instances this has been done very briefly; in the case of a few very important administrations the subject has been treated still more broadly, so as to include practice as well as policy. The work of Miss Salmon on the *Appointing Power of the President* has left me free to leave out constitutional questions, except when they become questions of politics; and the problem of civil service reform has been treated historically, and not from the standpoint of expediency.

I have had access to the collections of the Harvard College Library and the libraries of Boston, of Brown University, the American Antiquarian Society at Worcester, the Rhode Island Historical Society, the Wisconsin Historical Society, the Library of Congress, and the departmental libraries at Washington; and I desire to express my thanks to the officials of these institutions for their uniform interest and assistance. Thanks are particularly due to the owners of private collections of manuscripts and newspapers, whose courtesy in opening them for research evinces the general interest felt in historical studies. Most of all, I wish to record my appreciation of the kindness of Professor Albert Bushnell Hart and Professor Edward Channing, to whose inspiration and guidance the inception and development of this monograph are chiefly to be attributed.

CARL RUSSELL FISH.

MADISON, WISCONSIN,
    May 30, 1904.

CONTENTS.

CHAPTER I.

ESTABLISHMENT OF THE NATIONAL CIVIL SERVICE, 1789–1801.

CHAPTER II.

JEFFERSON'S POLICY AS TO PUBLIC OFFICE, 1801–1809.

CHAPTER III.

THE PATRONAGE QUESTION UNDER DISCUSSION,
1809–1829.

CHAPTER IV.

GENESIS OF THE SPOILS SYSTEM, 1700–1828.

CHAPTER V.

ESTABLISHMENT OF THE SPOILS SYSTEM UNDER JACKSON, 1829-1837.

CHAPTER VI.

IMMEDIATE EFFECTS OF THE NEW POLICY, 1837-1845.

CHAPTER VII.

THE SPOILS SYSTEM TRIUMPHANT, 1845-1865.

CHAPTER VIII.

MACHINERY OF THE SPOILS SYSTEM.

CHAPTER IX.

A STRUGGLE FOR THE PATRONAGE, 1865-1887.

CHAPTER X.

PERIOD OF CIVIL SERVICE REFORM, 1865-1901.

CHAPTER XI.

PRESENT STATUS OF THE CIVIL SERVICE REFORM MOVEMENT.

APPENDICES.

THE CIVIL SERVICE AND THE PATRONAGE.

———◆———

CHAPTER I.

ESTABLISHMENT OF THE NATIONAL CIVIL SERVICE.
1789–1801.

THE makers of the constitution fully realized that the adjustment of the power of appointment to office required careful consideration. From their youth up they had seen the rivalry for office, they had felt the influence of the patronage, in the politics of colony and state. John Adams complained that Governor Hutchinson of Massachusetts passed over proper candidates in order to advance members of his own family; and, while this particular charge may be unjust, it is certainly true that in most cases colonial governors owed their positions wholly to favoritism, and that one of their chief duties was to use the offices within their gift for the upbuilding of a British party.[1] All Americans were familiar, moreover, with the power wielded in England by the "King's Friends," the most mighty faction ever based almost solely on the distribution of offices, and the source to which the colonies attributed much of the evil treatment which had estranged them from the mother country.[2] While they knew, however, the evil possibilities of the patronage, they regarded the disease as peculiarly characteristic of monarchy, and were unacquainted with the new conditions presented by a democratic form of government.

A mechanical system for the choice of public servants existed at that time in no considerable country except China, to whose example the convention at Philadelphia was not likely to turn;

---

[1] Greene, *Provincial Governor*, ch. 3.   [2] Elliot, *Debates*, iii. 371.

nor in the ancient civilizations could any precedent for such a scheme be found. The responsibility for appointments must be personal, and the question to be decided was, in what person or persons it should reside. The national civil service under the Confederation was so small, and the conditions were so exceptional, that the experience to be drawn from its history was slight. It was practically certain, moreover, even before the convention of 1787 met, that the old system must be changed. The call for a constitution was largely the result of a reaction against the extreme democracy and decentralization of the Revolution; and it is not strange, therefore, to find in the earliest plans for "a more perfect union" the proposal to transfer the appointing power from Congress to the executive.[1] In other words, the question of the civil service was part and parcel of the more general problem of the extent of the executive power, and was itself scarcely drawn into debate.

While it was thus tacitly admitted that the power of appointment should be taken from the legislature, the feeling was by no means universal that the executive could be safely intrusted with it. The idea of a council, one of whose duties should be to aid and limit the president in making appointments, was pertinaciously pressed. Its chief supporter was George Mason, who could point for authority to the constitutions of several states, and particularly to that of New York, which provided for a special council of appointment.[2] It was urged, however, that the Senate could perform these functions; and it was said by Davie of North Carolina that this proposition was strongly supported by the smaller states because of their equal representation in that body.[3] Opposition arose from those who feared the power, not of the executive alone, but of the whole central government; and Dickinson, supported by Randolph, suggested that officers be selected by the president with the advice and consent of the Senate, "except where by law the appointment

---

[1] Pelatiah Webster, *Dissertation on the Political Union*, art. ii. § 6. In his *Political Essays*, 221.

[2] *Madison Papers*, ii. 1130, iii. 1522; Ford, *Pamphlets on the Constitution*, 341; *Federalist* (Ford ed.), 513.

[3] Elliot, *Debates*, iv. 122.

shall be vested in the Legislatures or Executives of the several States."[1] This plan, so foreign to the spirit of the convention, was dropped by unanimous consent; and the two following clauses were finally framed, and have stood unchanged to the present time.

The president "shall nominate, and, by and with the advice and consent of the Senate, shall appoint ambassadors, other public ministers and consuls, judges of the Supreme Court, and all other officers of the United States, whose appointments are not herein otherwise provided for, and which shall be established by law; but the Congress may by law vest the appointment of such inferior officers as they think proper in the president alone, in the courts of law, or in the heads of departments.

" The President shall have power to fill up all vacancies that may happen during the recess of the Senate, by granting commissions which shall expire at the end of their next session."

In the debates on the adoption of the constitution, these clauses received a fair share of attention, though in all probability no single vote was changed because of them. In Pennsylvania the power of the Senate was most feared. " Centinel," the strongest Antifederalist writer, predicted that the Senate would control appointments; and it was argued that, since that body was to judge officials when they were impeached, it should not share in their election. Thomas McKean replied that in practice the president would name the successful candidate in nominating him; and James Wilson relied upon the president's power to fill vacancies during the recess of Congress, to secure him his proper share of influence.[2] In New York the Antifederalists occupied different ground from those of the neighboring state; and George Clinton, who was perhaps of all Americans the man best fitted by experience to judge, feared lest the president, by choosing subordinates from his own circle, should build up " an imperfect aristocracy, bordering on monarchy."[3] Similar differences of opinion existed among Federalists, and John Adams

---

[1] *Madison Papers*, iii. 1423, 1434.

[2] McMaster and Stone, *Pennsylvania and the Federal Constitution*, 366, 375, 401, 673.

[3] Ford, *Essays on the Constitution*, 264.

and Roger Sherman carried on an interesting correspondence with regard to the subject in 1789. Adams graphically depicted the chances for combination and corruption opened by the participation of the Senate; and, while he perhaps underrated the danger of according the full power to the executive, he certainly grasped the nature of the problem better than his correspondent, who argued that the senators would in general be the most respectable citizens of their respective states, and deduced therefrom that they would be diffident about recommending even friends and kindred of other members, "lest they should be thought unduly to favor a person who is related to a member of their body."[1]

On one point there was widespread criticism: it was claimed that the president would be able to control the action of Congress by appointing its members to offices, and that congressmen should therefore be made ineligible during their terms. Roger Sherman answered this objection boldly by declaring that for many places they would be best fitted, and that all danger was prevented by the provision that they could accept no positions which had been created, or the emoluments of which had been increased, during their terms.[2] Such arguments did not fully meet the issue; and three state conventions, those of New York, Virginia, and North Carolina, included a clause providing for such a restriction in their suggested amendments to the constitution.[3] It will be found that at a later period this question assumed a peculiar importance.

While these discussions were progressing, it was claimed that in the very struggle then being waged instances of the evils dreaded were present. The Antifederalists, particularly in Pennsylvania, asserted that the Federalist mail authorities curtailed the circulation of newspapers hostile to the proposed constitution. These charges are made with great particularity, and may contain a kernel of truth; for the carriage of newspapers was not a part of the regular mail service, but was arranged

---

[1] John Adams, *Works*, vi. 433–442.

[2] Ford, *Essays on the Constitution*, 234.

[3] *Federalist* (Ford ed.), 637, 644, 648. Virginia debate in Elliot, *Debates*, iii. 369–375.

for by special bargain with the riders, a system which afforded opportunity for favoritism. A change in postal regulations made about this time may, however, explain the facts presented.[1]

More extensive and more telling were the charges made by the Federalists. James Wilson of Pennsylvania pointed out that the transfer of the customs from the states to the national government, and the establishment of many new judicial and administrative offices, would turn the stream of patronage into a new channel, and that the constitution would therefore be opposed by all those who profited by existing conditions. Francis Hopkinson, in his famous satire, *The New Roof*, depicted the old woman who led the opposition to the improvement as using the cornice of the old roof for a cupboard, and as boiling her pot with the shingles that blew off. Specific charges were also made. The fact that Elbridge Gerry held no office in Massachusetts did not prevent the Federalists from attributing his opposition to a desire to retain one; and Luther Martin was accused of refusing to sign the draft of the constitution because he despaired of receiving under it an office that he desired.[2]

The charges of interested opposition seemed most reasonable in New York. There the patronage was particularly valuable, owing to the commercial importance of New York City, where goods destined for a large part of New Jersey and of Connecticut paid duty.[3] It will be remembered that New York had been willing that the Congress of the Confederation should lay certain customs dues, if the state government might retain the appointment of the collecting officers. In the state convention of 1788 the charge was definitely made that Governor Clinton was using this patronage to defeat the constitution. A prompt denial was made; it was pointed out that some of the state officials supported the new plan, and the charge was partly

---

[1] McMaster and Stone, *Pennsylvania and the Federal Constitution*, 530, 637, 650–654, 666–668; Harding, *Federal Constitution in Massachusetts*, 18.

[2] Ford, *Pamphlets on the Constitution*, 161; McMaster and Stone, *Pennsylvania and the Federal Constitution*, 440, 511 ; Ford, *Essays on the Constitution*, 129, 187, 188.

[3] *Massachusetts Centinel*, January 5, 1788 ; *Federalist* (Ford ed.), 37, note.

withdrawn. Undoubtedly the state machine formed the chief prop of the opposition; but Clinton, as will be shown later, was moderate in his use of the appointing power, and it is extremely improbable that he made any direct threats of removal or promises of reward.[1] The more serious accusation made by the Federalists, that the governor was chiefly influenced in his opposition by fear of loss of prestige, must be dismissed as entirely unfounded. It was perfectly natural that the men in office should oppose the constitution: they represented the ideas of the Revolution; they had been the active agents in destroying the governmental control of Great Britain over the colonies; and by their type of mind they were opposed to centralized government and vigorous administration. The adoption of the constitution marked a change of party dominance; and many of the men prominent in 1787 by 1790 had retired, some to be restored by the Democratic wave of 1800.

When the new government was installed, almost the first task with which it had to deal was that of filling the offices, in order that the constitution, and the laws as they were passed, might be executed. The question of qualification was left entirely to the discretion of President Washington, who formed his plans with the punctilious exactness which was characteristic of him. Early in May, after his inauguration, he wrote to Edward Rutledge, "I anticipate that one of the most difficult and delicate parts of the duty of my office will be that which relates to nominations for appointments;" and in the same letter he remarked that he had made it a rule to say nothing definite on particular appointments until his mind was made up. In 1796 he said that his plan was "to lay the recommendations . . . by, until the hour comes when nominations are to be made, and then after reference to them and an attention to other circumstances (which is often essential) prefer those who seem to have the greatest fitness for the office."[2]

There can be no doubt that Washington considered fitness for the post to be filled a *sine qua non* for appointment. His

[1] Elliot, *Debates*, ii. 220 ; Hammond, *Political Parties in New York*, i. 85.
[2] May 5, 1789, Washington, *Writings* (Sparks ed.), x. 1 ; Rowland, *Charles Carroll*, ii. 204.

letters constantly repeat this, and he was a man honest even with himself. An excellent example is a letter of May 21, 1789, to Mary Wooster: "MADAM, I have duly received your affecting letter, dated the 8th day of this month. Sympathizing with you as I do in the great misfortunes, which have befallen your family in consequence of the war, my feelings as an individual would forcibly prompt me to do everything in my power to repair those misfortunes. But as a public man, acting only with reference to the public good, I must be allowed to decide upon all points of my duty, without consulting my private inclinations and wishes. I must be permitted, with the best lights I can obtain, and upon a general view of characters and circumstances, to nominate such persons alone to offices, as in my judgment shall be the best qualified to discharge the functions of the departments to which they shall be appointed." [1] This absolute requirement of capacity seems to have been generally understood, and nearly every existing application for office under Washington dwells on the applicant's ability.

There is a broad difference between appointing only fit men to office, and appointing those who are most fit; and Washington pursued this second aim also. It was a difficult task. There were many applicants who appealed to his benevolence; [2] and it must have been particularly hard to turn away soldiers of the Revolution, great numbers of whom urged their sufferings upon him as just ground for reward. Yet he always answered that these considerations could not offset superior efficiency. He refused to make public office a bounty, though in some cases he did assist such applicants with his private means. One class of seekers he cut off from all hope of office by writing to his nephew, Bushrod Washington, that relationship must be an absolute bar to preferment. So clear did he make the honesty of his attempt to fulfil his difficult task impartially, that sometimes even disappointed candidates acknowledged the justice or the necessity of his selections. [3]

---

[1] Washington, *Writings* (Sparks ed.), x. 6.

[2] *American Historical Review,* i. 275, 278.

[3] *Ibid.* i. 276, 278; Boutell, *Roger Sherman,* 223–224; Washington, *Writings* (Sparks ed.), x. 23, 24; Webb, *Correspondence,* iii. 141.

Into Washington's idea of fitness, however, several elements entered. The ability to perform the functions of the post was, of course, essential; but that alone was not a sufficient qualification. A large and loose-jointed federation, such as the United States was in 1789, made geographical considerations of special importance. From the very beginning of the attempts at union, honors had been distributed with anxious care among the several states and sections, the nice balance maintained between Virginia and Massachusetts being particularly noticeable. Washington himself was indebted to such considerations for a part of his prestige, as it is scarcely possible that he could have been chosen commander-in-chief in 1775 had he lived in Delaware. As president, he prudently consulted geography in making his general appointments:[1] his cabinet at first contained two men from Virginia, one from New York, and one from Massachusetts. When party lines came to be drawn more closely, the task became more arduous. John Adams wrote to his wife, January 7, 1796, "There seems to be a necessity of distributing the offices about the States in some proportion to their numbers; but in the southern part of the Union, false politics have struck their roots so deep, that it is very difficult to find gentlemen who are willing to accept of public trusts, and at the same time capable of discharging them."[2] Still, a certain balance of sections was always preserved in the cabinet. After the retirement of Jefferson and Hamilton, it consisted of one member from Virginia, one from Pennsylvania, and two from New England; afterward Maryland was substituted for Pennsylvania. The balance would appear more nearly perfect if Timothy Pickering were counted as from the West, where he lived when appointed, and not as from New England, where he was born and died.

In addition to this attempt to prevent jealousies between the several sections was the desire to make each choice acceptable to the section especially concerned. The constitution was as yet but an experiment; and Washington, who was responsible for

[1] Washington, *Writings* (Sparks ed.), x. 26 ; Jefferson, *Anas*, August 6, 1793, in his *Writings* (Ford ed.), i. 256–258.

[2] John Adams, *Works*, i. 483.

its success, wished it to be put in force, not only by competent men, but by men known and respected in the localities in which they were to serve : he preferred to have the federal authority represented by men who had been esteemed and honored by their neighbors. He therefore considered the previous career of the various men whose names were presented, and allowed any marks of the confidence of their fellow-citizens to count in their favor.[1] To have previously held an elective office was considered the best recommendation. Some administrative officers were transferred from the State to the national service, — as Oliver Wolcott, comptroller of public accounts for Connecticut, who was made an auditor.

This qualification was particularly insisted upon for judicial appointments. The new judiciary had much to contend against. Legal changes are always looked upon with disfavor ; and Washington wished to draw into the national service, so far as possible, judges from the benches of the states. This plan would serve to create a judiciary tried and therefore trustworthy, would indicate that the line of promotion lay from the State to the nation, and would tend to lessen the rancor of the disappointed. His letters to Madison show the solicitude with which he applied himself to the filling of the judicial list ; and it is largely owing to this care that the national courts so soon acquired the confidence of the public.[2]

To Washington's anxiety that the officers of the general government should be men of established reputation, was added a desire that they should be sound supporters of the new system ; that is, political orthodoxy was considered as one of the elements of fitness for office. The supreme importance of this qualification in later periods lends special interest to the

---

[1] Richardson, *Messages and Papers*, i. 58–59.

[2] He wrote to Madison, August 10 (?), 1789 : " My solicitude for drawing the first characters of the Union into the judiciary is such, that my cogitations on this subject last night, after I parted with you, have almost determined me, as well for the reason just mentioned, as to silence the clamors, or more properly, soften the disappointment of smaller characters, to nominate Mr. Blair and Colonel Pendleton as associate and district judges, and Mr. Edmund Randolph for the attorney-general, trusting to their acceptance." Washington, *Writings* (Sparks ed.), x. 26 ; Gibbs, *Memoirs of the Administration of Washington and Adams*, i. 165, 22–27.

attitude of the first president in regard to it. It is, however, a subject so elusive that his policy can be made clear only by a somewhat detailed account of the conditions existing, and a study of some characteristic instances of his practice.

In one sense, Washington had a clear field before him in the creation of a civil service : there were absolutely no hold-over officers ; the servants of the Confederation became private citizens the moment the new government was established. Justice demanded, however, that the men thus legislated out of office should be considered as having a special claim to the new offices that involved similar functions, and Washington recognized these claims whenever he was convinced that the old occupant possessed the requisite qualifications. John Jay, who had been president of the old Congress and was in 1789 secretary of foreign affairs, was given his choice among the new offices,[1] partly because of the new president's esteem for him, but partly, doubtless, because of his official position. Jefferson, who held the ministry to France, the most important post in the diplomatic service after that to England, which Adams had vacated to become vice-president, was made secretary of state. Samuel Osgood, who had been commissioner of the board of the treasury, was appointed postmaster-general; Charles Thomson, the secretary of the old Congress, might have been secretary of the Senate, but declined, as he expected a higher office; and Washington broke his rule of not interfering with departmental appointments, to recommend Thomson's assistant secretary, Roger Alden, to Jefferson for a place in the state department. In addition, the governor and judges elected by Congress for the Northwest Territory were reappointed, with the exception of General Varnum, who had died in the interregnum.[2]

A similar policy was pursued with regard to the state offices. Richard Henry Lee, writing early in June, 1789, says : " Conversing on the subject of these appointments [those in the

---

[1] Pellew, *Jay*, 262 ; he cites no contemporary evidence.

[2] Harley, *Thomson*, 128–134 ; Washington, *Writings* (Sparks ed.), x. 40; *Journals of Congress*, xii. 174 (October 5, 1787); *Executive Journal*, i. 18 (August 18, 1789); *Appleton's Encyclopædia of American Biography*, Varnum.

revenue service] lately with the P., I mentioned two principles which I had the pleasure to hear him approve of. The first that State officers in similar lines who had behaved well, deserved preference in the service of the United States; and that having discharged these duties undivided, now that they become divided, the same officers were entitled to the best." Many applications for office were grounded on these principles, and such statistics as can be obtained tend to show that the rule was adhered to. There were 136 offices in the customs service as at first established under the new government: in 42 cases the old occupants were reappointed; in 4 cases they received some office in the service; in 15 cases they were not appointed; and in 75 cases either there is no record or the office was a new one.[1]

The fact that such was the general policy gives peculiar importance to one case in which it was not carried out, — that is, in Rhode Island. The struggle for the adoption of the constitution was particularly bitter in that state, and even before it was finally decided Washington began to receive applications for office. John Brown and John Francis, great merchants who favored the new establishment, sent him a letter of advice: they describe the iniquities of the opposition, and "sincearly Hope that none of these carrectors may be promoted to Aney office," and "take the Libberty of Recommending a core of Honest Faithfull and Vigilent Custom House Officers for this Department Such as will cause Every Copper of the Revenew . . . to be punctually paid to the Treasury of the United States."[2] While the Antifederalists were yet in control of the state, they had elected a board of customs officers with but one of their opponents upon it. When the constitution was at last adopted, it was fully expected that a change would be made; and one of the Rhode Island senators was asked to advise the president to divide the offices between the several parties.[3] The subject excited much local interest, and was most carefully considered

---

[1] Washington, *Writings* (Ford ed.), xi. 394 note; *American Historical Review,* i. 277; Appendix A, table ii.

[2] June 11, 1790, *American Historical Review,* i. 280.

[3] *Massachusetts Centinel,* September 30, 1789; *Foster Manuscripts,* i. 22, 23.

by the administration. The very pressure put upon it by the one side and the other showed how bitter the previous contest had been, and how important it was that the new officers should be such as would not only perform their duties well, but would strengthen the hold of the constitution on the people. Each case was minutely considered.

The list of customs officers finally made out contained ten new names, only two of those who had served under the state being appointed. One of those retained was Theodore Foster, naval officer at Providence, who has just been referred to as the single Federalist in office. As a matter of fact, Foster, though generally rated as a Federalist, had friends and enemies in both parties, and seems to have been reported to Washington as an Antifederalist. Immediately after his second appointment he was elected senator, and his successor as naval officer was Ebenezer Thompson, who had been collector under the state government and was avowedly opposed to the adoption of the constitution. Job Comstock, the other representative of the old corps of officials, declined to serve the new government; but on the declination of Aborn, the newly selected surveyor at Pawtuxet, Zachariah Rhodes, the old incumbent there, who had been passed over when the list was first made out, was chosen.[1]

The fact that two representatives of the state board of customs officials were thus persistently retained may indicate that Washington judged it proper to recognize to that extent the Antifederalist element. The remaining officers, both in the customs and in the judicial service, seem to have been all strong Federalists;[2] and at least three of them had previously held state offices, but had lost them during the " Know Ye " troubles. If the general government hoped to allay political rancor in Rhode Island by recognizing both factions, it was unsuccessful. Three years later, on occasion of a vacancy in Rhode Island, Henry Marchant wrote a letter to Hamilton carefully estimating

[1] *Massachusetts Centinel,* September 30, 1789; Jameson, in Rhode Island Historical Society, *Publications,* viii. 109, 131, 135.

[2] *Ibid.* 131, 133; Arnold, *Rhode Island,* ii. 525, 544. One of them, Jeremiah Olney, had been commissioner of the town of Providence at the time it proposed to secede from Rhode Island and join the Union (Greene, *Providence Plantations,* 64).

the several candidates, and adding, " It is indeed to be regretted that this affair should assume a Party Complection." [1]

A similar care was observed in making the North Carolina appointments, for the conditions were similar. So far as can now be discovered, there were no reappointments in the state. There exists in Jefferson's handwriting, under date of June 7, 1790, an annotated list of candidates for the judicial positions there, such as it has always been customary to prepare for the president's use in important cases ; in it one man is definitely recommended as being a " federalist." [2] The fact that Jefferson made this note shows that the term " federalist " was not used in its later party signification, but referred to those who had supported the adoption of the constitution. If ever political discrimination was justifiable, it was at this time; and fair-minded Republicans of a later date recognized that the conditions had been unusual, and that it was especially important that the constitution should be in the hands of its friends while receiving its trial. Nor should the sharpness of the distinction drawn be exaggerated. Washington wrote with regard to the district judgeship of Maryland: " Mr. Paca has been mentioned for that appointment, and, although his sentiments have not been altogether in favor of the general government, and a little adverse on the score of paper emission, I do not know but his appointment on some other accounts might be a proper thing." The important post of collector of New York was given to General John Lamb, a vigorous Antifederalist.[3]

When political strife grew hotter and the Republican and Federalist parties began to emerge, and when, too, the irascibility of old age came upon him, Washington became more of a party man. He made only seventeen removals,[4] and these strictly for the efficiency of the service ; but in 1795 he wrote to Pickering, " I shall not, whilst I have the honor of administrating the

---

[1] *American Historical Review*, i. 281.

[2] *Ibid.* i. 273–274.

[3] Amory, *James Sullivan*, ii. 94; Washington, *Writings* (Sparks ed.), x. 56; Leake, *Lamb*, 337. John Lowell (in his *New-England Patriot*, 21) says that Major Melville, appointed inspector at Boston, had also been an Antifederalist.

[4] C. R. Fish, *Removal of Officials by the Presidents*, in American Historical Association Reports, 1899, i. 69.

government, bring men into any office of consequence knowingly whose political tenets are adverse to the measures the general government is pursuing; for this, in my opinion, would be a sort of political suicide."[1] It was the popular charge of the Republicans that, in his second term, after the dismissal of Randolph, he confined his appointments to members of the Federalist party; and certainly in 1798 he advised McHenry to be cautious about enlisting Jacobins in the new army.[2]

Such seem to have been the ideals which Washington set before himself, and which he attempted, with his usual conscientiousness, to realize.   Like all his policies, they were proper and practical; but he was not omnipresent, he could not control his subordinates in all their actions, and his practice did not, therefore, accord wholly with his theory.   The members of the cabinet were given power to appoint their clerks, and how unrestricted that power was, the long employment of Freneau in the state department shows.[3]

By many avenues, intrigue and faction crept in.   The following extract from a letter exhibiting the political situation in Savannah shows what a part local politics played in the establishment of the civil service: "Col? Few will nominate me with the others. Our other Senator [James Gunn] I expect no Friendship from. . . . His Man will be a Wretch who now fills the Office of Collectorship at this place — his Name is Ruben Wilkinson — he is from our back Woods low and illiterate as possible, but served our Honorable Senator Gunn in geting him Votes."[4] In a similar way the other possible candidates were discussed. Theodore Foster, senator from Rhode Island, wrote February 17, 1791, of the difficulties of steering between the Scylla of favoritism and the Charybdis of ingratitude in making sugges-

---

[1] September 27, 1795, Washington, *Writings* (Ford ed.), xii. 107.

[2] *Oracle of Dauphin and Harrisburgh Advertiser*, August 10, 1801; alluded to in Coleman, *Examination of the President's Reply*, 24; Washington, *Writings* (Ford ed.), xiv. 104; see also Appendix B below.

[3] Washington, *Writings* (Sparks ed.), x. 40. See account of the Goddard papers, in *Facts*, July 12, 1902. Miss Mary K. Goddard was removed from the post-office of Baltimore in 1789. Washington's influence was sought, but he declined to interfere. She was reinstated by Osgood on petition of patrons of the office.

[4] Letter of Seagrave, February 22, 1789, in Webb, *Correspondence*, iii. 123.

tions to the president, and spoke of charges made against the former Rhode Island delegate of improperly using his influence.[1] It is said that in New York, where Hamilton's advice was naturally potent, the appointments were such as tended to aid the Schuyler faction and weaken Clinton, but the force of this charge is weakened by the appointment of Lamb. The Livingston family, so great an influence in that state, felt slighted; and perhaps their turning to Jefferson is to be thus accounted for.[2] It lies not in man to give universal satisfaction; and small as was the part which politics played in the selections of the first administration, the government did not escape the charge of intolerance. John Tyler, Sr., was one of the judges of the admiralty court of Virginia, the functions of which, under the constitution, fell to the United States district court. Tyler was not the only admiralty judge; and Cyrus Griffin as judge of the federal Court of Appeals in Cases of Capture had as high, if not higher, claim, and was appointed. Yet Tyler was displeased and wrote, long after the event, "This kind of conduct began the strong distinction which has embittered the cup of life, and, in a great measure, produced a spirit of retaliation."[3]

The constitution of the consular service, moreover, was unsatisfactory. The law provided that a consul be appointed for the Barbary coast at a salary of not more than two thousand dollars. This post involved semi-diplomatic functions, and for that reason, and because there was little legitimate trade in the region, was made an exception to the general rule that the service support itself by fees. The system of paying consuls by fees is a very wasteful one: the agents at a few great posts are overpaid, while in many places where the trade may be important, though small, the fees do not afford a living. Washington found it impossible to secure proper candidates for many minor posts,[4] and was thus forced to appoint natives of the country, or at

[1] *Foster Manuscripts,* i. 36.

[2] Hammond, *Political Parties in New York,* i. 30; H. Livingston, March 29, 1791, complains of Washington's appointments from the South, and adds, "I wish to see a change." Webb, *Correspondence,* iii. 172, 176.

[3] Tyler, *The Tylers,* ii. 171, 246.

[4] Even for Lisbon proper candidates did not apply. Jefferson, *Writings* (Ford ed.), v. 344; *Statutes at Large,* i. 254–257.

least Americans residing abroad for business purposes, whose administration of their duties might be affected by their private interests. This expedient was, however, the result of conditions rather than of policy; and the evils resulting from it have only recently been eradicated from the service.

Such facts should not obscure the wisdom of Washington in laying down the proper general qualifications for office, and his unusual skill in applying them. His success in quietly and satisfactorily organizing the new government is indicated by the fact that the press of the day contains so few references to the change in administration. One of the few allusions to it, aside from the mention of local appointments, is the simple change under " Ship News," of the heading, " Naval Office " to " Custom House," and a notice in the *Massachusetts Centinel*, in fancy type, of the location and office hours of the new board of officers.[1] The constitution was quietly launched and was manned with a good crew. Washington was perhaps the only president who could write, after passing through the ordeal of appointing a new staff of officers, " I have the happiness to find, so far as my information extends, that they are highly acceptable to the good people of this country."[2]

John Adams became president in 1797 under circumstances quite different from those of 1789. The constitution was now fully accepted, at least as a basis for development; but while this question was out of politics, the country was more distinctly divided into two parties than before, and Adams had been definitely elected as the representative of one of them. Further, he found a well-established civil service, and had to deal with the question of appointments only as vacancies occurred from time to time. As the total number of public officers was then small, he had comparative freedom from the irritating task of selection, a freedom which he increased by

---

[1] August 19 there appeared the following notice : " *The* COLLECTOR, NAVAL-OFFICER, *and* SURVEYOR, *of this district, have opened their respective offices, at the house next door to* Mr. Paine's *Insurance-Office in State-Street — Constant attendance will be there given by the several officers, each day in the week, from* Nine o'clock *in the morning, until* One, *and from* Three *in the afternoon until* sunset — *Sundays, Saturdays in the afternoon, and Publick Days of Thanksgiving and Fasting excepted.*"

[2] Washington, *Writings* (Sparks ed.), x. 51.

leaving most minor appointments to the members of his cabi-net.[1] No president has enjoyed such immunity from this vexa-tious task as did he; still he found opportunity to develop a policy which is significant as marking a transition from the principles of Washington to those of Jefferson.

The war with France rendered the military appointments the most important of the administration. The pressure brought to bear upon Adams to make Hamilton second in command is too well known to need description; but there was then, as there has been ever since, a conviction that the army should stand on a different footing from the civil service, and that the two parties should unite to defend the country. In response to this sentiment, Burr and Muhlenberg were placed on the list of generals.[2] Although the Republicans received representation, the control remained in the hands of the Federalists : probably Washington's caution to McHenry against enlisting Jacobins indicates the general attitude of the war department. The same policy was advocated with regard to critical diplomatic missions. Hamilton, in 1797, advised that either Jefferson or Madison be sent to France to conciliate the republic, but that Federalist colleagues be joined with them to control their action;[3] he did not wish a repetition of the Monroe episode. The plan was carried out, but Elbridge Gerry, who was not fully identified with any party, was substi-tuted for the Republican leaders suggested.

Turning to the ordinary appointments, we miss the careful statements of policy which are found in Washington's letters. Adams wrote to Wolcott, in October, 1800, strenuously denying that he had told any one that " political creed would be an in-superable bar to promotion." He added, however : " Washing-ton appointed a multitude of democrats and jacobins of the deepest die. I have been more cautious in this respect; but there is danger of proscribing, under imputations of democracy, some of the ablest, most influential, and best characters in the Union."[4]

[1] *American Historical Review,* ii. 242.
[2] C. F. Adams, *John Adams,* 529; Muhlenberg, *Muhlenberg,* 324.
[3] Hamilton, *Works* (Lodge ed.), viii. 445, 449, 450.
[4] John Adams, *Works,* ix. 87.

This letter is rather an omen of the coming break between Adams and the more extreme Federalists than an indication of political tolerance. With one wing of the Republicans, — with men like Elbridge Gerry, — Adams had more in common than with the Essex junto, but the active and dominant members of that party he would include under the name "Jacobin"; and while there are repeated requests for office from his political opponents, no instance has been noticed in which a "Jacobin" was appointed.

Not only was a bar placed against Jacobins, but there is a sus-picion of the influence of personal prejudice on appointments. The collectorship of New York fell vacant in the first year of the administration. Hamilton wrote a letter (apparently to Wolcott) suggesting and carefully characterizing seven men, and recommending four of them. If one may judge by what is known of the relations between the three men, these recom-mendations were pressed upon the president by Wolcott, secre-tary of the treasury; yet no one of the men recommended was appointed.[1] This can hardly be construed otherwise than as a slight to Hamilton; but it should be attributed rather to per-sonal dislike than to the ulterior purpose of undermining the latter's influence in New York. Adams had too few supporters there to form even the nucleus of a personal faction.

Adams was also charged with nepotism. Washington had explained to General Webb, in 1789, that it was necessary for him to find a post for Colonel Smith, the vice-president's son-in-law; but it is not known whether Adams urged the suit by personal solicitation. In 1798 Colonel Smith was again a can-didate.[2] Washington, as commander-in-chief, suggested that he be made a brigadier-general, and also mentioned him as third choice for adjutant-general. The president promptly nomi-nated him for the latter more lucrative position. When Timo-thy Pickering, the secretary of state, heard of this action, he hastened to the Senate and secured a rejection of the nomination, claiming afterward that his step was an act of kindness toward

---

[1] *American Historical Review*, ii. 245, 247; *Executive Journal*, i. 240.

[2] Webb, *Correspondence*, iii. 141; Washington to Hamilton, July 14, 1798, Wash-ington, *Writings* (Sparks ed.), xi. 265; *Executive Journal*, i. 292, 293; Pickering, *Pickering*, iii. 465.

Adams. The kindness is open to doubt; but certainly few things tend more to hurt a man politically than a reputation for feathering the family nest with the salaries of public offices. Even the transfer, by his father, of John Quincy Adams from the post of minister to Portugal to that of minister to Prussia, so amply justified by the event, furnished material for detractors.[1]

In Adams's letter to Wolcott, quoted above, mention is made of the fact that Washington appointed many violent Republicans to office. The break between the Federalists and the Republicans did not follow quite the same lines as that between the Federalists and the Antifederalists; hence, in spite of Washington's policy of excluding most of the latter from the service, many vigorous supporters of Jefferson were in office. It would have been indeed surprising, considering the bitterness of party spirit at the time, if they had remained unmolested. One of the most obnoxious was Tench Coxe, commissioner of revenue, an intense partisan and very useful to the opposition. In 1797 he received his dismissal from Wolcott, who based it upon the ground of deliberate misconduct in office. This misconduct was the giving of aid to the opposition, and it may be that Coxe used his official position to make this aid more effective; but that does not alter the fact that the removal was made for party purposes, and that a precedent was set which might prove dangerous. The Federalists were exceedingly gratified, and warmly congratulated Wolcott on having finally expelled the traitor from the treasury.[2]

This may be considered the first case of removal for party reasons. It was not the only one under Adams. In June, 1798, Jeremiah Smith wrote to Wolcott complaining of Joshua Whipple and William Gardner, the collector at Portsmouth and the commissioner of loans for New Hampshire. He said: "They have been it is generally said faithful and punctual in the discharge of the duties of their offices. They have some property and I believe are pretty free from debts and speculations. Their political conduct has been disrespectful to the Government and offensive to good men in the extreme." He

---

[1] Callender, *Sedgwick & Co., or a Key to the Six Per Cent Cabinet.*
[2] *American Historical Review,* ii. 261.

described at length their methods of instilling jacobinical ideas into the minds of their fellow-citizens, and concluded : " I have no hesitation in saying that I think Justice to the public requires the removal of these men. They surely cannot complain if that Government which is the object of their execrations should weaken their means of injuring and abusing it." The next day Eliphalet Ladd wrote, complaining particularly of Whipple, and adding charges of unjust exactions. On June 30, successors to both of these accused men were nominated.[1]

Here we have an indubitable case of political removal; for of course no credence can be placed in the vague eleventh-hour tales of injustice. Callender writes that the removals of Gardner and Whipple were made because they would not sign one of the eulogistic addresses to the president that were so numerous at the outbreak of the French war ;[2] and the conjunction of these first removals with the Federalists' high hopes based on the war, and with the Alien and Sedition Acts, is indeed striking. The *Columbian Centinel* had previously asked : " Why does not the President tumble headlong from their places the collector, loan-office commissioner, and commander of the revenue cutter at Portsmouth ? These ingrates ought not for a moment to be suffered to eat the bread of the public, when they wait only for a safe occasion to betray our country to France." [3] Pickering, who as secretary of state chose the newspapers that should print the laws of the United States, deprived Freneau of that privilege, which in those days of scanty circulation was much prized ; and General Knox apparently voiced the desires of many Federalists when he urged the president to make a general sweep of all the more pronounced Republicans.[4]

That Adams resisted the pressure for a general proscription is made evident by the statistics of removals during his administration. The total was only nineteen, and most of these seem

---

[1] *American Historical Review,* ii. 254–256; *Executive Journal,* i. 283.

[2] Callender, *The Prospect before Us,* 31–32.

[3] *Ibid.* quoting Wood.

[4] Jefferson, *Anas,* March 14, 1800, in his *Writings* (Ford ed.), i. 286; Lodge, *Cabot,* 230 ; Duane, *Examination of the Question who is the Writer of Two Forged Letters,* 18.

to have been for some cause connected with the efficiency of the service.[1] The dismissal of Pickering, the secretary of state, was due to the break in policy between Adams and the more extreme elements in the Federal party. After this removal had been made, Stephen Higginson accused Adams of using his patronage to help the Republicans elect Gerry to the governorship of Massachusetts;[2] but he did not cite any specific instance, and this was undoubtedly only a vague charge caused by personal spleen. On the whole, Adams seems to have developed no such systematic policy of appointments as Washington, but to have yielded more to influence, time, and circumstance; he was more moderate than some of his advisers, but more proscriptive than the first president; the line of division that he drew was not exactly between the Federalist and Republican parties, but rather between those with whom he agreed, as Gerry and Marshal, and those with whom he differed, as Pickering, Hamilton, and Jefferson.[3]

The constitution assigned to the president the duty of nominating public officers; but, in a country so extended as the United States, even a man with the wide personal acquaintance of Washington needed assistance in finding proper men. A machinery for presenting names to the executive therefore grew up outside of the constitution. This was based in part on experience, and was in part the natural result of conditions; it has grown in scope and importance with every increase in the civil service, but for almost a century from the foundation of the government no essentially new elements were introduced into it.

Under the Confederation, appointments were made by Congress. Often the delegates from a single state, or from several

---

[1] See, for example, Pickering to Cabot, June 16, 1800, *e.g.* the consul at Cape St. Francis had attacked Pickering's honesty, and had interfered with the consul-general at San Domingo. If the facts are as stated, the reason was good. Lodge, *Cabot*, 275.

[2] Fish, in Tables of Removal, in American Historical Association, *Reports*, 1899, i. 70, table ii.; *Report*, 1896, i. 836.

[3] The relations between Adams and Hamilton are not discussed here, because to bring anything new to light would demand a long chapter devoted to that subject alone.

states, would agree upon a candidate, and would press his appointment with their combined votes.[1] This precedent, and the fact that under the new constitution the Senate shared the appointing power, led to a belief in many sections that officers would actually be elected by that body. James Seagrove of Georgia wrote to General Webb, January 2, 1789: " As the new government of the United States will soon take place, and of course all appointments be made, it behoves us all to look round and try what we can get. I am advised by all my friends this way to offer for the Collectorship of the Import for Georgia and have little doubt of being Nominated by our Senators to Congress — But this alone will not do. It will also be necessary to have as many friends as possible in the Senate." On February 22 he wrote, " There will be four Candidates for that office from Georgia so that it must be determined by a Vote of the Senate." [2]

The senators, who were burdened with numberless applications for the few offices within their respective states, differed broadly in their interpretation of their duties. George Cabot was apologetic when he made recommendations. Roger Sherman understood that the method to be employed by those desiring office was to write a letter to the president, " mentioning the office to which they wish to be appointed, and their past services and sufferings as a ground of claim, — and if the President is not personally acquainted with their character, their letter is accompanied with a certificate from persons of distinction, certifying their qualifications, and they sometimes in their letters refer the President to members of Congress, or other persons residing at the Seat of Government for information." [3]

Republican senators were more insistent on their rights. Monroe boldly protested against the rumored appointment of Hamilton as special envoy to Great Britain in 1794;[4] and Davis, in his life of Burr, asserts that, after the recall of Gouverneur Morris from France, it being conceded that some promi-

---

[1] Austin, *Gerry*, i. 294–295.   [2] Webb, *Correspondence*, iii. 121–124.

[3] McRee, *Iredell*, i. 275 ; *FosterManuscripts, passim*, for Foster's term as senator; Lodge, *Cabot*, 43, 94 ; Boutell, *Sherman*, 223–224.

[4] Monroe, *Writings*, i. 291–292.

nent Republican must be sent to succeed him, the Republican members of Congress held a caucus, and decided to press the appointment of Burr. This statement is confirmed by Monroe's letters of the period; for he positively refused to accept the mission until assured that Burr would, under no circumstances, be appointed.[1]

The famous debate of 1789, on the subject of the removing power, lies outside the field of this monograph; but one incident of it is worthy of note in this connection. In the House of Representatives the supporters of the president's power won by votes of thirty to eighteen, and thirty-one to nineteen, on the crucial points; in the Senate the casting vote of the vice-president was needed, indicating that the latter body was already alert and jealous of its rights.[2]

Washington recognized that the word of a member of Congress should have special weight with regard to local appointments because of his local knowledge.[3] He insisted, however, in a communication to a committee of the Senate upon his right of nomination, presenting all names to the Senate by a

[1] Davis, *Burr*, i. 408–409 (given on the authority of Burr, and of "a gentleman of high standing"). See also Parton, *Burr*, 196. Monroe wrote to Jefferson, May 26, 27, 1794, that Burr is sole candidate "under auspices very favorable to his success," that "of course he goes as a Republican," that the New Jersey members are in his interest; then that Monroe has accepted, after being assured that Burr could not be appointed, and after consulting friends. Monroe, *Writings*, i. 298, 299–301.

[2] Lucy M. Salmon, *Appointing Power of the President* (American Historical Association, *Papers*, i. No. 5), ch. ii.

[3] The following notes of the opinions of the new congressmen from North Carolina are in Jefferson's handwriting, and were to guide the president in making the North Carolina appointments (*American Historical Review*, i. 273-274) : —
"District judge. Col° Davie is recommended by Steele.
Hawkins says he is their first character.
Brown sais the same.
    Samuel Spencer.
Steele sais he is a good man, one of the present judges, not remarkeable for his abilities, but deserves well of his country.
Bloodworth sais Spencer desires the appointment, but sais nothing of him.
    John Stokes.
Steele names him at his own request, he is a Virginian, was a Capt^a in the late war, lost his right hand in Beaufort's defeat, practises law in S. Carolina with reputation and success; has been frequently of the legislature, was a member of the

written message;[1] and he did not suffer himself to be coerced. Monroe received a rebuff for his interference in regard to Hamilton, and the president himself selected the Republican who should go to France. When the Senate rejected one of the nominations presented to it, Washington sent a dignified letter of protest, asking that, in the future, the senators make sure what reasons he had for presenting a name before they rejected it.[2]

During the first administration the influence of the senators was simply that of men with special opportunities for information. Other prominent men sent advice, and Washington's broad acquaintance resulted in his receiving directly many requests for offices, particularly from army officers. In addition to these and to the applications sent to members of Congress, many were sent to the heads of departments and to other prominent officials. The administration, moreover, like any intelligent employer of labor, refused to confine its selection to those who sought employment either directly or indirectly, but searched out able men from all over the country.[3]

Methods were unchanged under Adams, but conditions were somewhat different; for the Senate was less friendly to him than to his predecessor, and his smaller personal acquaintance left him more at the mercy of advisers.[4] One case of competition for office can be closely followed, and illustrates very well

convention, a federalist, is now a Col° of Militia cavalry and additional judge of the Supreme Court.

Hawkins has understood he is a worthy man.

Ashe names him."

Davie was appointed, declined, and Stokes was selected (*Executive Journal*, i. 50, 53). See also Oliver Wolcott's application for office and reliance in the decision of the Connecticut delegation (Gibbs, *Memoirs*, i. 20).

[1] Washington to a committee of the Senate, August 8, 1789, Washington, *Writings* (Ford ed.), xi. 417.

[2] Monroe, *Writings*, i. 292 note, 301 ; *Executive Journal*, i. 16 ; Richardson, *Messages and Papers*, i. 58.

[3] Higginson to Adams, July 4, August 10, 1789, American Historical Association, *Report*, 1896, i. 767 ; Washington, *Writings* (Sparks ed.), x. 3 ; *American Historical Review*, ii. 241, 271, 276; Monroe, *Writings*, i. 227; Washington, *Writings* (Sparks ed.), x. 25–26 ; Lodge, *Cabot*, 107, 109.

[4] Note the rejection of his son-in-law mentioned above, and Pickering's success in securing the rejection of General George Mathew's nomination as governor of

the conditions of the period. A certain Colonel Lindsay, collector of Norfolk, Virginia, early in Adams's term became mortally ill. Since the deputy of the collector, Francis Taylor, was engaged to Lindsay's daughter, it was felt by Colonel Lindsay's friends that it would be pleasant for Taylor to succeed to the collectorship, marry the daughter, and so provide for the family. In April, 1797, a citizen of Norfolk wrote to some one in authority, probably a member of the Virginia delegation in Congress, in regard to the case. He said that Lindsay had for some time been disabled, would soon die, and that Taylor was well qualified to succeed to the position, as he had for some time performed its duties. This letter was supported, within a few days, by a petition of merchants.

The surveyor, Mr. Bedinger, who had had several contests with Lindsay himself for the post, naturally felt aggrieved at seeing a new rival rise from the grave of the old. He appealed at once to the representative of the district in Congress, a Mr. Parker, who had at one time been collector with Bedinger as his deputy. "I cannot say," he writes, "but it seems to me that a *death-bed* resignation looks too much like a *bequest* — that this kind of *succession in office* has too greatly the appearance of the *inheritance of office*, ever to be countenanced by the President of the United States, should he be truly informed of all the circumstances attending this Case." Bedinger secured the support of Parker, who warmly recommended him to Wolcott. In May, Lindsay was still alive; but the news of his condition seems to have become public, for two new candidates appeared. One of these, a man by the name of Byrd, was brought forward by General William Heth, to whom Wolcott seems to have applied for a suggestion. Byrd was also supported by General Carrington, and was appointed. Parker attributed his success over Bedinger to political reasons. Doubtless these counted, as they usually did under Adams; but probably General Heth's charges of wholesale mismanagement in the Norfolk custom-

Mississippi (Massachusetts Historical Society, *Collections*, 6th series, viii. 322); *American Historical Review*, ii. 241.

house had some weight in deterring the administration from selecting any of the incumbent officers.[1]

This controversy illustrates the machinery for the distribution of offices as it existed under Adams. One candidate, it is noted, presented his claims through his congressman; another supported his with personal letters and petitions. These latter do not seem to have been very highly regarded: there is on one the marginal note, "I should not consider it a *very great* compliment to be highly recommended as a Collector by the Merchants, owners and Masters of vessels of Norfolk — or indeed any other District." The general government did not, however, rely on these suggestions and simply take what was offered; it sought for the best men. The details also show how strongly, in spite of the removals that Adams made, the idea of property in office was held, and how much greater, at this particular time, seemed the chance that a place would be held too long, become hereditary, than that it would change hands too often. In fact, the idea set forth by John Cotton, in his famous election sermon, that even elected officers should not be changed so long as they properly performed their duties, seems not to have entirely disappeared.[2]

On the whole, the civil service under the Federalists seems to have been exceptionally honest. With the loose business tone prevailing in the country, a certain amount of loss was to be expected; but while there were defalcations, some attributable to dishonesty and some to bad management, they scarcely bear so large a proportion to the amount of money handled as they did in the succeeding period. The best proof of the general integrity of the service is that Gallatin, when directed by Jefferson to conduct a searching investigation of the Federalist financial administration, was able to find no evidence to its discredit.[3] Honesty and efficiency are not entirely

---

[1] This account is taken wholly from the documents printed by Mr. Gaillard Hunt, in the *American Historical Review*, ii. 247–254.

[2] "It is the height of ingratitude, says a correspondent, to endeavor to remove the Honorable Mr. Dunbar from the Senate" (*Massachusetts Centinel*, April 4, 1789).

[3] Leake, *Lamb*, 353–354; *Senate Documents*, 16 Cong., 1st sess., ii. No. 89; J. A. Hamilton, *Reminiscences*, 121–122.

synonymous, and government reports cannot tell how well the various officers of the government performed their duties — whether they were polite and abreast with the progress of the age or not; but the general impression that one carries away from the correspondence and press of the time is that the people were satisfied. It must be borne in mind, however, that official duties were simple as compared with the functions of the modern public officer, and that, in the absence of foreign travel, standards of comparison were lacking. The only branch of the public service that closely affected the mass of the people was the post-office. Jefferson complained that he dared not use the office most convenient for him, lest his mail be tampered with;[1] but this sensitiveness was perhaps exaggerated for political purposes. The continuance of Mr. Lindsay in office until death, in spite of his long sickness, shows that the civil service was not kept constantly pruned; yet one of the very few cases in which an officer has been requested to resign because disabled by permanent ill health occurred in Washington's administration.[2] On the whole, it seems probable that the administration of public business bore a better relation to the business standards of the country under the Federalists than at any subsequent period.

In a summing up of the whole policy of the Federalists toward the civil service, this point should first of all be insisted upon, that fitness was always an essential requirement; other qualifications were often looked for, but these were ever subsidiary to the ability to perform the duties of the office. Of these subsidiary qualifications, correct political opinion was one of the most important both under Washington and under Adams. Political service, however, was never seriously reckoned by them: requests for office made no parade of services at caucuses and polls, and it cannot, therefore, be said that the spoils system had then come into existence.

---

[1] Jefferson, *Writings* (Washington ed.), iv. 230–231, 256 ; *Massachusetts Spy,* October 9, 1799.

[2] But Pickering, in 1796, advised William Lithgow, district attorney of Maine, to resign (Massachusetts Historical Society, *Collections*, 6th series, viii. 281). Lithgow resigned (*Executive Journal,* i. 217).

The Federalist policy of excluding the opposition from office, however, inevitably entailed a policy of removals upon their opponents when the latter should come into power; while the few removals they actually made furnished their enemies with the *tu quoque* argument, always so telling in political conflicts.[1] In the very last weeks of their power, moreover, they laid themselves distinctly open to the charge of using the patronage for party purposes. The hasty creation of an extensive judiciary in the very death hour of the administration, and the filling of the places created with ardent Federalists, would, if the act were that of a modern legislature, be generally considered as a job. Gouverneur Morris looked upon it in that way at the time.[2]

One feature of this act, especially, gave opportunity to suspect the good faith of its framers: among the offices created were those of twenty-four justices of the peace for the District of Columbia; these positions were not to be held during good behavior, that practice having become unpopular, but for a term of years, which, out of all analogy with the other fixed terms for national officers, was to be five years.[3] Republicans could not refrain from the reflection that this provision would protect the justices until another election, which might give the patronage to the Federalists once more. Politically these minor sins of the Federalists almost offset the general decorum of their administration, and must be held, at least in part, responsible for the evil times into which they were soon to fall.

[1] " Every person holding office must either quit it, or think and vote exactly with Mr. Adams." The hope was also expressed that on March 4, 1801, Gardner and other "expelled public servants" would be replaced (Callender, *The Prospect before Us*, 32–33). See also Coleman, *Examination*, 27. As late as 1808 the charge was repeated (*Address to the People of the American States who Choose Electors*, 13).

[2] "That the leaders of the federal party may use this opportunity to provide for friends and adherents is, I think, probable ; and if they were my enemies, I should blame them for it. Whether I should do the same thing myself is another question. . . . They are about to experience a heavy gale of adverse wind ; can they be blamed for casting many anchors to hold their ship through the storm ?" (Roosevelt, *Gouverneur Morris*, 333).

[3] *Statutes at Large*, ii. 107.

CHAPTER II.

JEFFERSON'S POLICY AS TO PUBLIC OFFICE.

1801–1809.

WHEN Jefferson became president, he found nearly all the offices filled by his opponents.[1] Was it right, when the people had expelled the Federalists from the elective offices and put Republicans in their places, that the old occupants of the appointive offices should be left in their positions merely because the people could not reach them? Should the government be administered, should the national salaries be enjoyed, by representatives of a minority of the population? Most of the Republicans agreed that it was not right, and that it should not be tolerated. Gideon Granger, Jefferson's postmaster-general, wrote: "Upon entering on the duties of this office, my mind was impressed with an unusual anxiety and solicitude. Knowing as I did that most of the officers under me, from their official stations, had been in the habit of associating and corresponding, as well on politics as on business, with those lately in authority, from whom the people had withdrawn their confidence; and elevated to office men whose political principles they believed better calculated to preserve the constitution and public prosperity, and having a general knowledge of the most pronounced recent events, it occurred to me that some removals would become necessary, as well to effect an equal participation and enjoyment of office by the two great classes of citizens who are designated by the terms Federalists and Republicans, as to maintain and preserve confidence in the Department."[2] The

---

[1] February 18, 1803, Jefferson, *Writings* (Ford ed.), viii. 212–213.
[2] *New York Evening Post*, March 4, 1802.

bitterness of the preceding contest sharpened this call for action. The judiciary act was viewed in the worst possible light, the few removals made by Adams were magnified into a searching proscription, charges wholly false were fabricated, and cries for the punishment of the Federalists mingled with demands for a just recognition of the Republicans.[1]

The Federalists foresaw the danger, and a story was circulated at the time, that some of their leaders attempted to ward off the blow by sowing dissension between Jefferson and his followers. Certainly during the early months of his term some of the well-known Federalist newspapers praised him and disparaged his party.[2] The *Columbian Centinel*, August 12, 1801, told how, when a list of men to be appointed to office because of their services in the campaign of 1800 was presented to the president, he remarked, " Yes, yes, I have read that Rome was saved by geese; but I do not remember that these geese were made Revenue Officers or Marshals." Jefferson was too clever to be caught by such chaff. Three days after his inauguration he wrote to Monroe : " I have firmly refused to follow the counsels of those who have advised the giving offices to some of their leaders, in order to reconcile [them]. I have given, and will give only to Republicans, under existing circumstances."[3]

The question of the patronage was of special importance to Jefferson because of his desire to win over the bulk of the Federalist party, and its delicacy was enhanced by the fact that his own party was not united ; while the majority expected vigorous action, some desired that removals be made sparingly.[4] He felt that efficiency was not the sole object to be kept in mind in administering the civil service ; and wished so to con-

[1] *American Historical Review*, iii. 276–280. For instance, it was said that Congress gave special power to the secretary of state to make contracts with the newspapers by which the printing was secured to the " aristocratic presses " for " the term of one year " (*Columbian Centinel*, April 11, 1801).

[2] Jefferson to Gerry, March 29, 1801, Jefferson, *Writings* (Ford ed.), viii. 41; *American Historical Review*, iii. 274 ; *Columbian Centinel*, May 23, 1801 ; *Massachusetts Spy*, July 15, 1801.

[3] Jefferson, *Writings* (Ford ed.), viii. 10.

[4] P. Butler to Burr, September 19, 1801, " On the subject of removal from office, it appears to my finite judgment that it should be done sparingly " (Davis, *Burr*, ii. 153–154).

duct it as to bring about the best political results for country and for party. He wrote to Monroe, March 7, 1801, that he believed, as did others, "that deprivations of office, if made on the ground of political principles alone, would revolt our new converts, and give a body to leaders who now stand alone. Some, I know, must be made. They must be as few as possible, done gradually, and bottomed on some malversation or inherent disqualification. Where we shall draw the line between retaining all & none, is not yet settled, and will not be till we get our administration together; and perhaps even then, we shall proceed *à talons*, balancing our measures according to the impression we perceive them to make."[1] On the next day he wrote to Horatio Gates about the patronage, "If we can hit on the true line of conduct which may conciliate the honest part of those who were called federalists, & do justice to those who have so long been excluded from it, I shall hope to be able to obliterate, or rather to unite the names of federalists & republicans."[2]

With these ideas in mind, — of conciliation for the opposing party, and of justice for his own, — Jefferson sought out classes of officers for whose removal some special reason might be assigned. First, he treated as null and void all appointments about the validity of which there was any legal doubt. The best known of these cases was that of the justices of the peace for the newly organized District of Columbia, — the "midnight appointments."[3] Although the supreme court decided against the president in the famous case of Marbury *vs.* Madison, it declined to issue any writ;[4] and the men whom he appointed to take the place of Adams's nominees retained office. The

---

[1] Jefferson, *Writings* (Ford ed.), viii. 10; a letter of March 23, *Writings* (Washington ed.), iv. 380.

[2] Jefferson, *Writings* (Ford ed.), viii. 11-12. He expected that there would not be more than twenty removals. Randall, *Jefferson*, ii. 656.

[3] Jefferson seems to have felt that the appointment of these officers by Adams was a personal unkindness. See letter to Mrs. Adams, June 13, 1804, Jefferson, *Writings* (Ford ed.), viii. 307. On the judiciary, see Max Farrand in *American Historical Review*, v. 682-686.

[4] I. *Cranch*, 137; *Columbian Centinel*, May 23, July 1, 1801; *Gazette* (Charleston), September 9, 1801.

eagerness with which Jefferson seized on every opportunity to get an opponent out of office without removing him is illustrated by an incident in Rhode Island. After the judiciary act of 1801 was passed, Adams had nominated Mr. Bourne for one of the new circuit judgeships and Mr. Ray Greene for the district judgeship that Mr. Bourne was to vacate. The latter did not resign his post until March 23, 1801 ; and Jefferson held that, as Mr. Greene had been nominated to a position which was not vacant, and which was held on the tenure of good behavior, his appointment was not valid, and he refused to recognize him. This action was violently attacked by the Federalists ; and the president, in an apparent attempt to ward off their criticism, selected Mr. Barnes, a moderate Federalist, for the position of district judge thus made vacant.[1]

The number of these so-called illegal appointments was small, and Jefferson was soon obliged to look beyond them for means to satisfy those of his followers who desired to serve their country in lucrative places. A class of officers subject to removal was soon discovered in those appointed by Adams after the Federalist defeat of 1800 became evident,[2] on the ground that Adams should not have chosen men to positions in which he knew they would serve another president. The Federalists, of course, would not acknowledge that Adams was under any such obligations of law or courtesy ; they saw no reason why customs officers need be in political sympathy with the president, and violently attacked this action, in which they foresaw the prelude to a promiscuous proscription. Jefferson was not the man to be silent under attack, and he spun out those persuasive arguments which always flowed so readily from his pen, and which provoked a full discussion of the problems of the civil service.

The particular case that called forth this discussion was the removal of Chauncy Goodrich from the collectorship at New

---

[1] *New York Evening Post,* March 24, 1803.

[2] See Jefferson to Giles, March 23, and to Rush, March 24, 1801, Jefferson, *Writings* (Washington, ed.), iv. 381, 383. However illogical his position, Jefferson stood by it. December 27, 1808, he wrote to Dr. Logan, "I shall make no new appointments which can be deferred till the fourth of March, thinking it fair to leave to my successor to select the agents for his own administration."

Haven. Connecticut, Jefferson considered as the fortress of the " monarchial party," the one state whose conversion to republicanism was problematical. From the first the *Connecticut Courant* had led the press of the state in a fierce denunciation of every instance of proscription. With several other papers it followed the ingenious device of printing conciliatory sentences from the inaugural, and under them, in fancy type, the heading " Practice," followed by all the instances of removals that could be accumulated.[1] Jefferson was probably not sorry to have an opportunity to fight out the question in the home of the enemy : there was little to lose, and much might be learned of popular sentiment.

The collector at New Haven had died in February, 1801, and Adams, about a week before the inauguration of Jefferson, appointed Goodrich,[2] who therefore fell under the ban which Jefferson had established. The president consulted his supporters in the state ;[3] and from them he received bitterly partisan letters calling for the removal of Goodrich and a clean sweep throughout the state.[4] Gideon Granger urged that " The principle cannot be controverted, that it is just, fair and honorable that the friends of the Government should have at least as great a proportion of the honors and offices of the Gov-

---

[1] *Columbian Centinel*, March 28, August 1, 8, 1801 ; *Connecticut Courant*, July 20, 1801 ; *New York Evening Post*, December 18, 1801.

[2] Austin died February 5, and Goodrich was appointed February 19 (*Columbian Centinel*, August 1, 1801).

[3] Jefferson to Gideon Granger and to Pierrepont Edwards, March 29, 1801, Jefferson, *Writings* (Ford ed.), viii. 44–45 and note.

[4] Granger wrote: " As to the case of Mr. Goodrich and the general questions affecting removals from office in this State, I have had a full consultation with Messrs. Edwards, Thirby and Wolcott and a few other tried friends. They are all agreed that the cause requires the removal of Mr. Goodrich immediately, and of various other principal officers as soon and in such manner, as the Executive should deem proper; for my own part I have yielded to the same opinion so far as respects the principal officers in Newhaven, Hartford, Middletown, and Litchfield though reluctantly and with some apprehension. . . . Premising that I am fully sensible of the agitations which will be produced by removals from office, that I have no connections for whom I wish office, and that I sincerely lament the existence of a state of things which require acts calculated to affect individuals, and to give pain to the feelings of the executive — I proceed to state the reasons upon which I have founded my opinion " (*American Historical Review*, iii. 272–273).

ernment as they are of the whole people. . . . The general depression of the Republicans in this State, who have suffered everything, combatting a Phalanx vastly superior to what can be found in any other part of the union forms a strong reason. Nothing can be lost here, and something may be gained : how far this applies to other parts of the union is not for me to judge. A knowledge that we had the real confidence of the Executive I think would have a happy effect, for already it is used as an argument to affect our elections that the President used the Democrats to ride into office, that now seated there he has evinced his contempt for them, and will rely solely on the federalists for support. . . . Lastly, the sacred rule that no man shall be persecuted for his opinions decently and reasonably maintained will not apply to any of our official Characters. I believe without a single exception All, and I know most have been bitter persecutors." [1] Pierrepont Edwards reiterated the charge that the Federalists expected Jefferson to look to them for support in Connecticut, and told stories of the violent hatred with which they nevertheless regarded him : how the "collector at Middletown . . . violent, irritable, priest-ridden, implacable, a ferocious federalist, and a most indecent enimy to you and your administration," drank the toast "*Thomas Jefferson* may he receive from his fellow Citizens the reward of his merit," adding, "*a halter.*" He suggested Samuel Bishop as the proper man to receive the New Haven collectorship,[2] and the appointment was made.

At first Bishop's name was well received by the Federalist press, though the removal of Goodrich was condemned. New Haven Federalists, however, immediately raised a cry of indignation, the merchants sent a protest to Jefferson, and the party press rallied to their support. "The office," they said, "while filled by Mr. Goodrich, was conducted with a promptness, integrity and ability . . . not to be found in his successor." [3] Jefferson

---

[1] *American Historical Review*, iii. 274.

[2] *Ibid.* 276. Jefferson also received a letter from twenty-four Connecticut Republicans asking for removals. *Congressional Record*, 47 Cong. 2 sess. 276.

[3] *Columbian Centinel*, June 10, July 29 (exceptionally fancy type), August 1, 8, 1801; *Connecticut Courant*, June 15, 1801; *Massachusetts Spy* and *Worcester Gazette*, October 7, 1801; *American Historical Review*, ii. 277.

seized this opportunity to give expression to his views on the question of the patronage, embodying them in a reply (July 12, 1801) to the petition of the merchants. "The removal, as it is called, of Mr. Goodrich," he writes, "forms another subject of complaint. Declarations by myself in favor of *political tolerance*, exhortations to *harmony* and affection in social intercourse, and to respect for the *equal rights* of the minority, have, on certain occasions, been quoted and misconstrued into assurances that the tenure of offices was to be undisturbed. But could candor apply such a construction?" He goes on to quote the usual arguments, that the Federalists had excluded from office those "not of a particular sect of politics," and that, as a consequence, office was a monopoly in the hands of the minority. "Does it violate their *equal rights*," he continues, "to assert some rights in the majority also? Is it *political intolerance* to claim a proportionate share in the direction of the public affairs? . . . If the will of the nation, manifested by their various elections, calls for an administration of government according with the opinions of those elected; if, for the fulfilment of that will, displacements are necessary, with whom can they so justly begin as with persons appointed in the last moments of an administration, not for its own aid, but to begin a career at the same time with their successors?" Could the preference for another as successor to Mr. Austin be justly considered the removal of Mr. Goodrich? "If a due participation of office is a matter of right, how are vacancies to be obtained? Those by death are few; by resignation, none. Can any other mode than that of removal be proposed? This is a painful office; but it is made my duty, and I meet it as such. I proceed in the operation with deliberation and inquiry, that it may injure the best men least, and effect the purposes of justice and public utility with the least private distress; that it may be thrown, as much as possible, on delinquency, on oppression, on intolerance, on ante-revolutionary adherence to our enemies. It would have been to me a circumstance of great relief, had I found a moderate participation of office in the hands of the majority. I would gladly have left to time and accident to raise them to their just share. But their total exclusion calls for prompter corrections. I shall correct the procedure; but that done, return with joy to that state of things, when the only questions concerning a candidate shall be, is he honest? Is he capable? Is he faithful to the Constitution?"[1] With a zest and an analytical keenness worthy of the *New York Evening Post* of to-day, its first editor, William Coleman, probably with the assistance of Alexander Hamilton, dissected this programme of proscription, enunciated the Federalist doctrine, and imagined the president, "Gazing round him with wild anxiety, he furiously enquires, 'How are vacancies to be obtained?'" He pointed out the absurdity of the contention that Goodrich had not been removed, but was less convincing when he endeavored to show a distinction between refusing to appoint opponents, as the Federalists had done, and removing them; nevertheless he acutely remarked in this connection that, if the first were proscription, it could not be cured, as Jefferson was trying to do, by more proscription. Enunciating his own principles on the subject, he said: "Every man who accepts an office, takes it under an implicit contract from the Government, that he shall be continued in it, as long as he exercises it with fidelity and capacity. On this reliance he relinquishes his regular business, . . . and devotes his time and talents to his public employment." In marked contrast with a later famous utterance is the following statement: "There are few offices, with the duties of which a person can, till after a considerable length of time, so far familiarize himself, as to perform with accuracy all the necessary details . . . if every change of a chief magistrate is to produce a similar change of subordinate officers . . . their places are to be supplied by a new set of men who have everything to learn . . . : the means of improvement being thus rejected, Government will be entirely deprived of all the benefits of experience, and the management of public offices, perpetually shifting from one tyro in office to another, will forever be kept in infancy and weakness." He goes on to point out that in America most men have to support themselves, that it is difficult to resume a business once laid aside, and that consequently the best men will not take office unless its tenure is fairly stable. The latter part of the pamphlet is taken up chiefly

[1] Jefferson, *Writings* (Washington ed.), iv. 402–405.

with a discussion of some of the intricate constitutional questions of the civil service, and with an exhortation to the Senate to review carefully all removals and appointments made during the recess.

This discussion [1] has been treated at considerable length, because it illustrates the contemporary idea of the civil service. It is noticeable that Jefferson did not put forward the idea that long tenure of office is unrepublican; and that Coleman, in spite of his general sanity, fell into the fallacy of commending an appointment made in order that the recipient, a veteran, might "spend the evening of his days in ease and competence;" [2] that is, he sanctioned the popular view that the civil service was a pension fund for meritorious public servants, a view mistaken and baneful.

Samuel Bishop was a man of repute, and so much respected that he was at this very time holding office under the Federalist legislature; and Jefferson doubtless hoped that he would reflect his respectability on the Republican party in his state. Yet it was an altogether bad appointment. Bishop was deacon in one of the established churches, mayor of New Haven, justice of the peace, chief judge of the court of probate. He was seventy-seven years of age, and so far as the collectorship was concerned merely a figurehead. The office was really given to his son Abraham, an active Republican leader and pamphleteer,[3] who acted as his father's clerk in nearly all his capaci-

---

[1] Coleman, *Examination*, 12, 49, *et passim*. Particularly as to the power of the president to commission officers in the place of men removed during the recess of the Senate, a question which the *Columbian Centinel* (September 9, 1801) wished to be fully discussed in the Senate.

[2] Coleman, *Examination*, 45.

[3] *Massachusetts Spy*, July 29, 1801; *American Historical Review*, iii. 276; Jefferson to committee of merchants, July 12, 1801, Jefferson, *Writings* (Washington ed.), iv. 403; Noah Webster to Jefferson, July 18, 1801, *Good Government*, October 15, 1894; *New York Evening Post*, March 13, 1804; *Columbian Centinel*, June 10, 1801. The following words show Jefferson's appreciation of the younger Bishop's work: "Bishop's pamphlet on political delusions has not yet reached the book stores here. It is making wonderful progress, and is said to be the best anti-republican eye-water which has ever yet appeared. A great impression of them is making at Philadelphia to be forwarded here" (Jefferson to T. M. Randolph, November 30, 1800, Massachusetts Historical Society, *Collections*, 7th series, i. 78).

ties, and performed the functions of the collectorship not
without causing complaint.[1] Samuel Bishop died in 1803, and
Abraham was appointed to succeed him.[2]

Although Jefferson, in his answer to the New Haven remonstrance, hinted at a more general proscription if he could not by
other means bring about the desired equality in the civil service
between the parties, he continued to seek for special classes
that seemed peculiarly proper subjects for removal.　Charles
Pinckney was nominated minister plenipotentiary at Madrid,
"vice David Humphreys, recalled on account of long absence
from the United States."[3]　William Jarvis, hearing while in
Lisbon that Jefferson had said that any well-qualified citizen of
the United States who desired a consulate held by a foreigner
might have it for the asking, wrote to General Dearborn
requesting the place in that city, and obtained it.[4]　The president found that, although in general "good men" of no undue
political activity were not "proper subjects of removal," the
principle did not apply to attorneys and marshals.　"The
courts being so decidedly federal and irremovable," he wrote
to Giles, March 23, 1801, "it is believed that republican attorneys and marshals, being the doors of entrance into the courts,
are indispensably necessary as a shield to the republican part
of our fellow-citizens;" and he strengthened his case by prefer-
ring charges of partiality and jury-packing against the officers
then holding.[5]

Having thus proceeded carefully step by step, observing the
effect of the removals made, and particularly watching the
masses of the opposition, whom he wished to ween from their
leaders, Jefferson felt encouraged by the end of the first year
of his administration to go farther.　He wrote to Elbridge
Gerry, August 28, 1802: "After a twelve months' trial I have
at length been induced to remove three or four more of those

---

[1] *Connecticut Courant,* June 17, 1801; *Columbian Centinel,* September 12, 1801.

[2] *Executive Journal,* i. 453 (November 11, 1803).

[3] *Ibid.* 404 (January 6, 1802); Jefferson to William Short, October 3, 1801,
Jefferson, *Writings* (Ford ed.), viii. 95–99.

[4] Cutts, *Jarvis,* 129.

[5] Jefferson, *Writings* (Washington ed.), iv. 381 ; Jefferson to Rush, March 24,
1801, *ibid.* 383.

most marked for their bitterness and active zeal in slandering and in electioneering. Whether we shall proceed any further will depend on themselves."[1] In fact, the policy of removing his opponents was a political success, and had alienated from the Republican administration none of the elements upon which it counted for support. The Federalists had, in the beginning, hoped that Jefferson's action might meet with popular resentment. So suicidal did it seem, that they imagined that Burr, while endeavoring to dissociate himself from the proscription, was urging it on the president with a view to rendering him unpopular.[2] Yet before the end of 1801 all were forced to acknowledge that their prognostications were unwarranted.[3]

The Federalists, moreover, continued to give the administration some little ground for countercharges. June 13, 1801, the *Columbian Centinel* noted with satisfaction that after the election in New Hampshire "all the vacancies" were "filled by federal men." The dismissal of the clerk of the court of common pleas in Massachusetts by Federalist superiors gave the *Aurora* an opportunity to speak of "tyranny."[4] The *Columbian Centinel* asserted that much of the material for the Republicans' countercharges was cleverly manufactured by their politicians;[5] but, whether these allegations were genuine or not,

[1] Jefferson, *Writings* (Ford ed.), viii. 169.

[2] *Columbian Centinel*, August 5, 1851. This rumor reached London, but was there attached to the name of Madison. *London Traveller*, quoted in *Massachusetts Spy*, December 16, 1801.

[3] See, for example, Theodore Sedgwick to Rufus King, December 14, 1801: "I do not think that Mr. J——n has lost any influence by his removals from office. There is nothing more mischievous & monstrous than the principle, and it is avowed, on which this conduct rests. It is, palpably, rendering the aggregate of the emoluments of all the offices, holden at the pleasure of the president, a mass of electioneering corruption. And yet there is a wonderful tranquillity prevailing on the avowal and practice of this conduct. There was a time when the resentment of the people of Connecticut would have been roused, almost to a frenzy, by removing such men as Chester, Goodrich and Whittlesey, from important offices, to fill them with such as Thirby, Bishop, and Wolcott, let the motive have been whatever it might ; but on this occasion, tho' a most detestable motive is declared, no great degree of sensibility seems to be excited among even good men " (King, *King*, iv. 35).

[4] *Columbian Centinel*, June 13, 1801.

[5] "Certain sly-boots," it said, June 6, 1801, recommend worthless persons to Governor Strong for justices of the peace, and when he rejects them, say it is on party grounds.

the unthinking reader of newspapers at that time must have believed that it was six of one party and half a dozen of the other. At the same time, some of the Republican elements were growing restive. The state committee of Republicans, appointed to correspond with the committees of the several counties in the state of Pennsylvania, signed an address in 1802 in which it referred to "the slow, but we trust, certain progress of the executive, to restore the Republicans to that share in the public patronage, of which they have been so long, and so unjustly deprived."[1]

These circumstances probably helped give Jefferson courage for bolder acts than any he had yet attempted. The repeal of the judiciary bill of 1801 involved much broader issues than we are concerned with in this monograph, but it involved the question of the patronage also. Jefferson at an early date expressed a determination to cut off the "excrescences from the judiciary"; and in the debate on the measure Mr. Thompson of Virginia denounced the act because it had created sinecures.[2] Jefferson, much to the amusement of the Federalist press, divided the number of cases by the number of judges, and so arrived at the decision that the system provided for was too expensive for the country.[3] Of course, as the offices were abolished, Republicans could not obtain what was taken from the Federalists; and while the enemy was punished, friends were not rewarded.

The debate on this proposition brought out some facts which neither side relished. In the Senate, Giles showed that, while none of the congressmen who had voted for the judiciary act could constitutionally be appointed to the offices created, two senators had been made district judges in the place of men promoted to the new circuit judgeships, and thus the intent of the constitutional clause was violated.[4] Bayard pointed out that

---

[1] *Address of the State Committee* (published by Duane, 1802).

[2] To Levi Lincoln, August 26, 1801, Jefferson, *Writings* (Washington ed.), iv. 401; Bayard, *Speech in Opposition to the Repeal of the Judiciary Act of 1801*, 33.

[3] *New York Herald*, January 2, 1802. "Then by another operation you will readily see whether the *justice done* is worth the money" (*New York Evening Post*, December 29, 1801).

[4] *Annals of Congress*, 7 Cong. 1 sess. 598. One of the senators whose appointments are here referred to was Mr. Ray Greene, who, as we have already seen (above, p. 32), failed to secure his new office.

every man who "had any distinguished means in the competition for the presidential office, of deciding the election," received some valuable appointment.[1] It is probable that neither of these particular facts revealed any conscious corruption; yet the very fact that, without dishonest intention, questionable action had been taken by both parties, forced many to the conclusion that under the most honest men unworthy motives inevitably enter into the distribution of the patronage, and that the hands of those dispensing it are almost sure to be soiled. Both parties had now held the reins, and the purity of neither was untouched. There was about this time an appreciable change of tone in speaking of the civil service; speakers and writers while evincing more comprehension are more despondent; for the first time they begin to doubt the ability of their own party to deal with the question in an altogether satisfactory manner.[2]

The repeal of the judiciary act was effected March 9, 1802, and just about this time began an active proscription of postmasters. The *New York Evening Post* of March 4 contains a letter which Postmaster-general Granger, in accordance with the Jeffersonian penchant for explaining the motives of the administration, wrote to a postmaster to be removed. "From repeated complaints from the country, and from opinions which are entertained by persons who have been long in office, together with the reasons upon which those opinions are founded, I was soon convinced that as a general rule the printers of newspapers ought not to be employed as postmasters, because they have a special interest." This interest lay in their opportunities for suppressing rival papers, and in the possibility of extending their won circulation by abusing the franking privilege, which enabled postmasters to send free of charge letters and packages not exceeding two ounces in weight.[3] Armed with such reasons, Granger began what seems to have been a general sweep in his

---

[1] *Annals of Congress*, 7 Cong. 1 sess. 641.

[2] For example, a pamphlet of the year 1806 (*Who shall be Governor* [of Massachusetts], 22) praises the administrations of both Washington and Jefferson, but fears that favoritism has a place "even in the best regulated republic."

[3] *Statutes at Large*, v. 362.

branch of the service. It is not surprising to find complaint that the Republican editors were allowed to hold postoffices in spite of their special interests.[1]

Jefferson, in the course of his administration, removed 109 out of a total of 433 officers of the presidential class. This does not by any means show the total changes in personnel. In July, 1803, Jefferson wrote to Duane that, of 316 officers in his appointment, 130 were still held by Federalists; probably he meant that there had been 186 changes. From March 4, 1801, to July 16, 1803, there were 59 changes in the 165 offices of the external revenue service; 8 were due to death, 4 to resignation, 9 to misbehavior,[2] and the remaining 38 were doubtless cases of political removal. Except for the last item, this would be but a normal list of changes, though possibly there would not have been so many removals for misbehavior if all the officers had been supporters of the administration. During Jefferson's first term there were, in all, 164 changes in 334 offices.[3]

These figures do not adequately represent the severity of the proscription. In some localities the sweep was much more complete than in others: Jefferson wrote to Governor McKean of Pennsylvania, who had just turned out his opponents in that state, "Some states require a different regimen from others."[4] In Massachusetts alone there were almost as many removals as in the whole South, and in general the proportion of changes was greater in the North.[5] Jefferson told John Quincy Adams

---

[1] *New York Evening Post*, February 12, 13, 25, March 4, 6, 24, 31, April 6, 8, 16, 22, 1802, March 31, 1803 ; *New York Herald*, February 17, 1802.

[2] Fish, *Removal of Officials*, in American Historical Association, *Reports*, 1899, i. 70, table ii.; August 21, 1802, Gouverneur Morris wrote to Livingston, "Indeed, some officers have resigned, because they felt a kind of dishonor in remaining as exceptions to the proscription" (Sparks, *Morris*, iii. 171); *American Historical Review*, iii. 281.

[3] Five district judges out of 17, 14 district attorneys out of 22, 15 marshals out of 22, 41 collectors out of 82, 4 naval officers out of 11, 18 surveyors out of 30, 67 miscellaneous out of 150. American Historical Association, *Papers*, ii. No. 1, p. 51.

[4] July 24, 1801, Jefferson, *Writings* (Ford ed.), viii. 78.

[5] There were 15 removals from offices local in the South, 12 in Massachusetts, 8 in New Jersey, 6 in New York, 5 in Pennsylvania, 4 each in Connecticut and New Hampshire, 3 in Vermont, and 2 in Rhode Island. Of the southern removals the greater number were in Virginia and North Carolina, a fact somewhat surprising, as

that not one request for appointment involving a removal had come from Virginia.   This extreme statement was probably due to a lapse of memory; [1] but it is true that the southern states, particularly those south of the Potomac and east of the Alleghanies, did not take kindly to the proscriptive system, and that it never really flourished in that region until after the Civil War. The small number of removals there at this time is further explained by the fact that Jefferson found some supporters in office, [2] and that his conciliatory programme was so successful that the Federalist party in the South almost ceased to exist.

In estimating the severity of this first proscription, as of all later epochs of removal, it must always be remembered that if the lists of removals were made out on the basis of salary, or of the influence which the various offices carried with them, the proportion of changes would be very much greater. [3]   Among the removals are always found the collectors of the great cities, the postmasters, the great territorial and foreign officers, and, under Jefferson, the supervisors of the revenue.   These officers had subordinates under them and carried on minor proscriptions. It is difficult to secure information with regard to local and departmental removals at this period; there are no figures, and the policy was vacillating.   July 25, 1801, Gallatin sent Jefferson the draft of a proposed circular to the collectors, particularly intended for those of them who were Federalists.   In it they were ordered " no longer to shut the door to the offices under them to any man merely on account of his political opinions," and were told that an electioneering collector was necessarily a bad one.   Jefferson expressed qualified approval; he thought that the circular should be delayed until his answer to the New Haven remonstrance had been published, and said that he had

South Carolina was the stronghold of the Federalist party in the South.   See *Executive Journal.*

[1] February, 1805, J. Q. Adams, *Memoirs,* i. 344.   He wrote to Pierce Butler, August 26, 1801 : " The Southern republicans [have] been really magnanimous.   In Maryland little has been asked, in Virginia, North Carolina, Georgia, not one " (Jefferson, *Writings* (Ford ed.), viii. 82); *American Historical Review,* iii. 280.

[2] *Ibid.*

[3] See Jefferson to Duane, July 24, 1803, Gallatin, *Writings,* i. 130-133.   He figures this point out carefully.

intended to have the collectors produce " an equilibrium " before the non-partisan régime went into effect. The circular was never sent.[1] At Boston, Dearborn, the new collector, made removals. Jefferson wrote to John Burke that there was a "redundancy of applications" for departmental places; and Duane prepared lists of the clerks holding such positions, appending to each name reasons for removal. As the president, however, left to each head of a department much freedom of action,[2] the treatment of the patronage differed in the various localities and in the various branches of government.

In the summer of 1803 Jefferson apparently decided that the desired equilibrium had been attained, and removals ceased. At that time the balance of office-holding weighed down considerably on the Republican side; but it should be borne in mind that the Federalists no longer constituted half the population, and were therefore, according to the Jeffersonian rule, not entitled to half the offices. If Jefferson had lived up to his principles, the attainment of the equilibrium should have been followed by the adoption of a non-partisan standard for appointments. There was an abundant opportunity for this, as forty-six new appointments were made in the customs service alone;[3] but the opportunity was neglected, and by 1806 the civil service must have been as strongly Republican as it had been Federalist in 1801.

This proscription is pleasantly distinguished from later ones by the fact that it was conducted with a certain degree of courtesy. Reasonable notice was given to the victims, who, in their turn, often initiated their successors into the mysteries of the craft. One letter of removal reads in part as follows: "Accept, Sir, my thanks for all the faithful services you have rendered while in office. With esteem and respect, Gideon Granger."[4]

---

[1] Gallatin, *Writings*, i. 28 ; Adams, *Gallatin*, 279.

[2] *Columbian Centinel*, August 29, 1801 ; *American Historical Review*, iii. 285 ; Adams, *Gallatin*, 277–278 ; Jefferson to Burke, June 21, 1801, Jefferson, *Writings* (Ford ed.), viii. 66.

[3] *American Historical Review*, iii. 281.

[4] *Ibid.* 271; *Columbian Centinel*, August 5, 12, 1801 ; Adams, *Gallatin*, 277 ; *New York Evening Post*, February 13, 1802.

Jefferson did not plan to fill all the offices thus vacated. During a long period of our history, our civil service has been hampered by the popular prejudice against large salaries. The *Massachusetts Centinel* of September 17, 1789, pointed out that to people accustomed to deal in pounds a fair salary in dollars looked large, and urged that cheap rogues and dunces would cheat and lose more than could be saved on the salary account; but this argument did not appeal to the democracy of the time, and the liberal schedule established for the federal officers caused opposition.[1] Retrenchment, therefore, was a natural plank in the Republican platform. Not high salaries alone were attacked, but also the tendency to strengthen the central government, and particularly the executive, by creating an extensive patronage; and it was urged that the civil service must be reduced to the lowest terms.

Both of these objects had been in mind when the judiciary act was repealed, and Jefferson struck a popular chord when he lopped off two missions and saved about twenty thousand dollars a year in the diplomatic service.[2] More important was Gallatin's plan for the abolition of the internal taxes. Throughout the discussion of this measure, particularly in the House of Representatives, the Republican members repeatedly asserted that one of its main objects was the reduction of the patronage. The Federalists argued that, if this was the end desired, the taxes might be collected by the customs officers and the postmasters.[3] There were, of course, other motives for passing the bill; but there seems little doubt that the majority of the Republicans were sincerely pleased at the reduction of the civil service thus entailed. The actual annual saving effected seems to have been about one hundred and fifteen thousand dollars.[4] The only important offices abolished were sixteen supervisorships and twenty-

[1] *New York Evening Post,* September 26, November 21, 1789.

[2] *American State Papers, Miscellaneous,* i. 306; *Gazette and Daily Advertiser* (Charleston), September 9, 1801. This form of retrenchment long continued popular. See *Niles's Register,* xxiii. 225 (December 14, 1822).

[3] *Annals of Congress,* 7 Cong. 1 sess. 1032, 1053, 1061; Jefferson to Dickinson, December 19, 1801, Jefferson, *Writings* (Washington ed.), iv. 425.

[4] *Statutes at Large,* ii. 148. The figures are calculated from a list of officers in *American State Papers, Miscellaneous,* i. 280–288.

four inspectorships, together with the post of commissioner of the revenue. These officers could not be spared at once, as there were taxes already due that must be collected; but a year later provision was made that the president be authorized to attach their duties to those of any other officer in the district.[1] It was proposed also to discontinue the mint,[2] but the measure was never adopted.

In addition to the actual retrenchments, a number of useful regulative acts were passed. One of these fixed the maximum compensation for customs officials;[3] it did not save much money, but was a step toward the correct principle of fixed salaries as opposed to fees. While these measures tended to show the good faith of the Republicans, the sum total of the economies was not very great. One bill, the judiciary act of 1802, actually increased the patronage of the president by transferring to him, from the district judges, the appointment of commissioners of bankruptcy, thus giving Jefferson the opportunity to do the ungracious act of displacing John Quincy Adams.[4] What little reduction was made in the patronage of the president was soon offset by the increases made necessary by the growth of the country, and particularly by the annexation of Louisiana.[5]

Jefferson had, therefore, more offices to fill than had Washington, and he devoted himself to the task with great energy. The Federalist press represented him as overwhelmed by "strange beings continually . . . crying More, More, Give, Give."[6] Some cases presented little difficulty; he accepted as an axiom that all officers removed by Adams for political reasons should receive appointments, preferably to their old posi-

---

[1] *Annals of Congress*, 7 Cong. 2 sess. 1612 (March 3, 1803).

[2] *Ibid.* 7 Cong. 1 sess. 1036.

[3] *Ibid.* 1197, 1252, 1348. Collectors were to receive not more than $5000, naval officers $3500, surveyors $3000.

[4] *Statutes at Large*, ii. 21, 164 ; Morse, *J. Q. Adams*, 28.

[5] Seybert's *Annals* (p. 378) gives a yearly increasing number of officers from 1790 to 1812. These lists are probably incorrect, though, as the Blue Book was not published in this period, I have been able to check them only here and there, — as for 1794, 1795, and 1797, for which years I have used a semi-official register published in Philadelphia.

[6] *American Historical Review*, iii. 278 ; *Columbian Centinel*, August 29, 1801.

tions.[1] Gardner and Whipple went back to their posts, and Tench Coxe became supervisor for Pennsylvania. Two clerks claimed appointments as martyrs of the previous régime: one had been removed by Adams, the other had apparently been forced to resign. These men, in plain violation of good faith and actual legal regulation, had given Duane information which enabled him to bring charges of defalcation against Timothy Pickering and Jonathan Dayton. Gallatin wrote: "Whatever impropriety there might be in their conduct, I have reason to believe Gardner to be a man of honor. Campbell is very impudent, but as enthusiastic as his friends (the United Irishmen, I mean) commonly are." Gardner was made consul at Demarara; and Campbell, as the new auditor refused to restore him to his old position, was made an ensign in the army.[2]

Where no such special claim existed, the decision called for more consideration, and a procedure developed much like the old Federalist machinery. Members of Congress continued to be the main purveyors of information.[3] The New Yorkers, already becoming adept at businesslike politics, agreed upon a slate, to be submitted to the president by Burr in the name of the whole delegation in Congress.[4] This was accepted, but with a few changes. Although this form was not always followed, the successful candidate seems generally to have been the one who had the support of his state delegation;[5] and if congressmen did not take the initiative, the president usually consulted some of them in regard to names presented.[6] It was natural,

[1] Jefferson to Giles, March 23, and to Rush, March 24, 1801, Jefferson, *Writings* (Washington ed.), iv. 381, 383.

[2] *Executive Journal*, i. 403, 432 (January 6, 1802, January 11, 1803); *American Historical Review*, iii. 282–285; Gallatin to Jefferson, August 10 and September 14, and Campbell to Jefferson, October 12, 1801, Gallatin, *Writings*, i. 34, and note, 50; *New York Evening Post*, April 1, 1802. The *New York Herald*, January 9, 1802, says that Campbell was exonerated by a congressional committee.

[3] Jefferson to C. Pinckney, March 6, 1801, Jefferson, *Writings* (Ford ed.), viii. 6–7; to Gallatin, August 14, 1801, Gallatin, *Writings*, i. 36.

[4] *American Historical Review*, iii. 290.

[5] *Ibid.* 286; Gallatin to his wife, January 29, 1801, Adams, *Gallatin*, 258; Jefferson to George Clinton, May 17, 1801, Jefferson, *Writings* (Ford ed.), viii. 52; to Gallatin, September 18, 1801, Gallatin, *Writings*, i. 54; *New York Evening Post*, March 4, 1802.   [6] *American Historical Review*, iii. 282.

considering the democratic principles of the party, that petitions should be numerous.[1] The *Massachusetts Spy*, under Pennsylvania news, told how " A secret committee of accusation, established for the blackest purposes, in a neighboring commercial town, lately forwarded a memorial to President Jefferson against their Collector, a worthy citizen, . . . praying that he should be removed from office."[2] While petitions of unconnected individuals doubtless had full weight, Jefferson refused to be influenced even by those from organized bodies.[3] Certain prominent men, incipient political bosses, exercised much influence.[4] In New York the Livingstons, the Clintons, and Burr, in Pennsylvania, Duane and Dallas, struggled to gain advantage from the distribution of the patronage;[5] Dearborn seemed to control that of Maine without struggle, and Cæsar Rodney that of Delaware.[6] Burr fared ill in the conflict. Davis, his candidate for naval officer at New York, was not appointed, though he pressed the nomination on Jefferson in a personal interview, and wrote a most abject letter to Gallatin. Perhaps with a view of keeping up his hopes and so preventing a break in the administration no change was made in the office for two years, although the Federalist incumbent was guilty of " ante-revolutionary adherence to enemies." The post-office was given to a friend, but not the one selected by the vice-president ; nor could the latter secure the withdrawal of the printing from Cheetham, who was abusing him.[7] On the other hand, he was highly favored in the Louisiana appointments.[8] Jefferson apparently endeavored so to treat him as to

---

[1] *American Historical Review*, iii. 288; Jefferson to Rodney, June 14, 1802, Jefferson, *Writings* (Ford ed.), viii. 154.

[2] July 15, 1801.

[3] Jefferson to Duane, July 24, 1803, Gallatin, *Writings*, i. 130.

[4] *American Historical Review*, iii. 276, 280, 287, 291.

[5] *Ibid.* 277, 283, 290 ; Gallatin to Jefferson, September 14, 1801, Gallatin, *Writings*, i. 50–51; *New York Evening Post*, January 28, 1802.

[6] *New York Evening Post*, April 15, 1802 ; Jefferson to Rodney, June 14, 1802, Jefferson, *Writings* (Ford ed.), viii. 154.

[7] Adams, *Gallatin*, 282–289 ; Adams, *Administrations of Jefferson and Madison*, i. 296 ; Jefferson, *Anas*, January 26, 1804, in his *Writings* (Ford ed.), i. 301–302.

[8] Probably to secure his aid in the Chase impeachment. His stepson was made secretary, his wife's brother-in-law judge. Wilkinson also was his friend. See McMaster, *United States*, iii. 176.

avoid the danger of making him too powerful on the one hand, and of causing a premature break with him on the other. Although these men and many more exercised influence, there is no hint in the correspondence of the period that the administration felt itself in the least dependent on any individual or organization: no matter what its position or power, no dictation was allowed.[1] To Mr. Larkin Smith, who presumed to dictate on the ground that he was a presidential elector, Jefferson replied in a letter of admirable dignity and self-restraint, utterly dismissing the claim.[2]

It was Jefferson, therefore, who outlined the qualifications for office, although he did not as rigorously adhere to a fixed rule as had Washington. Fitness continued to be considered essential;[3] and while careful character studies are lacking, such as Henry Marchant sent to Hamilton and the latter to Wolcott, Jefferson and Gallatin sought out suitable candidates, not confining their choice to those who offered their services.[4] That these efforts were genuine is evinced by the many declinations they received; Jefferson wrote to Gouverneur Morris that he feared he should have to advertise for a secretary of the navy.[5] The majority of the appointees came from the same class of the population as those under the Federalists. The president wrote to Gallatin in regard to a man proposed for a New England position, "His family has been among the most respectable on that shore for many generations."[6] Some selections were even commented on by the Federalist newspapers as "judicious and proper."[7] The Jefferson Democracy, however,

---

[1] Gallatin to Jefferson, September 14, 1801, Gallatin, *Writings*, i. 50–51.

[2] November 26, 1804, Jefferson, *Writings* (Ford ed.), viii. 337.

[3] Correspondence between Jefferson and Gallatin, *passim.*

[4] Jefferson to George Clinton, May 17, 1801, Jefferson, *Writings* (Ford ed.), viii. 52 ; Gallatin to Jefferson, September 7, 1801, Gallatin, *Writings*, i. 44.

[5] May 8, 1801, Jefferson, *Writings* (Ford ed.), viii. 49 ; Gallatin to Jefferson, September 7, 1801, Gallatin, *Writings*, i. 45.

[6] November 12, 1801, Gallatin, *Writings*, i. 60.

[7] The *New York Evening Post*, February 12, 1802, said : "Mr. Gelston has been turned out of the post office in this city, . . . Alexander Coffin being appointed in his place. Federalism is the crime for which Mr. Gelston is removed. . . . The selection of Mr. Coffin was judicious and proper." See also *Columbian Centinel,* August 27, 1801.

brought new classes into politics, and, to the dismay of the conservative, these received some recognition. Especially the appointment of the foreign-born — "wild Irishmen" and French refugees[1] — called out such voluble criticism as to drown the occasional faint praise.

Among the elements of selection, geographical distribution may be regarded as permanent ;[2] but under Jefferson we find a markedly greater stress laid on politics than previously. Not only was the general political effect of appointments anxiously discussed, but party services were vigorously urged as paramount reason for receiving office, and very often were given recognition. There were some complaints that the new Republican office-holders engaged actively in politics ; General Lincoln, for example, was accused of causing an expense of three thousand dollars for extra clerk hire while he was electioneering in Massachusetts.[3] Such complaints, however, were not numerous, and there is no indication that such activity was required or expected.

Jefferson professed to be, and apparently was, free from nepotism ;[4] it was opposed to his character, and, moreover, he understood full well its political danger. To do a favor for a friend, however, was second nature to him, and his administration of the civil service is marred by favoritism. July 3, 1806, he wrote to John Page that, having consulted "the best medical judge" on the subject, he expected the early demise of the commissioner of loans for the Richmond district. "The office is a perfect sinecure," he wrote. "The introduction of one of your sons into the office [as clerk], besides adding the benefit of the additional thousand dollars to the family, would, by placing him as it were in possession of the office, secure his succeeding to it in that event which you and I ought now to consider as not

---

[1] *New York Evening Post,* March 13, 1804 ; "Tacitus," *Letters to Thomas Jefferson.*

[2] Jefferson to Gates, March 8, 1801, Jefferson, *Writings* (Ford ed.), viii. 11.

[3] *American Historical Review,* iii. 270–291; *Connecticut Courant,* June 15, July 27, 1801 ; correspondence of Jefferson and Gallatin for the period, *passim;* *New York Evening Post,* April 13, 1802.

[4] Jefferson to George Jefferson, March 27, 1801, Jefferson, *Writings* (Ford ed.), viii. 38. Mention is made of rumors of family influence. See Massachusetts Historical Society, *Collections,* 7th series, i. 90, 93.

very remote." The appointment was made; but Page's health failed, and Jefferson, solicitous lest he should overexert himself, wrote, "Would it be a relief to transfer the office to your son Francis . . . for the benefit of the family?" Francis did not succeed his father, but was later appointed by Madison as collector of Yorktown. Freneau, while editing the leading administration paper of Charleston, South Carolina, held one of these sinecures until 1810, when financial disaster forced him to relinquish paper and position.[1]

It is evident that, in spite of favoritism and politics, Jefferson succeeded in the main object which he placed before himself in dealing with the patronage, — that of satisfying the people. In this, as in many other cases, his sympathetic response to popular desire gave him unexpected victory; to satisfy his own followers, and at the same time not to alienate the masses of the opposition, was indeed a wonderful feat. So cleverly did Jefferson steer his bark that the patronage had ceased to be an issue by 1809. Technically one must assign to Jefferson the introduction of the spoils system into the national service, for party service was recognized as a reason for appointment to office, and party dissent as a cause for removal. It was not, however, the sole reason required; and, as has been shown, the character of the civil service was really not much changed.[2] The natural question, why this proscription, proportionately as extensive as that of Jackson, affected the civil service and subsequent politics so much less, can best be answered in the discussion of Jackson's administration.[3]

[1] Jefferson, *Writings* (Ford ed.), viii. 136–137, note; *Executive Journal*, ii. 123 (June, 1809); Thomas, *Reminiscences of the Past Sixty-five Years*, 78. Thomas bought Freneau's paper.

[2] There was very little complaint at loss of efficiency, and that chiefly in the spring of 1802, during the changes in the post-offices.

[3] I have not discussed the question of the reported attempts of Jefferson and Burr to obtain support for the presidency by offering places to members of Congress, as I have found nothing in regard to it that throws additional light on Jefferson's policy.

CHAPTER III.

THE PATRONAGE QUESTION UNDER DISCUSSION.

1809–1829.

WHAT Madison's policy would have been had he become president under circumstances similar to those which Jefferson encountered is uncertain. The Federalist press supposed that, as secretary of state, he opposed the proscriptive system,[1] and at one time announced that he was on the point of resigning because of it;[2] yet even if it were not to his liking, he might have been forced to practise it had he become chief magistrate in 1801. As it was, he succeeded an administration with which he was in complete harmony; there was as yet no loud call for rotation in office, and he was not even tempted to reconstruct the civil service.

Madison did not, however, find the apparently simple task of filling the natural vacancies an easy one. His lack of personal force gave hostile factions an opportunity, and they attempted to control, through the Senate, the distribution of the patronage. A threat of opposition forced the president to relinquish his project of nominating Albert Gallatin for secretary of state; and this victory did not make his opponents more considerate. The nomination of General Dearborn as secretary of war was defeated; there was a contest over the confirmation of Monroe as secretary of state in 1811, and another in 1813 when Jonathan Russell was nominated as minister to Sweden. We have some interesting notes, taken by Pickering, on the debate which took

---

[1] Quincy, *Quincy*, 74; *Massachusetts Spy*, July 29, 1801; *Columbian Centinel*, August 5, 1801.

[2] *Columbian Centinel*, July 22, 1801.

place when the name of Joel Barlow, for minister to France, was sent in. Pickering sarcastically defended the nomination, saying that Barlow was no mere poet, for he had made too much money,[1] — an allusion probably to the Ohio Company frauds. The War of 1812 brought unexpected patronage to the executive; but the administration escaped much of the toil involved by leaving military nominations almost wholly to the state delegations. William Lowndes wrote to his wife that he should have liked a commission, but that he felt a scruple about asking for one, as the delegation of which he was a member really made the appointment.[2] The advice of the state delegation was not always followed, however. Gallatin complained that a Mr. Chrystie, selected by the New York members for a lieutenant-colonelcy, was nominated for a majority only, because of the hostility of the secretary of war.[3] The nomination of Thomas Pinckney, a South Carolina Federalist, received some opposition in the Senate,[4] and caused general surprise. Even Lowndes, an extremely liberal man, wrote to his wife regarding it, " The Republican party, having so large a proportion of the population of the State, has enough of talents and of virtue to serve the country, if the administration knew how to select and employ them." [5] Madison, however, adhered to the policy of the Federalists, in making the war a national and not a party measure. He recognized the opposition, not only in the military but also in the diplomatic appointments, by making James A. Bayard a member of the peace commission at Ghent. This was in no sense an erasure of party lines; it was merely a call for the

---

[1] Adams, *Administrations of Jefferson and Madison*, v. 4–8 ; 359–360; Madison, *Letters and Other Writings*, ii. 598. A vote was not taken ; the name was withdrawn. *Executive Journal*, ii. 626, March 2, 1815 ; Monroe, *Writings*, v. 194 ; *Niles's Register*, iv. 409–412 ; *William Winston Seaton* (1871), 100. Another notable rejection was that of Alexander Wolcott, nominated for associate justice of the Supreme Court.

[2] Ravenel, *Lowndes*, 105 ; Monroe, *Writings*, v. 201.

[3] Gallatin to Madison, 1812, Gallatin, *Writings*, i. 500.

[4] Lowndes wrote to his wife, March 23, 1812, "There is some little objection in the Senate to the confirmation of his appointment, the result of that illiberality of faction from which no public body can be expected to be altogether exempt " (Ravenel, *Lowndes*, 103).

[5] Ravenel, *Lowndes*, 105.

assistance of the minority, an assistance then much needed. In the selection of individuals from both parties, political motives played the usual prominent part.[1] It was bi-partisan, not nonpartisan.

Vastly more difficulty was experienced in reducing the army when the war was over than in creating it, for every hero wished a reward, and his claims were vociferously urged by his admirers. The work of selecting the officers to remain in the regular army was largely left to a board of officers, but a liberal discretion was retained in the executive, and was sometimes used.[2] This part of the task is said to have been easily accomplished, owing to the good sense of General Ripley;[3] but many who could not thus be provided for cast an eye on the civil departments. Dallas wrote to Madison, August 3, 1815: "The cases of General Wilkinson, General Cushing, and General Boyd are urged upon me. The vacancies at Castine, etc., are too humble for these gentlemen; and I am requested to ask your authority to create vacancies of a higher kind in the collectorships of New York, New London, Newport, etc. There is no delicacy used on the occasion."[4] On August 10, Madison replied with a touch of irony: "The cases of the three generals you name are embarrassing, but the mode of relief merits serious consideration also. The principle of it is entirely new, and the extent of it not easily limited." Boyd, he says, is not in need, and Wilkinson is dangerous. "Cushing's situation is probably urgent, and his conduct strengthens his claims. But is not the foundation of them the same with those on which the actual collector of New London received and has retained his appointment? . . . It is true, his political conduct has been justly exceptionable, but it is not on that ground that his removal is required. Ellery [at Newport] . . . was a revolutionary patriot in high public trusts, and on that ground also has been retained . . . notwithstanding frequent charges of political misconduct. . . . I am disposed to take into fair consideration the

---

[1] Ravenel, *Lowndes*, 113.
[2] Madison to Dallas, April 14, 1815, Dallas, *Dallas*, 398; memoranda, *Ibid.* 414.
[3] Madison to Dallas, and Dallas to Madison, April 20, 1815, *Ibid.* 401.
[4] *Ibid.* 436.

mode proposed for rewarding or alleviating the cases to which it would apply; but I should be glad to learn, before it be adopted, some practicable rule for designating the officers to be displaced, and for selecting those to be provided for. If the deciding consideration be the wealth of the former and the poverty of the latter," the rule would not be popular. " These remarks do not exclude the resource in favor of meritorious and indigent officers, which may be found in special removals pointed out by legitimate causes." [1] General Cushing was appointed collector at New London; [2] how Huntington, the incumbent, was disposed of does not appear on the Senate journal. [3] The twenty-seven removals made by Madison [4] would seem to show that not many of these "indigent officers" could have been relieved in the way suggested; and the correspondence between Madison and Dallas would indicate that some reason, at least nominally valid, was required in all such cases. [5] The official record is not, however, entirely truthful, for pressure was sometimes brought to bear which caused officials to resign. On June 18, 1816, Dallas wrote to Madison that the removal of Mr. Du Plessis from the collectorship at New Orleans was asked for, but on general grounds. September 11 he told him that Beverly Chew was recommended for the place, but was insolvent. Madison answered, September 15, that as Du Plessis's accounts were satisfactory and Chew's financial situation was not the best, it would be well to delay, at least until Congress met. Eventually Du Plessis resigned and Chew was appointed. [6]

There is not much evidence that office sought the man under Madison. The death of an officer was looked on with regret, as entailing numberless applications, in deciding between which political quiet would seem to have been the effectual motive, so far as one can judge from Madison's rather vague statements. [7]

---

[1] Dallas, *Dallas*, 440.   [2] *Executive Journal*, iii. 20 (January 8, 1816).

[3] *Appleton's Cyclopædia* gives his death as two years later; he may have retired, or have been retired, for infirmity.

[4] Fish, in American Historical Association, *Report*, 1899, i. 71.

[5] Memoranda, March 14, 1816, Dallas, *Dallas*, 449.

[6] *Ibid.* 454, 473, 474; *Executive Journal*, iii. 72 (January 21, 1817).

[7] See Madison to Dallas, June 30, and Dallas to Madison, July 1, 1816, Dallas, *Dallas*, 456–457.

William Plummer was made successor to Gardner as loan officer
in New Hampshire, because he was recommended by his father,
the governor, and because he had planned a history of the War
of 1812 to counteract the Federalist publications.[1]   Henry
Wheaton was made judge advocate, because his "talents are
unquestionable, and it is desirable, on many accounts, to gratify
him;"[2] and Madison was very sure that the selection of a certain Albany appointee would be "more agreeable" to Albany,
and to the state in general, than that of any of his competitors.
He could not, however, escape the toils of state politics; and
there can be no doubt that the appointment of Dr. Leib to the
post-office at Philadelphia, by Granger, still postmaster-general,
and the subsequent removal of both of them, were due to political machinations in the faction-ridden state of Pennsylvania.[3]

The abuse of the patronage was a subject much discussed
during this period; but, so far as the national civil service was
concerned, it consisted rather in lack of vigilance in guarding
against favoritism and the influence of local faction, than in any
direct misuse for the purpose of party or personal advantage.
One practice was gaining ground, however, which was regarded
as distinctly dangerous.   It has been shown that, because of
their local knowledge, the advice of congressmen had from the
first been considered important; it is obvious that the congressmen themselves would be better known to the president than
any other citizens of the more distant states, and that he would,
therefore, often appoint them to office.   Jefferson gave places to
twenty, and Madison to twenty-nine.[4]   The dangers anticipated
from this custom led to the first reform movement.

In January, 1811, Nathaniel Macon introduced an amendment
to the constitution, by which it was provided that no senator
or representative should be appointed to any civil office or
"employment, under the authority of the United States, until
the expiration of the presidential term in which such person

---

[1] Dallas, *Dallas*, 456, 459, 460 ; Madison, *Letters and Other Writings*, ii. 607 ;
Executive Journal, iii. 72 (January 21, 1817).

[2] Memoranda, 1815, Dallas, *Dallas*, 414.

[3] J. Q. Adams, *Memoirs*, v. 481 ; *Niles's Register*, v. 414, vii. 320.

[4] *House Documents*, 19 Cong. 1 sess. ix. No. 164, p. 11.

shall have served as senator or representative." It has been seen that such a clause was proposed in the Constitutional Convention;[1] and the twenty years of experience had brought the danger more clearly before men's minds. Roger Sherman's idea, that modesty would prevent the presentation even of the name of a relative of a colleague, had been proved delusive. Josiah Quincy moved to amend Macon's amendment by adding, "and no person standing to any Senator or Representative in the relation of father, brother, or son, by blood or marriage, shall be appointed to any civil office under the United States, or shall receive any place, agency, contract, or emolument from or under any department or officer thereof," a suggestion which Mr. Wright sought to render ridiculous by further amending that every member be required to furnish a genealogical table. The amendments were rejected; the original suggestion received seventy-one votes against forty, but was thrown out, as this was not the two-thirds majority required for a constitutional amendment.[2]

As a reform measure this movement seems aimless and ineffective. It was truly pointed out that it would seriously hamper the president by removing from the list of eligibles those who were presumably the most able and with whom he was best acquainted. The key to the movement lies in the fact that the object was not to secure a more efficient civil service, but to guard against a political danger. Macon was a Republican of the old school, and, in the appointment of members of the legislature by the president, foresaw the destruction of that separation of powers which was so highly prized. Quincy condemned that "consolidation, which has grown and is strengthened under the influence of the office-distributing power, vested in the Executive. A consolidation perceptible to all, and which is the more fixed and inseparable, inasmuch as the cement is constituted by the strongest of all amalgams: that of the precious metals."[3]

[1] Lucy M. Salmon, *Appointing Power of the President* (American Historical Association, *Papers*, i. No. 5), 13; *Niles's Register*, xix. 193.

[2] For the whole discussion, see *Annals of Congress*, 11 Cong. 3 sess. 454, 840–854, 897–900, 904–905 ; Quincy, *Quincy*, 219–223.

[3] *Annals of Congress*, 11 Cong. 3 sess. 454, 841, 846.

In 1811 there was special reason for dreading this danger, because of the development of the congressional caucus for the nomination of candidates for the presidency, a device which seemed calculated to break down utterly the barriers which separated the departments of government, and to open a wide breach for corruption. In 1808 the caucus for the first time had been really influential in selecting the successful candidate. Opposition at once appeared;[1] and now in 1811, when a new election was approaching, Macon introduced his bill, though he disavowed the intention of attacking the caucus. An amendment to his amendment was introduced, extending the disqualification to any senator or representative "who shall have been such at the time of the election of any President."[2] Macon objected to this as too broad. He said that the caucus, at which it was aimed, should have no weight in the discussion, as it was unknown to the constitution, and hence could not be a subject of legislation. He would not dignify it by direct attack; but Quincy, who delivered the main speech in favor of the original amendment, was openly fighting the caucus. "The Constitution," he said, " prohibits the members of this and of the other branch of the Legislature from being Electors of the President of the United States. Yet what is done? The practice of late is so prevalent as to have grown almost into a sanctioned usage of party. Prior to the presidential term of four years, members of Congress having received the privileged ticket of admission assemble themselves in a sort of electoral college, on the floor of the Senate or of the House of Representatives. They select a candidate for the Presidency. To their voice, to their influence, he is indebted for his elevation. So long as this condition of things continues, what ordinary Executive will refuse to accommodate those who in so distinguished a manner have accommodated him? Is there a better reason in the world why a man should give you, Mr. Chairman, an office worth two or

[1] A pamphlet of 1808 said that, if the public could know Washington, "They would say with us, that of all the places on the continent none was so unfit as the seat of Government, for commencing the election. They would duly appreciate the volunteer, the forbidden services of the Representatives, they would duly *reward* their *services*" (*Address to the People of the American States who Choose Electors*).

[2] *Annals of Congress*, 11 Cong. 3 sess. 841.

three thousand dollars a year for which you are qualified, and
which he could give as well as not, than this, that you had been
greatly instrumental in giving him one worth five and twenty
thousand for which he was equally qualified? It is in vain to
conceal it. So long as the present condition of things continues,
it may reasonably be expected that there shall take place regularly between the President of the United States and a portion
of both Houses of Congress an interchange, strictly speaking, of
good offices." [1] When the time came for the caucus of 1812,
"Messrs. D. R. Williams, Cheves, and Lowndes from South
Carolina, and Macon of North Carolina, all Democrats, refused
to attend the . . . meeting of members of Congress to nominate
a President . . . on the ground that it was improper, inexpedient, indelicate, unconstitutional, and a monstrous usurpation of
the rights of the people."

This attack perhaps tended to make the executive a little
cautious. A Mr. Smythe of Virginia, who had voted for the
establishment of a new judicial district in that state, was proposed, at the close of his term as congressman, for the new
judgeship thus created. President Monroe refused to nominate
him, solely because such action seemed against the spirit,
though not against the letter, of the constitution. Nevertheless,
the appointment of congressmen continued, fostered by the fact
that they were such persistent applicants. In 1821 John Quincy
Adams said that one-half of the members of Congress were
seeking office, and that the other half wanted something for
their relatives. In the same year Niles stated that sixty members were applicants, and threatened to publish the names
of those who were successful; five senators and forty-five
representatives are said to have applied for one auditorship.[2]
From time to time congressmen were successful in obtaining
places ranging from an important diplomatic mission to a post-
office worth one hundred and fifty-five dollars a year.[3] This

[1] Quincy, *Quincy*, 222 ; *Niles's Register*, xxvi. 129.

[2] Ravenel, *Lowndes*, 111; *Niles's Register*, xx. 102, xxvi. 37, 129 ; Benton, *Thirty
Years' View*, i. 84 ; J. Q. Adams, *Memoirs*, v. 238.

[3] Noted in *Niles's Register* are the following appointments between 1812–1828: 3
ministers (xviii. 17, xxv. 229, xxvi. 16), 1 secretary of the legation (x. 125), 1 attorney (xxvii. 16), 1 fourth auditor (xxvi. 37), 2 receivers of public monies (xviii. 128),

appetite for office, far keener among congressmen than it is to-
day, was caused in part by the very small pay that they received
for their legislative services. The six dollars a day voted by
the first Congress was still the legal rate of compensation, and
when the fourteenth Congress changed this to fifteen hundred
dollars a year, the popular disapproval was shown by the defeat
of many of its members on that issue alone.[1] Clay had to retire
from the speakership to recoup his fortunes. To a friend who
was thinking of running for Congress he sent a rather dismal
picture of the monotony of the life and the expense involved :
after the first few months, he said, it retained the interest only
of the rival leaders.[2] It was not strange, then, that members
were eager to exchange their legislative for civil positions.

Thus fed, the agitation for a constitutional amendment similar
to that proposed by Macon continued active. Jackson declared
himself emphatically in favor of an amendment, and from 1820
to 1840 almost every session of Congress saw a bill introduced
to recommend one. The movement attained its greatest height
between 1820 and 1830, and was constantly connected with
attacks on the caucus. When the latter was superseded by the
convention, the issue became less important and the discussion
perfunctory. It was used as an election bogie ; many sincerely
reprobated the custom, but popular interest had subsided.[3]

When James Monroe became president, he seemed face to
face with the vision of universal good-will which Jefferson had
seen as through a glass darkly. Only thirty-four Federalist

1 collector (xvii. 223), 1 district judge (xviii. 240), and 2 deputy postmasters (xxxvi.
118, 161). The following is an official list of the totals for each administration to
April 25, 1826 : Washington, 10 ; J. Adams, 13 ; Jefferson, 25 ; Madison, 29 ; Monroe,
35 ; J. Q. Adams, 5 (*House Documents*, 19 Cong. 1 sess. ix. No. 164, pp. 11–12).
Niles affirms that Adams appointed to temporary positions numbers of congressmen
who had voted for him in the contest for the presidency. *Niles's Register*, xxxvi. 267.

1 Schurz, *Clay*, i. 138–140 ; *Niles's Register*, x. 415 ; Crawford to Gallatin, October 9, 1816, and March 12, 1817, Gallatin, *Writings*, ii. 11, 28.

2 Schurz, *Clay*, i. 202. Crawford thought that Clay's dissatisfaction was for political reasons. Crawford to Gallatin, April 23, 1817, Gallatin, *Writings*, ii. 35.

3 December 8, 1829, Richardson, *Messages and Papers of the Presidents*, ii. 448 ;
See Rufus King on Benton's bill to amend the constitutional method of choosing
president and vice-president, *Annals of Congress*, 18 Cong. 1 sess. 32, 355–375 ;
Ames, *Amendments to the Constitution*, 30–31. Amendments were proposed in 1793,
1808, 1810, 1818, and the last in 1850 ; 33 in all.

electors cast their votes against him; and the project of completing the affiliation of parties, by treating all citizens as alike worthy of the favors of the government, seemed feasible. Even before the election had actually taken place, urgent pressure was brought to induce Monroe to adopt such a policy. Andrew Jackson wrote to him, October 23, 1816, recommending Colonel William H. Drayton for the expected vacancy in the position of secretary of war. " I am told," he said, " before the war he was ranked with the Federalists, but the moment his country was threatened he abandoned private cares and a lucrative position for the tented field. Such acts as these speak louder than words. ' The tree is best known by its fruits,' and such a man as this, it matters not what he is called, will always act like a true American." In another letter, written November 12, before he had received a reply to the first, Jackson again recommended Drayton, and added: " Now is the time to exterminate the *monster* called party spirit. . . . Consult no party in your choice; pursue the dictates of that unerring judgment which has so long and so often benefited our country and rendered conspicuous its rulers. These are the sentiments of a friend. They are the feelings — if I know my own heart — of an undissembled patriot."

To these letters, Monroe replied, December 14, with a long dissertation setting forth the rise and growth of the Federalist party, and affirming his belief that government could be conducted without an opposition. He asserted that the administration should rest strongly on the Republican party, using toward the other a spirit of moderation, and evincing a desire to discriminate between its members and to bring the whole into the Republican fold as quickly as possible. He avoided, however, the expression of any opinion distinctly favoring the appointment of any Federalist to office. Cabinet officers, he thought, should certainly be " decided friends, who stood firm in the day of trial." Moreover, except in " great emergencies " and in case of " transcendent talents, the four heads of departments should represent the four great sections of the country." [1] In the last month of his administration he did appoint a Federalist

[1] Parton, *Jackson,* ii. 358-364.

to an important office, — George Izard, to be governor of Arkansas, — and told Adams that he regretted that he could not have done so oftener, but that he had gone as far as he could without forfeiting the confidence of his own supporters and thereby defeating the very object he had at heart.[1]

Monroe was not a man from whom we should expect innovations; and the rather abundant evidence that we possess in regard to the detailed working of his administration shows a careful adherence to the traditional methods of securing the names of candidates, and of judging between them. While this was undoubtedly the intention, it could not, by reason of changed circumstances, be followed in every particular. Though parties seemed dead, politics were not; and three opposing political leaders, three rival candidates for the succession, were members of the cabinet. Under such conditions it is natural that the heads of departments should have played a more prominent part in the distribution of the patronage than ever before or since. The president attempted to avoid friction by giving to each head complete control of his own department. Adams gives an account of the appointment of Solomon Van Rensselaer to the post-office at Albany. The news that Meigs, the postmaster-general, intended to appoint him got abroad, and objections were made ; whereupon the case was referred to the president. Crawford and Wirt thought that Meigs should have assumed full responsibility, but that, as the case was now before the president, the latter must act on it, or ground his refusal upon the general principle that he would never interfere in such appointments. Adams differed with them on both points. In the end the president refused to interfere, although he apparently had no high idea of Van Rensselaer.[2] Crawford complained that his appointing power was sometimes interfered with. He wrote to Gallatin that the Florida appointments, even those " connected with my own Department have been made without regard to my wishes, or rather without ascertaining what they were "; and said he surmised that the rumor that

---

[1] J. Q. Adams, *Memoirs*, iii. 494.

[2] *Ibid.* v. 479–482, 484; Monroe to Madison, February 25, and to Jefferson, June 7, 1813, Monroe, *Writings*, v. 247, 261.

he had influenced the Senate to reject certain military appointments had "soured" Monroe, who favored Calhoun in these new selections.[1] These appointments were doubtless of the presidential class, and were decided upon in cabinet meeting when Crawford happened to be absent. No instance appears where a strictly departmental office was interfered with.

When the question of offices came before the cabinet, the president endeavored to hold an even hand. At one time he announced that he was thinking of Mr. Southard for the vacant post of secretary of the navy; he said that Southard was a good man and that his state had never had a cabinet officer, but added that in view of the rivalry between the members of the cabinet, he would not make the nomination if any of them objected. This seems eminently fair, and that Monroe's intentions were good is beyond question; but Adams, who tells the story, adds that Southard was a Calhoun man.[2] It was, in fact, an impossible task to suit all three of these ambitious men; and the cabinet, with its rivalries, so graphically revealed in Adams's diary and the contemporaneous letters of Crawford and Calhoun, must have been a disagreeable body during the "era of good feeling."

The relations between the cabinet and the Senate during the administration are illustrated by a further study of the case of Solomon Van Rensselaer. On January 3, 1822, Rufus King and Martin Van Buren, the New York senators, wrote to Postmaster-general Meigs that they heard that a change was necessary in the Albany post-office, and desired "a fit and full opportunity for all concerned to make their representations" to him on that subject. He replied that the name of General Van Rensselaer had been presented and was before the president for consideration, and that a speedy appointment was desirable; and he continued to resist all attempts to delay action. It was a delicate affair, for the general was recommended by twenty-two representatives from New York belonging to both parties. Meigs threw the responsibility on Monroe, who, as has been seen, refused to shoulder it. King dropped out of the contro-

---

[1] May 13 and June 26, 1822, Gallatin, *Writings*, ii. 242, 249.
[2] J. Q. Adams, *Memoirs*, vi. 174.

versy; but Van Buren induced many of the representatives who had signed for Van Rensselaer to change sides, and on January 7, 1822, a long letter with many signatures was sent to Meigs, summing up the views of the opposition. They wanted delay; they wanted to consult the citizens of Albany; they recommended Mr. Lansing, a destitute patriot of the Revolution; they accused Van Rensselaer of being a violent partisan; but they rested their case mainly on the question, "Lansing's capacity and integrity are at least equal to Van Rensselaer's; should not preference be given him because he is a Republican?" There is evidence that, when this letter was written, the appointment was known to have been already made, but that the letter was sent to record their opinion that appointments should in the future be confined to Republicans. The administration was able in this instance to resist pressure and appoint the man of its choice.[1] It should, of course, be observed that the appointment, as it was in the post-office department, did not require the confirmation of the Senate; if it had, it might have met with more difficulty.

In 1820 a startling attack was made on the conduct of the civil service. DeWitt Clinton, in what is known as the "green-bag" message to the legislature of New York, and in a subsequent message of January 17, 1821, charged that the officers of the general government were an "organized and disciplined corps." Speaking of one of them, he said, "When the situation, connexion, education, and political principles of this officer of the United States are considered, there can be no doubt but that he had previously ascertained the sense of his political superiors, and that he was instructed to act accordingly." He accused Adams of partiality in selecting the newspapers which were to publish the laws, and the postmaster-general of making nine removals for factional reasons. A committee was appointed to investigate, or rather, as the lower house was hostile to the governor, to disprove these charges. The report shows

[1] The material for the above statements is from letters in an article called "A Political Coincidence," by A. H. Joline, in the *Collector*, vi. 39–40. See also J. Q. Adams, *Memoirs*, v. 479–482, 484, vi. 495; *Niles's Register*, xxxvi. 161; *Appleton's Cyclopædia of American Biography*, an article, "Solomon van Rensselaer."

that a certain amount of political activity on the part of the government officials was considered proper; and when the question is thus one purely of degree, we certainly cannot presume to pass judgment at this distance of time. The removal of the postmasters is shown to have been at the request of the representatives from their respective districts, the presumption being that, in most cases, the government would not look behind the reports. In at least one case the cause for dismissal was stated to be that the incumbent had lost the confidence of the people, which is another way of saying that he was politically opposed to the person who asked for the change. Several of these removals were secured by Mr. Van Buren on the ground that the incumbents were improperly using their influence against him by tampering with the circulation of certain newspapers.[1]

The general impression left by a study of the papers relating to these charges is that the national offices in New York were being drawn into the whirlpool of state politics. That this was chiefly the work of state politicians, rather than of the national administration, seems clear. Monroe and William Wirt tried to be, and actually were, above faction. Adams, Calhoun, and Clay took a lively interest in New York politics, and were quick to believe in the vices of their enemies and the virtues of their friends; but their letters show little real understanding of local conditions — from a political point of view they are decidedly amateurish.[2]

The case of William H. Crawford, secretary of the treasury, demands more detailed consideration. About no man of equal prominence in American history do we know so little; and the most definite contemporary testimony in regard to his political character is that given by his rival, John Quincy Adams, who was at the time tremblingly eager for the presidency and

[1] Hammond, *Political Parties in New York*, i. 552–564; see Van Buren to Meigs, April 4, 1820, in the pamphlet, *The Van Buren Platform* (1848), 7. For the general subject, see *Niles's Register*, xix. 376–380; xx. 66–72, 97.

[2] J. Q. Adams, *Memoirs;* Clay, *Private Correspondence;* Gallatin, *Writings* (letters of Crawford); *Calhoun Correspondence* (American Historical Association, *Reports*, 1899, ii.). For Calhoun, see also *Edwards Papers* (Chicago Historical Society, *Collections*, iii.); and Edwards, *Illinois.*

nervously imputing to others motives of which he knew himself incapable. Adams certainly thought that Crawford was using the influence of his position to build up a faction, and he was not alone in that opinion;[1] but Crawford believed somewhat the same thing of Adams.[2] In tone, however, they are quite different: Adams is shocked, and seems to say, "God, I thank Thee, that I am not as other men are"; Crawford speaks of such action on Adams's part, as a matter of course, a difficulty to be guarded against, and one might readily suspect Crawford himself of adopting the tactics he so easily takes for granted in the case of his rival.

The special charge against Crawford is that he obtained, for unworthy purposes, the passage of the famous Four Years' Law. This act was passed in 1820. It established a fixed term of four years, in place of the previous tenure at the pleasure of the president, for district attorneys, collectors of customs, naval officers, and for surveyors of customs, money agents, receivers of public money for lands, registers of land offices, paymasters in the army, the apothecary-general, his assistant, and the commissary-general of purchases.[3] It was introduced into the Senate by Mahlon Dickerson of New Jersey, but Adams says that Crawford acknowledged the authorship. Its ostensible object was to compel the regular submission of accounts; but according to Adams its real purpose was to elect Crawford president by turning all office-holders, their families and friends, and "five or ten times an equal number of ravenous office-seekers," to his support. This charge was not made until 1828, and Adams then added that the sickness of Crawford during the last eighteen months of Monroe's administration prevented his active use of the weapon he had forged.[4] Fortunately we have Crawford's own statement of the purpose of the bill, in a letter of June 12, 1820, evidently written to the

---

[1] J. Q. Adams, *Memoirs*, v. 483, vi. 387.

[2] Crawford to Gallatin, October 27, 1817, Gallatin, *Writings*, ii. 55.

[3] *Statutes at Large*, iii. 182. The commissions were to fall in from time to time, beginning in September, 1821, and allowing every one in office to complete four years of service.

[4] *Annals of Congress*, 16 Cong. 1 sess. 26 (December 16, 1819); J. Q. Adams, *Memoirs*, vii. 424–425.

president. He said that he had told inquirers that reappointment would take place — when there were no reasonable grounds of dissatisfaction — unless some one was found with stronger claims than the incumbent; and that one advantage of the new system lay in the possibility of discontinuing unsatisfactory public servants without putting any stain upon their characters.[1] The dissimilarity of these two statements demands examination.

Little is to be gleamed from the contemporaneous discussion. The debate in Congress, at least the report of it, is barren ; and there was practically no public comment. Jefferson and Madison, however, corresponded rather vigorously on the subject. About this time Tench Coxe applied to both of them for their influence in securing a post. Jefferson, in forwarding Coxe's letter to Madison, said : "This is a sample of the effects we may expect from the late mischievous law vacating every four years nearly all the executive offices of the government. It saps the constitutional and salutary functions of the president, and introduces a principle of intrigue and corruption, which will soon leaven the mass, not only of Senators, but of citizens. It is more baneful than the attempt . . . to make all officers irremovable but with the consent of the Senate"; it puts all appointments under their control every four years, and "will keep in constant excitement all the hungry cormorants for office." Madison replied, agreeing with Jefferson and claiming that the law was unconstitutional. He wrote also to Monroe in a similar strain, deprecating particularly the increase in the power of the Senate ; and Adams says that Monroe regretted that he had signed the bill, and resolved to renominate the incumbent in every instance in which there was no misconduct.[2] This criticism, however, only slightly touches the question of the purpose of the bill ; no reflections were cast on Crawford, who was, in fact, the special representative of the old-fashioned Republicans, and a particular friend of Macon,

---

[1] Fragment of a manuscript letter from the Bureau of Rolls, Washington, loaned to the author by Dr. U. B. Phillips.

[2] Jefferson, *Writings* (Ford ed.), x. 168–169 ; Madison, *Letters and Other Writings*, iii. 196, 200 ; J. Q. Adams, *Memoirs*, vii. 424.

the watch-dog of the patronage. Madison feared an encroachment on the appointing power of the president, and Jefferson apprehended corruption in general.

The question now arises, Did the bill have any legitimate object? Certainly, in 1820, some method of securing more regular accounts might have seemed advisable. A special report presented at this time by Crawford showed many defalcations; some dating from Washington's administration, and amounting in all to $929,390 uncovered by bonds. This is not surprisingly bad considering the lax business methods of the country, nor yet is it strikingly good.[1] The military accounts showed a deficit of about a million dollars, part of which, it was supposed, could be accounted for. Although there was some general distrust of the integrity of the public service, bills to secure a greater accountability did not pass readily;[2] Crawford refused to accept the secretaryship of the treasury until one that he then prepared had been adopted.[3]

Was this bill, then, calculated to secure a greater sense of responsibility? It was certainly a crude method, one quite inapplicable now; but in a service scattered as was that of 1820, when means of communication were so slow and unreliable, and the individual officer had so large a degree of independence, the prospect of a thorough overhauling at definite periods might well have served as a spur to accuracy and promptness.[4] It would also enable the administration to freshen and invigorate the service by dropping the old and incapable without fixing upon their characters the stain of removal. An especially significant fact, which will be developed at length in the next chapter, is that this practice of limiting the term of office was very common in the states at this time, and was found in both Georgia and South Carolina — states with which Crawford was

---

[1] *Senate Documents,* 16 Cong. 1 sess. ii. No. 89. This total is obtained by a comparison and combination of the figures for the several departments of the civil service.

[2] *Annals of Congress,* 18 Cong. 1 sess. 236–241 ; *National Intelligencer,* May 20, 1820.

[3] *Statutes at Large,* 14 Cong. 2 sess. ch. 45 ; Crawford to Gallatin, March 12, 1817, Gallatin, *Writings,* ii. 24–25.

[4] *Niles's Register,* xxii. 99.

most familiar and in which the limited tenure did not lead to actual rotation in office.

It is evident that the law would serve equally well as an incentive to continued political activity, if that was likely to be of account in the day of reckoning, and that it was as aptly framed for the easy dropping of political rivals as for ridding the service of decrepit members. Who were the persons that Crawford mentioned as having stronger claims upon the nation than the incumbents? Were they simply necessitous military officers, such as secured recognition from Madison? were they prominent Republicans? or were they the political supporters of William H. Crawford? It is impossible to answer fully all the questions thus suggested, but some light may be thrown upon them. James A. Hamilton wrote to Crawford, February 25, 1823, that he had just had an interview with Governor Gibbs of Rhode Island to discover the cause of the latter's dissatisfaction with Crawford. Gibbs said that it was based on Crawford's refusal to make certain removals in the customs service of that state, and added that this small matter was likely to turn Rhode Island to Clay in the coming contest. Hamilton argued that it was improper to remove subordinate officials merely because of their political opinion; whereupon Governor Gibbs replied that one of the men complained of not only held incorrect political views, but used the influence of his position to induce others to support them.[1] The man thus mentioned still retained his position in 1825; but part of his duties had been taken from him, and his emoluments had been reduced by a half.[2]

This case is certainly not conclusive as to Crawford's methods of dealing with the patronage; hence resort must be had to indirect evidence. Would the law of 1820 work advantageously to Crawford? Not all the offices affected by it fell within his department, and, as he believed that his rivals were intriguing against him, he might well have feared lest it prove a boome-

[1] From a manuscript letter in possession of Miss F. Crawford of Dunbar, Mississippi, lent by Dr. U. B. Phillips.

[2] From a comparison of the Blue Books of 1823 and 1825. Cogswell, the name mentioned by Hamilton, is not found in either; but Hamilton must have mistaken the name. Doubtless the man referred to was Coggeshall, weigher and gauger at Newport.

rang. To be sure, the largest share fell to him; but as all presidential appointments were discussed in cabinet meeting, how could he expect to carry on an extensive campaign of personal aggrandizement under the noses of two avowed rivals and President Monroe? As a matter of fact, many of the men appointed to such positions under the secretary of the treasury favored the election of Calhoun.[1] Crawford might reap some slight profit from the law, in that he had a high probability of success; and those who believed that he might be the next president would be nerved to more active service, while those who did not so believe would not support him under any circumstances. Possibly, too, he might have intended thus to bind the New York politicians to him, as his supporters there were men who practised the spoils system in their own state and afterward helped to introduce it into national politics. They would seem, however, for some time after the passage of this act, to have made no real agreement to support him. No definite conclusion seems safe, except that serious doubt is thrown on Adams's statement as to the purpose of the bill. It is a safe conjecture that Crawford expected it to be of value in the conduct of public business, particularly because it increased the flexibility of the service to the profit both of the nation and of the Republican party; that he intended to transform it into an instrument to secure his election and to introduce the spoils system seems distinctly improbable.

As the election of 1824 approached, and the closeness of the contest became more and more apparent, the supporters of the several candidates made efforts to attract the Federalist vote, which, though small, might prove decisive. In the interest of Jackson, his correspondence with Monroe advocating the appointment of Federalists was brought to light and published.[2] The enemies of John Quincy Adams made public his father's correspondence with Mr. Cunningham, filled with invectives

---

[1] See Crawford's complaint about the Florida appointments (above, p. 62). Also a letter from James Latham to Edwards, November 12, 1823, "Colo. Cox, Mr. Enos [who had just been appointed land officer, after a close contest], and Maj'r Iles has purchased Springfield and have altered the name to Calhoun with the general satisfaction of the people" (*Edwards Papers*, 211).

[2] Parton, *Jackson*, ii. 359.

against the Essex junto.[1] Both of these publications had great effect; and when the election by the House of Representatives drew near, there were persistent reports that Adams would proscribe his father's enemies. Under these circumstances, Mr. Warfield of Maryland wrote to Webster that, as the vote of that state might rest with him, he desired certain information with regard to Adams's attitude on the subject.[2]

Webster replied that his own vote would be for Adams, and that this would not be the case did he "not believe that he [Adams] would administer the government on liberal principles, not excluding Federalists, as such, from his regard"; he deprecated the desire to see any particular man in office, and the "portioning" of offices among men of "different denominations," but thought it "just and reasonable to be expected" that "by some one clear and distinct case, it may be shown that the distinction above alluded to does not operate as cause of exclusion. Some such case will doubtless present itself, and may be embraced, probably, *in proper time and manner.* . . . It will then be understood that the field is open." He added a note to the effect that he wrote this letter on his own responsibility, but before sending it showed the draft to Adams, who approved but was afraid that it might seem to refer to a cabinet appointment, a difficulty which Webster obviated by underlining it as above. Adams says that he told Webster that Clay or Crawford would probably pursue the same course as he.[3] On February 16, Webster wrote to his brother: "If there is any faith in man, we shall have a liberal administration. I think it not unlikely that if it were pressed, there might be a Federalist in the cabinet, but our friends are not at all satisfied that such a measure would be discreet. . . .

---

[1] *Correspondence between the Hon. John Adams . . . and . . . William Cunningham* (Boston, 1823).

[2] February 3, 1825, Webster, *Private Correspondence*, i. 377.

[3] February 5, 1825, *Ibid.* 378–380 ; J. Q. Adams, *Memoirs*, vi. 492–493, vii. 539. In regard to Crawford, Adams was doubtless mistaken, as Gallatin, his intimate friend and candidate for the vice-presidency, had written, just after the publication of the Monroe-Jackson letters, strongly disapproving the doctrine " of paying no regard to party in the selection of the great offices of government " (May 22, 1824, Gallatin, *Writings*, ii. 259).

We may be deceived, but if we are, it will be a gross decep-
tion." The "clear and distinct case" was the appointment
of Rufus King as minister to Great Britain.[1] In 1827 Webster
declared himself satisfied that Adams was fairly living up to
the policy thus outlined. The latter could not go as far as
he wished, however, because of the opposition of the rank and
file of his own party; and he often lamented the fact that he
could not appoint more Federalists, as they were usually the
best men presented for the various vacancies.[2]

President Adams carried political tolerance to an extreme,
even offering to continue Crawford in the cabinet. The latter
had the good sense to decline; but Postmaster-general McLean
was retained throughout the administration, in spite of Adams's
firm belief that the whole patronage of that department was
being used to promote the interests of Jackson. The retention
of McLean under these circumstances was hardly consonant
with the president's determination that offensive partisanship,
whether for or against the administration, should be sufficient
cause for removal; and as only twelve removals altogether
were made during his term, it is quite evident that this determination was not carried out.[3] Adams abhorred the task of
selecting officials; and it is not surprising to find him, when
first elected, summarily closing an interview with certain senators
who urged him not to renominate those whose terms were about
to expire under the new Four Years' Law, but to initiate "a
principle of change or rotation in office." The purity of his
conduct of the civil service is illustrated by the prominence
given to the charge that he interfered with the appointment
of a postmaster.[4]

[1] Webster, *Private Correspondence*, i. 381 ; J. Q. Adams, *Memoirs*, vi. 523.

[2] Webster, *Private Correspondence*, i. 415, 417, 421. Rufus King was sent as
minister to England, and afterward the post was offered to Webster ; Van Tyne,
Webster, 135–136. In March, 1827, Webster recommended that, when the district
judge for Pennsylvania should die, Mr. Hopkinson be appointed to placate the Federalists (*Ibid.* 122–124). December 11, 1828, Hopkinson was nominated (*Executive
Journal*, iii. 621); J. Q. Adams, *Memoirs*, vii. 207.

[3] *Ibid.* vi. 508; vii. 277, 281 ; viii. 163, x. 447. See also Schurz, *Clay*, i. 259–
261, 281 ; Fish, in American Historical Association, *Reports*, 1899, i. 73.

[4] J. Q. Adams, *Memoirs*, vi. 514, 520–521 ; *Daily National Journal*, March 24,
1829.

The ferret eyes of the opposition press were a little better re-warded in the case of Henry Clay. Clay advised the president, probably wisely, to remove the most active of his opponents among the office-holders; and himself struck a few newspapers from the list of those paid for printing the laws. The number, however, was very small: a comparison of the last list under Monroe with the first under Adams shows, out of seventy-five papers, ten changes, four being a usual number,[1] and only one was of importance. In the District of Columbia the printing was taken from Gales and Seaton, publishers of the *National Intelligencer*, and given to Peter Force, who was editing the *National Journal*. The reason for this change was doubtless political, as the *Intelligencer* had supported Crawford; but if such a change is ever justifiable, it was in this instance. The printing in the District of Columbia gave a certain prestige to the paper receiving it, which thus became to a certain extent an official organ; it was therefore expedient that this paper should be in hearty sympathy with the administration. That Clay did not exclude opponents in general is seen by the fact that one of the papers he selected was the *Jackson Republican* of Nashville; he seems, indeed, to have continued the custom of giving the printing to at least one opposition paper in every state.[2]

While the administration gave its enemies but slight basis for criticism, the lack of sympathy between Congress and the executive afforded an excellent opportunity to those who wished to effect a reform in the civil service. Macon, who had never lost sight of the matter since his futile attempt in 1811, once more, in 1826, introduced the subject; but, as his health was poor, Thomas H. Benton was made chairman of the committee appointed to consider it, and was ably assisted by Judge White of Tennessee, who was to be conspicuous in a similar movement ten years later.[3] The report of this committee shows a much broader comprehension of the problem than is found in any of the speeches of fifteen years before, and a vastly more

[1] *Senate Documents*, 19 Cong. 1 sess. iv. No. 88, pp. 30–45, 149.

[2] J. Q. Adams, *Memoirs*, vi. 50, 399; Jefferson, *Writings* (Washington ed.), ix. 206; Quincy, *J. Q. Adams*, 193.

[3] Benton, *Thirty Years' View*, i. 80–82.

ambitious attempt to handle it. Accompanying the report were documents showing the value of each office under the government, and indicating to whom the appointment belonged. From these figures, and from predictions as to the future, which have proved not extravagant, the committee deduced the proposition that the appointing power of the president should be reduced.[1]

With this general object in view, six bills were introduced. The first was directed against the control of the press; the number of papers in the several states to which the printing of the laws should be assigned was to be limited to one-half the number of representatives from each state. The essential point of this proposition lay in the provision that these papers were to be selected by the congressional delegation from each state, a majority ruling; if they neglected to make the selection, the secretary of state might do it as before. It is significant that the committee did not show itself eager to reduce the amount of the patronage, but only to shift the control: the first bill would allow, in some states, a considerable increase of subsidized newspapers, three being the customary number. By other bills the president was required to state the cause of each removal of a presidential officer; the appointment of postmasters receiving compensation above a fixed amount was to be subject to the advice and consent of the Senate; and a blow was struck at the executive by the provision that military and naval commissions should read "during good behavior" instead of "at pleasure." The Four Years' Bill was to be repealed, and in its place was to be substituted a regulation that collectors and disbursers of the public revenues should submit their accounts to Congress once in four years, on penalty of losing their commissions.

This report is certainly not without merit. The repeal of the Four Years' Law was highly desirable, and there was certainly no good reason why the larger post-offices should remain outside the list subject to confirmation while the collectorships and naval offices were on it. It is evident that the ultimate object of the reformers was still not so much to improve the service

[1] *Senate Documents,* 19 Cong. 1 sess. iv. No. 88, pp. 1–12.

as to reduce the power of the president, which they rightly judged was liable to great extension. Their method, however, was different from that advocated by Quincy. In 1811 the functions of the president were respected ; the aim then was to reduce his power to control Congress : now the design was to divide the patronage between the executive and legislative departments. This was the first distinctly aggressive act on the part of the Senate in the great struggle between that body and the president for the control of the patronage. There had been friction before : [1] the Four Years' Law Madison believed to be a usurpation on the part of the Senate. In the first Congress the claims of the Senate had been advocated. Now for the first time, however, was presented a well-considered programme of encroachment. The bills reported by this committee were tabled by Macon himself, as he was too feeble to conduct the debate necessary before they could be adopted ; [2] but they were not lost sight of. They remained a tangible threat held over the head of any president who should fail to recognize the prerogatives of the Senate.

During no administration before 1828 was there so much contemporary criticism of the civil service as in that of John Quincy Adams, and none has received more praise from posterity. Part of the praise is doubtless due to the fact that Adams was the last of the presidents sometimes called " statesmen" in rather invidious distinction from the "politicians " who succeeded ; most of the criticism is explained by the conditions of the time, which will be discussed in the next chapter. A detailed study of actual conditions shows that there was some ground for both.

The efficiency of government service cannot be expected long to maintain a standard much higher than that of the community in which it works. Principles of business promptness and responsibility were not highly developed in the United States during the first fifty years of its existence, and the common belief that the administration of the government before 1828

---

[1] In Washington's, Adams's, and Madison's administrations, above, pp. 22, 23, 53. See also *Niles's Register*, v. 276; Gallatin, *Writings*, ii. 242.

[2] Benton, *Abridgment of Debates*, viii. 533–540, 560.

attained a level of efficiency which it has since sought in vain to recover, seems to be unfounded. Yet of the central offices it was to some extent true ; one able, honest man succeeded another in the chief positions of state, and by many years of unbroken service was enabled to master fully the details of his duties. It was impossible, however, to find men of exceptional character for all the minor and local offices. The annual reports of the comptroller of the treasury, and occasional special reports, as that of Crawford in 1820, bring to light a record far from brilliant. Defalcations are shown, beginning with the time of Washington, and amounting in 1820 to $927,390 in the civil service and to about the same in the military ; for these, causes are assigned varying from the dishonesty of a trusted clerk to the absconding of the officer himself to the West Indies. It is evident that even the " Fathers " could not wrench the government entirely away from its environment. Under Adams the service was probably more honest than it had been at any time since the War of 1812, as it was able to stand the fiery test of investigation by the Jackson leaders and to reveal only one defaulter ; but there was enough irregularity to furnish the small spark that alone was necessary to raise a great smoke of accusation.[1]

Emphasis must again be laid on the fact that honesty and efficiency are not entirely synonymous, and that the latter is not so easily measured as the first. That there were active, able men in office under Adams is evinced by the careers of some of them after they were turned out by Jackson ;[2] but it is probable that there was also a certain amount of dead timber. Although Jefferson was the only president as yet to abuse the removing power, none of the others seem to have used it with proper vigor. The neglect to remove officers who were dragging through long sicknesses sure to end in death is certainly to be

---

[1] *Niles's Register*, i. 320–321, xvi. 71, xvii. 426, xxii. 251, xxxvi. 238, 298, 309, 315, 322, 358, 373, 384, 421, xxxvii. 399, xxxii. 5 ; *National Intelligencer*, May 20, 1820.

[2] One was appointed to office by the governor of Virginia (*Niles's Register*, xl. 345) ; another received a service of plate from the merchants of the port for which he was collector — a dubious compliment (xxxviii. 292) ; others obtained elective offices (xxxvii. 275, xxxix. 156).

condoned;[1] but the continuance of this practice gave strength to the popular impression that officials were beginning to feel a property in office. Less excusable was the failure to prune the service of superfluous officers, of which there was at least one well authenticated case, — that of the Norfolk custom-house, where, with a constantly diminishing revenue, the full staff was retained from the days when its trade had promised to make it the peer of any port in the country.[2] The retention of men whose usefulness had passed was due to the fact that it was inhumane to discharge them without adequate provision, which, in a country as democratic as the United States was at the time, could not be given except in the form of salary. Thus the civil service became a pension fund for its disabled members. This policy would not have been so disastrous if the notion had not extended. Instances have been related already where civil posts were bestowed to reward distinguished success in war or politics ; and they might be multiplied, with many a contemporary note of commendation.[3] Thus the idea was gaining ground, among the most intelligent classes too, that past service rather than future efficiency should be the primary reason for appointment.

From the political point of view, the question of efficiency was of little moment ; there were few complaints of the manner in which the service was conducted,[4] and some of its very best features contributed most to its unpopularity. During the period of twenty-eight years, from 1801 to 1829, there was something like a system of promotion : consuls were transferred to more and more important ports, to become in time, perhaps, chargés d'affaires ; naval officers became collectors of customs, and district attorneys, judges.[5] Commendable as this practice was,

---

[1] *Niles's Register*, xxvi. 16 ; *Senate Documents*, 16 Cong. 1 sess. ii. No. 89.

[2] *Senate Documents*, 19 Cong. 1 sess. iv. No. 88, p. 9 ; *American Historical Review*, ii. 247.

[3] *Niles's Register*, v. 207, xiii. 160, xvii. 428, xxvi. 16 ; Madison to Monroe, November 19, 1820, Madison, *Letters and Other Writings*, iii. 187–188.

[4] *The National Republican and Ohio Political Register*, October 28, November 4, December 6, 1825, contains a few such complaints.

[5] Judicial promotions are mentioned in *Niles's Register*, xxvii. 32, 304 ; and in Coleman, *Chittenden*, 60–76 ; consular, in *Niles's Register*, xxix. 192, xxxiii. 208, 322 (double promotion), and in *Executive Journal*, i. 121 ; customs service, in *Niles's*

it did foster in the service a bureaucratic feeling, and in the public an apprehension lest government officers should consider themselves a class. An examination of the various Blue Books shows, moreover, that sons were often appointed to succeed fathers, which increased the disapprobation. A bureaucracy is always aristocratic ; [1] and this tendency was strengthened by the custom, established by Washington and continued in general by his successors, of appointing citizens rather prominent in their communities. Men originally of standing, holding life offices, and with the hope of placing their sons somewhere in the national service, are not likely to be popular in the heat of a democratic revolution ; and when the people voted in 1828 that John Quincy Adams should leave office, they undoubtedly intended to vote that most of the civil servants should go with him.

Register, xxxii. 75 ; miscellaneous, *Ibid.* xvi. 50, xxviii. 44, and in *Jackson Gazette*, June 28, 1828.

[1] See, for instance, McDuffie's speech, September 2, 1826 ; *Niles's Register*, xxxi. 124.

CHAPTER IV.

GENESIS OF THE SPOILS SYSTEM.

1775–1828.

THUS far the national civil service alone has been considered; but it is no longer possible to ignore the states, inasmuch as many national officers were appointed from the states to act in the states, and much of the service was thus affected by local political ideals. It has been seen that members of Congress possessed great influence over appointments. Many members chosen in New York and Pennsylvania owed their election to a skilful abuse of the patronage at home, and few abandoned their arts at the threshold of the capital. Thus it happened that, while the main fountain remained fairly pure, the stream of the patronage was mudded by the soil through which it flowed. It is to the states, too, that we must look for prophecies of the future; for nearly all our great national political movements have grown slowly and unevenly, appearing first in one state, then in another, and remaining for many years local in their manifestation.

Slowly but persistently there were found developing in the states, during the period we have been studying, two tendencies that burst suddenly and violently into national politics: first, the custom of using the public offices openly and continuously as ammunition in party warfare; second, the evolution of the idea of rotation in office. These together constituted the spoils system. It has not seemed expedient to treat at length the history of every state, or to study transitory tendencies or inchoate theories in such states as are taken up; attention will be confined to those states and those phases of state history which are typical and suggestive.

Rotation in office is said to have been an old Dutch custom, brought over to New Amsterdam and continued in New York.[1] It is to be found also in colonial New England;[2] but perhaps the most significant instance of its early use in America was its incorporation by William Penn in the Pennsylvania " Frame of government" of 1682, which provided that no councillor should hold his office for more than three years continuously, being then obliged to retire for one year, " that all may be fitted for government and have experience of the care and burden of it."[3] This, then, was what the colonists ordinarily meant by rotation ; it was to be applied to the lawmakers, and its objects were to educate the people and equalize the burdens of office-holding. With the quickening of political life, office ceased to be a burden ; but the notion that it was a means of education persisted, and was welcomed by the democratic sentiment of the Revolution.

Although the " frame of government " had been discontinued in 1696, this particular provision was revived in the radical constitution devised for Pennsylvania in 1776. A similar regulation was adopted by the neighboring state of Maryland with regard to the delegates to Congress. New Hampshire followed Maryland's example,[4] and this restriction was finally incorporated in the Articles of Confederation. In the Philadelphia convention of 1787 a debate arose over a proposition to apply rotation to the office of senator. Doubtless the unfavorable experience of the Confederation had much to do with the defeat of the proposal; but the persistence with which it was urged is evinced by the fact that it is found among the amendments to the constitution proposed by various state conventions.[5]

[1] A. E. McKinley, *Transition from Dutch to English Rule in New York*, in *American Historical Review*, vi. 712.

[2] In the New England Confederation of 1643, and many other instances.

[3] Poore, *Charters and Constitutions*, ii. 1520.

[4] *Ibid.* ii. 821, 1291, 1531, 1544.

[5] Mrs. Catharine Macaulay Graham to Washington, June, 1790, " It is true, that, in that sketch of a democratical government, I endeavoured to keep out corruption by enforcing a general rotation ; but I must acknowledge to you, that the corruptions, which have crept into our legislature since the revolution, with the wise caution used by the French patriots in the rules to which they have subjected their National Assembly, have led me to alter my opinion " (Washington, *Writings* (Sparks ed.),

The weakness of the argument that rotation would educate the public in the business of government was brought out by Pelatiah Webster, who said that, instead of making many men experienced in affairs, it made " many jacks at all trades, but good at none." The idea of its educational value, however, was not dropped, but was transmogrified. Elbridge Gerry said of rotation that it " keeps the mind of man in equilibrio, and teaches him the feelings of the governed, and better qualifies him to govern in his turn." This version of the benefits of rotation, that it was intended to educate the office-holder in the virtues of the people, grew in popularity during the first quarter of the nineteenth century, when it was not supposed that the people needed instruction in the arts of government.[1]

Education was not, however, the only motive for the adoption of rotation during the revolutionary period. The Massachusetts constitution of 1780 provided, " In order that the people may not suffer from the long continuance in place of any Justice of the Peace, who shall fail of discharging the important duties of his office with ability or fidelity, all commissions of Justices of the Peace shall expire and become void, in the term of seven years." The New Hampshire constitution of 1784 gave them tenure for five years instead of during " good behavior," " in order that the people may not be oppressed." Elbridge Gerry had this conception also in mind, for he spoke of the practice as a " check to the overbearing insolence of office." [2]

This new theory led to an extension of rotation from legislative to executive offices, and in this form it continued to gain ground until 1830. By that date, fifteen states had some such regulation in regard to the office of governor; that is, he should have a definite term, could serve a definite number of terms, and then, either forever, or for some fixed period, could not serve again. Nineteen states had similar regulations in their con-

x. 71, note); Elliot, *Debates,* ii. 34; *Federalist* (Ford ed.), 644. New York, Virginia, and North Carolina wished to apply it to the presidency.

[1] Pelatiah Webster, *Political Essays,* 205; Ford, *Pamphlets on the Constitutions,* 11; *Niles's Register,* xxiii. 162, xxvii. 216.

[2] Poore, *Charters and Constitutions,* ii. 1290; Ford, *Pamphlets on the Constitutions,* p. 11, § 9.

stitutions in regard to some offices, and included in this number were nearly all the states that had new constitutions.   The
states differ interestingly in details.   Even conservative Massachusetts distrusted the officer in charge of the public funds,
and Maine followed her example in 1820 by providing that the
treasurer should not hold continuously.   Pennsylvania and
the states that copied her contented themselves with restricting
the eligibility of the chief executive, and did not see fit to apply
rotation where it might have proved a more practical safeguard.

In eleven states the office of sheriff or marshal was made
rotative, a fact which is significant because of the light it
throws on an otherwise anomalous provision in one of the
laws for the organization of the national government.   Of all
the officers provided for by the great administrative acts of the
first Congress, the marshals alone were to serve a fixed term ;
all the others, even the district attorneys, created by the same
act, were to serve during the pleasure of the executive.[1]   The
reappointment of the marshals was not forbidden, and seems
to have taken place as a matter of course ; but, standing as a
solitary exception to the general rule, this limitation attached
to one class of commissions could not have been the result of
oversight, but must have had some object, although a search
for direct evidence as to its cause has been in vain.   In 1821
Madison had quite forgotten it, and supposed that the only
precedents for the Four Years' Law of 1820 were to be found
in the case of the territorial offices, the regulations for which
were carelessly adopted *in toto* from the Confederation.[2]

The indirect evidence to which one naturally first turns is
the practice of the colonies and of England.   Virginia and
Pennsylvania at one time chose their marshals or sheriffs annually,[3] and so, apparently, did New Hampshire ;[4] in the other
colonies, either they served indefinitely or the practice is ob-

---

[1] *Statutes at Large*, i. 87, 92.

[2] Madison to Jefferson, January 7, 1821, Madison, *Letters and Other Writings*, iii.
202.

[3] Channing, *Town and County Government* (Johns Hopkins University, *Studies*,
ii. No. 10), 46; E. R. L. Gould, *Local Government in Pennsylvania* (*Ibid.* i.
No. 3), 21.

[4] *New Hampshire Colonial Records*, i. 21.

scure.[1] English precedent may have had unusual weight in this case, for several of the framers of the judiciary act were close students of English law. Blackstone, whose work was certainly consulted, says that the under-sheriffs, whose functions would most resemble those of the marshals, could serve but one year, under heavy penalty. These precedents may explain the provision of the national law, but the widespread application of rotation to this particular office must have rested on some living principle. The fact seems to be that the sheriff or marshal was regarded with suspicion because of his relation to the court, particularly for his part in the selection of the jury. It was this latter function that rendered him more dangerous than the attorney, whose term is seldom regulated.[2]

Rotation, therefore, meant to the men of the formative period the limitation of the number of years during which a man might continuously hold an elective office. Its main objects were to educate as many of the people as possible in the business of political life, and to protect them from the usurpations of men habituated to office. It did not in strictness apply to the appointive offices of the civil service, nor could it logically be extended to very many of them, as few were calculated to give much political experience, or conferred powers liable to become dangerous to the people. By association of ideas, however, rotation in office came to be regarded as an end in itself, and to be regarded as applicable to all offices. The first steps in this extension are apt to be overlooked, for formal rotation was never widely extended by legislative enactment. The simple fixation of a term of office, however, even when reappointment

---

[1] The Connecticut practice is very difficult to distinguish. In October, 1771, Oliver Walcott resigned his commission as sheriff, which was signed November 14, 1751 (*Connecticut Colonial Records*, xiii. 568); yet in 1676 the sheriff or marshal seems to have been appointed for but one year (*Ibid.* ii. 275). It is possible that each county had a separate custom (*General Laws and Liberties of Connecticut Colonie*, 18), or that it was the custom to reëlect the old incumbent without renewing his commission (*Connecticut Colonial Records*, iii. 252). The attorneys were chosen from time to time (*Ibid.* v. 48, vii. 279). The Connecticut practice is of importance because of the prominence of Oliver Ellsworth in framing the national judiciary.

[2] Note that the assembly of 1675 in Virginia provided that sheriffs hold one year and that the office rotate. Hening, *Statutes*, ii. 341.

was not forbidden, was caused by the same democratic feeling that led to rotation, and ultimately produced the same results; this introduction of the fixed term for general administrative offices should, therefore, be regarded as a stage in the evolution of the idea of rotation.[1]

The process of transition is illustrated by the case of the marshal which has just been considered. The office involved powers which might become dangerous to the people, and, as it was elective, rotation was applied to protect them; when appointment was substituted for election, a definite term was provided to take the place of rotation. The justices of the peace were not usually elective, and, as their functions were such as might possibly become dangerous, it was provided that they should be commissioned for fixed periods. In both these cases limitation of term was clearly a substitute for rotation. Associated thus closely with the popular doctrine of rotation, the limited term came to be regarded as essentially democratic, and was soon extended to offices which conferred no dangerous powers. As in the case of rotation, the form remained popular after the principle had been forgotten.

South Carolina was the first state to make this extension on a large scale. It is found in her first constitution of 1776, and was gradually extended, until by 1812 nearly all the offices were limited in term. In this state there were no swiftly succeeding party changes, and the limited term does not seem to have led to a real rotation in office. State politics were exceptionally pure, and there are no indications of an abuse of the patronage, except possibly at the time of the nullification troubles.[2] By 1820 the idea was gaining ground in Pennsylvania, where rotation had always been popular,[3] in Ohio, and in most of the newer states.

Such a movement could not advance far without affecting the national government, and a rapid survey of a few of the laws

---

[1] McMaster (*United States*, iii. 146–183) discusses the fixation of the term for judges.

[2] Poore, *Charters and Constitutions*, ii. 1625, 1632; Cooper, *Statutes*, v. 238, 352, 570, 674, vi. 60, 164, 189, 322; Grayson, *J. L. Petigru*, 129.

[3] S. B. Harding, *First Pennsylvania Constitution*. American Historical Association, *Report*, 1894, pp. 371–402.

relating to the tenure of office will, besides illustrating this fact, put in its proper relation Crawford's Four Years' Bill, the political aspect of which has already been discussed. The Northwest Ordinance, which was continued in force, and the governmental provisions of which were extended to the territory south of the Ohio, by the first Congress, provided a fixed term for governor and secretary, but allowed the judges to hold for good behavior. This precedent with regard to territories was always followed by the Federalists. In organizing the judiciary they made the singular distinction between marshals and attorneys which has already been noted, and the term of directors of the Bank of the United States they fixed in 1791 at one year. At the close of Adams's administration they provided that the justices of the peace in the District of Columbia should hold for five years.[1]

Under Jefferson the tendencies of the times readily found expression, and it is therefore not surprising to find that the demand for short terms was distinctly recognized. The law providing for the government of Louisiana limited the term of the judges to four years, a provision which remained in the various laws for that territory. Not so when Michigan was set off. There the older arrangement was followed, perhaps because the territory was already under the Ordinance of 1787, for in 1812, when Missouri was set off from Louisiana, the limited term was again employed. The practice continued to be irregular. In 1817 Alabama was provided with judges holding for good behavior; while in 1819 Arkansas, a portion of Louisiana, was to have them with a four years' term. In 1817 the office of reporter of the Supreme Court was created for three years only, and was so continued by successive acts until 1842.[2]

The law of 1820, then, did not fail to cast its shadow before, nor did the unfavorable comment which it excited prevent the more extensive application of its principles. In 1822 and 1823 new territorial acts limited the terms of the judges; the Michigan law was changed in this respect, and the surveyors-general were added to the officers holding with a limited tenure.[3]

[1] *Statutes at Large*, i. 123, 193, 549; ii. 107.
[2] *Ibid.* ii. 284, 309, 331, 746; iii. 371, 376; v. 545.
[3] *Ibid.* iii. 655, 657, 697, 769.

After the incoming of Jackson the idea of a fixed term seems to have been fully recognized. Indian agents, postmasters, some clerks, the judges for Iowa, were all to have commissions expiring at the end of four years. In 1840 a term of five years was fixed for certain receivers-general of public moneys. The office of commissioner of pensions was created for two-year periods only. A surprising exception occurred in 1836, when the act organizing Wisconsin provided that judges should be appointed to serve during good behavior. Possibly this exception was a result of the great discussion of the civil service which occurred in that year.[1]

Whatever may have been true of Crawford, it is certain that many other politicians wished this limitation to lead to actual rotation in the minor offices. When certain senators requested Adams to send in "different nominations, and to introduce a principle of change or rotation,"[2] they gave voice to a growing demand. It is evident that the end to be obtained was exactly opposite to that which made rotation popular, for every limitation of the term of appointive offices, every new nomination called for, increased the power of the executive; but, though its meaning had completely changed, the word "rotation" continued to have a true democratic ring in popular discussions. Later, a still further twist was given to its significance: offices came to be regarded simply as prizes; and the phrase "rotation in office" served to give a pleasing and respected form to the doctrine that they should be shared as widely and as rapidly as possible.

While the path of the spoils system was thus being prepared, and a theoretical basis for it established, the actual practice was keeping pace with the theory. New York was the first state in which the offices were openly and continuously used for partisan purposes. There the royal appointments had been conspicuously bad, and colonial politics especially active. This experience was probably responsible for the elaborate attempt, made in the first constitution, to limit the appointing power of the executive, and to secure proper recognition for the various

---

[1] *Statutes at Large*, iv. 736, 779 ; v. 13, 26, 88, 187, 238, 369, 388, 597, etc.
[2] J. Q. Adams, *Memoirs*, vi. 520–521.

geographical sections. The state was divided into four districts, each represented by an equal number of senators. One senator from each district was elected by the House of Representatives to serve in the council of appointment. With these four the governor was associated, but in exactly what capacity was not made clear by the constitution. The original idea seems to have been that the nominations should be made by the council, and that the governor was to approve or disapprove;[1] but later the governor claimed that the exact reverse was true.

The conditions which governed the working of this machinery of appointment were complicated, and do not readily admit of brief explanation. New York politics had been controlled in the colonial period by family groups or combinations, based largely on land and old manorial privileges. The power of some of these groups was broken by the Revolution, but a large part of the population lacked American political experience and ideals, and were still ready to follow leaders;[2] hence the influence of certain families remained. The Livingstons were the most conspicuous; the Van Rensselaers were prominent for years; and the Schuylers, united with Alexander Hamilton by marriage, dominated the Federalist party. Besides these older families, the long governorship of George Clinton seems to have created a strong permanent interest, which passed to his nephew, De Witt Clinton,[3] while in New York City the democracy was marshalled by such organizations and leaders as Tammany Hall and Aaron Burr. Although Republican formulas were used, politics continued to be a game played by a number of factions, some aristocratic, some democratic, by bosses and patrons. The political situation reproduced in miniature that of England during the eighteenth century.

[1] Poore, *Charters and Constitutions*, ii. 1336; *Federalist* (Ford ed.), 513; Assembly resolution, October 2, 1777, *Clinton Papers*, ii. 357.

[2] C. Becker, *Nominations in Colonial New York*, in *American Historical Review*, vi. 260–275 ; a delegation from German Flats, for example, laid a petition before Governor Clinton in 1779, "hoping your natural affection towards true and faithful Subjects will give us redress" (*Clinton Papers*, iv. 746).

[3] In 1804 sixteen members or connections of the Livingston and Clinton families held office in state or nation, and drew $60,500 in annual salaries. *Lancaster Journal*, Extra, March 21, 1804.

Probably no system of appointment could have been better devised to continue this condition than that just described for New York.   It successfully divested every one of any feeling of responsibility, and opened an opportunity for an endless variety of jobs and deals, combinations and recombinations.   The council, although requested by the House of Representatives, refused to publish its minutes.[1]   How completely the popular will could be thwarted may be seen later.

From 1777 until 1795 continuously George Clinton was governor.   His opponent at his first election was Philip Schuyler, whom he seems to have much respected, and whom he later appointed surveyor-general.[2]   Many of the offices had been filled before he entered on his duties, and he wrote that he would remove no man from office without a hearing.   Either he or the council of appointment did, however, distress one man by making him third, instead of second, on a list of judges.   In answer to some protest from Schenectady, he said that, so far as he had anything to do with appointments, the people of every part of the state should be equally represented.   The Tryon County people proposed that they be allowed to choose their own county officers, because three of the council of appointment are "unquainted with us, and the other hath but an imperfect knowlidge of us"; but Clinton would not accede to the request, although the method was actually used in the case of Vermont, the conditions of which were totally unfamiliar to him and his colleagues.   He urged the Vermonters to be impartial, and to have regard for merit and abilities; in particular he hinted that they give lucrative offices to refugees.[3]   During his first governorship, Clinton had little call to be proscriptive; almost the only opponents in office were those whom he placed there, and it should be said that these were numerous.   He closely controlled the council of appointment, and once when the Federalists secured it, he managed to delay a good deal of business until a new council was elected.   Although his use of the patronage was moderate, it was skilful, and was one of the chief means by which he maintained his hold on the state.[4]

[1] New York Council of Appointment, *Military Minutes*, i. 186–187.

[2] *Clinton Papers*, iv. 537, note.   [3] *Ibid.* ii. 552, 746–784 ; iii. 54, 165, 173, 217, 398.

[4] Hammond, *Political Parties in New York*, i. 53 ff.; 5, 33, 83, 104; 38.

The establishment of the national government weakened the influence of the state executive in New York, particularly as the new appointments were largely controlled by Hamilton. The latter, however, could not successfully cope with the governor in the use of offices for party purposes ; and the Livingstons were driven by the neglect of the national government into alliance with Clinton,[1] who, in spite of lost patronage and the strong government reaction of the early nineties, was able to keep his office until 1795. His successor, John Jay, announced in his first message to the legislature that he would " regard all his fellow citizens with an equal eye, and . . . advance merit wherever found." Appointments were, however, confined to Federalists. The few direct removals seem to have been made for cause, but some for party purposes were brought about indirectly as follows : the commissions of justices of the peace ran for only three years, but it was customary to recommission the incumbents ; under Jay, when the new lists were made out, the names of Clintonians were omitted.[2] It is probable that Jay was deceived into signing these commissions, and that the first intimation he received of their proscriptive character was from the denunciations of the opposition press.

In 1800 the New York Republicans elected a council of which De Witt Clinton was a member. The council promptly claimed for its members a nominating power concurrent with that of the governor, to whom it denied even a veto. This interpretation the Federalists had successfully maintained against Clinton in 1794 ; and, as has been mentioned, it seems to have been what was intended when the constitution was framed. Jay, however, rejected it ;[3] hence during the last part of his term the appointing power was dead-locked, and the curious spectacle

[1] Hammond, *Political Parties in New York*, i. 30. Lamb, collector of New York, seems to have been the only important exception, and he was not personally unfriendly to Hamilton. Leake, *Lamb*, 321 ; Hammond, *Political Parties in New York*, i. 107; Lodge, *Hamilton*, 82.

[2] Hammond, *Political Parties in New York*, i. 95, 119, 127, notes, 580 ; Poore, *Charters and Constitutions*, ii. 1337. See, however, *New York Evening Post*, January 14, 25, 1802.

[3] Hammond, *Political Parties in New York*, i. 81; Jay to New York legislature, February 26, 1801; Jay, *Correspondence and Public Papers*, iv. 289.

was presented of a Republican council maintaining the correctness of a Federalist precedent, while a Federalist governor, supported by the advice of Clinton, the Republican ex-governor, denounced it as unconstitutional. A constitutional convention called to pass upon the question in 1801 decided in favor of the council. From this time until 1821 the history of the patronage in New York coincides with that of the council of appointment.[1]

The establishment of the supremacy of the council greatly facilitated the growth of the spoils system. In 1801 George Clinton was again elected governor; but he was then old, and his nephew, De Witt Clinton, controlled the council and the appointments. He followed quite exactly the tactics of Jefferson, reinstating with a great flourish of trumpets the few who had been removed during Jay's term, and with this start carrying out a genuine proscription, so severe that his uncle refused, in some instances, to sign the minutes of the council. According to the *Evening Post*, it was still felt necessary to justify removals by traducing the character of those removed; but this sense of shame soon disappeared, and all parties acted openly on the belief that they were held together by the cohesive power of public office, and that to the victors belonged the spoils.[2]

The spoils system was particularly dangerous in New York, because of the enormous extent of the patronage. The council of appointment, according to a report presented in the constitutional convention of 1821, filled directly 8287 military and 6663 civil offices, and compensation was relatively high. It appointed nearly all the state officers, all mayors, and some minor city officers, militia officers, and justices of the peace.[3] The potentialities of this mass of patronage are illustrated by the machine created by Judge Spencer, one of the chief political

---

[1] New York Council of Appointment, *Military Minutes*, i. 555–563; Hammond, *Political Parties in New York*, i. 155, 168.

[2] *Columbian Centinel*, August 19, 1801; *New York Evening Post*, February 23, 1801, January 14, February 19, 1802; New York Council of Appointment, *Military Minutes*, i. 562. Hammond, *Political Parties in New York*, i. 134, 178, 227, 234, 236, 238, 315–327, 330, 442, 460, 469. See also the lives of the New York leaders, as Burr, Van Buren, Tompkins, De Witt Clinton, etc., *passim*.

[3] Hammond, *Political Parties in New York*, ii. 65. Niles says that there were 709 civil offices in New York City. *Niles's Register*, xxi. 128; *New York Evening Post*, January 26, 1802.

figures of the time. Apart from his abilities, which were very good, he owed his influence to his manipulation of the appointments of justices of the peace. In his circuits he would make friends of prominent local politicians, who would recommend to him persons to be appointed justices of the peace. He would obtain the desired commissions at Albany, and this would aid his friends in securing an election to the legislature. Once there, they would vote for a council of appointment which would listen to the suggestions of Judge Spencer.[1]

The danger to the political morality of the state was keenly appreciated, and was one of the chief causes for summoning the convention of 1821. In the new constitution then framed the council of appointment was abolished, and the appointing power was given to the governor by and with the advice and consent of the Senate. Only 28 military and 325 civil appointments, however, were left to be thus disposed of; for the vast majority of the minor offices, as those of justice of the peace and the militia offices, were to be filled by direct popular election. The spoils system, however, was too firmly established to yield to these measures. Indeed, the power of the governor was more increased by the abolition of the council of appointment than it was lessened by the withdrawal of the minor offices; and his power over the patronage that remained was still further extended by the fact that the convention fixed a definite term for many of the offices which had previously been held "at pleasure." The making of the minor offices elective, moreover, did not remove them from the realm of politics; it merely necessitated a new method of management. Manipulation of the legislature ceased to be sufficient; small elective and petty nominating bodies had to be controlled. The want was soon supplied; and the Albany Regency, whose members first perfected a caucus system, and acquired the art of managing directly the small subdivisions of the electorate, obtained as its reward a firm and lasting hold on New York politics.[2]

---

[1] Hammond, *Political Parties in New York*, i. 420.

[2] Poore, *Charters and Constitutions*, ii. 1336, 1345. Hammond, *Political Parties in New York*, ii. 66, 72, 429; Mackenzie, *Van Buren*, 112, 207, and *passim;* Weed, *Autobiography*, 108.

Almost contemporaneous with the establishment of the spoils system in New York was its triumph in Pennsylvania, but the conditions of its rise were very different. The revolution of 1776 in the latter state was preceded by a long and bitter triangular contest between the Quakers, the proprietary party, and certain democratic elements. The last named won, and in their hour of triumph, organized by George Bryan and advised by Benjamin Franklin, they framed what was probably the most democratic constitution the country has ever known. With a legislature of but one house and a multiple executive, it afforded none of those checks and balances that were considered essential by most statesmen of the period. From the first, therefore, the more conservative elements of the population, under the name of Republicans, fought for a revision. This struggle, which continued until the adoption, in 1790, of a constitution which provided for a stronger executive, served to divide the state into two distinct parties and to prevent the development of such factions as were found in New York; it accounts largely for the early development of party organization and nominating conventions, and, through these, of the spoils system.[1]

Under the first constitution most appointments in Pennsylvania were controlled by the legislature, either alone or in conjunction with the president of the commonwealth who also was practically elected by it. Though no instances of removal have been found, complaint was made that offices were used to win adherents, and it is mentioned as remarkable that Rittenhouse should have held his office of treasurer for thirteen successive years, under legislatures now of one party, now of the other. In 1783 the Council of Censors called the attention of the legislature to the low standard of the holders of public offices.[2] Mifflin, the first governor under the new constitution, began his term by refusing to reappoint certain officers who had served under the old. Although elected as a Constitutionalist, that is,

---

[1] Lincoln, *The Revolutionary Movement in Pennsylvania*, 286, and *passim ;* Christopher Marshall, *Diary*, 68 ; Graydon, *Memoirs*, 288, 332, 342.

[2] Lincoln, *The Revolutionary Movement in Pennsylvania*, 280 ; Poore, *Charters and Constitutions*, ii. 1540–1548 ; Graydon, *Memoirs*, 332 ; Barton, *Rittenhouse*, 339 ; Sharpless, *Two Centuries of Pennsylvania History*, 211.

as of the more democratic party, he soon turned Federalist, and apparently confined his appointments to members of that party.[1]

Such was the situation that Thomas McKean found when, in 1799, he was elected governor, first of the *fin de siècle* Republican victors. He accused of combination against him the "officers and expectants of office under the President of the United States, not only in Pennsylvania, but in neighboring states," and he wrote to John Dickinson, "I have been obliged (though no Hercules) to cleanse the Augean stable." To Jefferson, in July, 1801, he outlined his theory of the civil service. "It appears," he said, "that the anti-Republicans, even those in office, are as hostile as ever, though not so insolent. To overcome them they must be shaven, for in their offices (like Samson's hair-locks) their great strength lieth; their disposition for mischief may remain, but their power of doing it will be gone. It is out of the common order of nature, to prefer enemies to friends; the despisers of the people should not be their rulers." The whole tone of this letter indicates that already in Pennsylvania the civil offices were considered as ammunition for political warfare, — a fact which Jefferson must have seen clearly when he wrote to McKean, "Some states require a different regimen from others."[2]

It is impossible to say exactly how far McKean carried out the policy he sketched. The *Eagle* reported that, of twenty-one particular appointments, seven were reappointments, one a promotion, and thirteen were new. Probably most of the latter were occasioned by removals. The proscription did not stop with the limits of the governor's authority, for the mayor of Philadelphia is said to have swept all Federalists from office in that city. In making appointments, McKean seems to have consulted his own pleasure; he is said to have been guilty of nepotism and favoritism, and his conduct received much

---

[1] Charles Biddle, *Autobiography*, 243, 245; Hildreth, *United States*, v. 361; Buchanan, *McKean*, 98; *Philadelphia Gazette and Universal Daily Advertiser*, January 13, 1800; *New York Evening Post*, February 12, 1802.

[2] *Pittsburg Gazette*, December 7, 1799; Armor, *Lives of the Governors of Pennsylvania*, 302. Jefferson, *Writings* (Ford ed.), viii. 78.

unfavorable criticism.[1] When, in 1805, the Duane branch of
the party broke with him, and he was reëlected a second time
by a combination of the Quids and Federalists, he removed
from office men whom he had himself appointed. It is
unnecessary to follow the successive party changes; the only
point of interest is that henceforth the spoils system was
accepted in Pennsylvania. Here, as in New York in 1821,
the politicians took advantage of the democratical slogan of
"rotation in office" to effect a limitation of tenure, and thus to
make more easy the path of the spoilsman.[2]

The results of the spoils system in New York and Pennsylvania seem to have been as different as were the circumstances
of its growth. The average standard of men called into the
New York state service was certainly higher. Nearly always
some men of eminent ability were to be found in the civil list.
This was partly due to the system of family cliques which made
politics fashionable, and also partly to the fact that at first the
confusion of factions, and later the even balance of parties,
always afforded an opportunity for talent. Many other causes
might, of course, be enumerated. Besides this difference there
seems to have been more actual corruption in Pennsylvania than
in the neighboring state, if we except New York City. Cases
of actual sale of office are reported. Niles gives an instance
in which a note was actually sued out, the drawer of which had
promised to pay the holder a certain sum if he were appointed
to a post which the latter was about to resign,[3] the consideration

---

[1] *Pennsylvania Eagle*, January 25, 1800; *Lancaster Journal*, December 29, 1801;
Armor, *Lives of the Governors of Pennsylvania*, 302; Brown, *The Forum*, i. 343–
347; *Claypoole's American Daily Advertiser*, May 1, 1800; Buchanan, *McKean*, 90,
92, 97, 98; *Philadelphia Gazette and Universal Daily Advertiser*, January 13, 1800;
Gallatin to Jefferson, September 12, 1801, Gallatin, *Writings*, i. 48; *Pennsylvania
Magazine*, xvii. 474.

[2] *Niles's Register*, xvi. 157; xxxiii. 332–337; xxxvi. 67, 164. The *Connecticut
Courant*, January 27, 1801, contains an interesting letter of Samuel Bryan, register-
general, to a member of the legislature, accusing it of yielding to the "malignant
rage of Party Spirit," and also records the proposal of the House to have him arrested
for slander in consequence. The zeal for office is illustrated by the fact that there
were thirty candidates for the clerkship of the legislature. *Lancaster Journal*,
December 17, 1801; Poore, *Charters and Constitutions*, ii. 1345; *Laws of Pennsylvania* (edition of 1834), 162, 184 (edition of 1837), 143, 628, 898.

[3] *Niles's Register*, xvi. 107, 160; xvii. 157, 428.

presumably being the influence of the old occupant with the governor. Naturally the offices of the national government local to these states did not escape the contagion. The charges of Governor McKean and Governor Clinton, and the case of Dr. Leib, have been mentioned;[1] and it is to be presumed that New York and Pennsylvania appointments caused presidents before Jackson's day to pass sleepless nights.

While these two states are most noted and most notable for the abuse of the patronage during this period, they did not stand alone. In many localities where there was no complaint of proscription, the immunity was due to the long and continued domination of one party; the same process was going on, but took the form of the silent exclusion of one party from power. In New Hampshire there was nothing like a spoils system; but in 1801 it was stated that all the vacancies would be filled with Federalists, and again in 1815, when the governor and council belonged to different parties, the appointments were in deadlock.[2] Moreover, the Langdon family controlled and absorbed all the patronage which the Republicans could command.[3] Rhode Island was praised as the land of " steady habits "; attention was called to the fact that one treasurer had served for forty-five years, and that there had been only six secretaries in colony and state during one hundred and twenty-seven years. Our wonder somewhat diminishes when we find that the total annual state expenditure in 1828 was only $8010.75;[4] and the praise is not entirely deserved, for, when the Rhode Island Tammany Society succeeded in carrying the state for the Republicans in 1810, they made a partial sweep. When the Federalists came back the next year they acted magnanimously in leaving some of their opponents in office,[5] and so the evil was stayed.

Of the northern states, Massachusetts was perhaps the most exemplary in the conduct of the civil service; yet there, as in Rhode Island, an element existed eager for the spoils. Under

---

[1] *Niles's Register*, xvi. 107, 160, xvii. 428; *Pittsburg Gazette*, December 7, 1799.

[2] *Columbian Centinel*, June 13, 1801; *Niles's Register*, viii. 352.

[3] *Columbian Centinel*, March 1, 1801.

[4] *Niles's Register*, xvi. 239; xxxi. 222; xxxiv. 234.

[5] *Massachusetts Spy*, etc., May 15, 1811; Jernegan, *The Tammany Societies of Rhode Island*, 22.

the early state government there was practically no complaint as to appointments; but when the Federalists began to condemn Jefferson's removals, their opponents replied by accusing them of excluding all Republicans from office. The best vindication of their administration is found in the conduct of James Sullivan, the first Republican governor. He was a strong, conscientious man, and refused to make any removals. The radicals of the party under the lead of Levi Lincoln controlled the executive council and urged proscription, finally putting on file a protest in which they argued that to make no removals "would be arraigning the wisdom and justice of the national administration, a censure and reproach of its most deliberate acts." Had they been able to add that the conduct of the Federalist governors had been notoriously unfair, Sullivan could hardly have resisted. The next year the executive council was composed of Federalists, who worked harmoniously with Sullivan; and when the succeeding election brought in once more a Federalist governor, no removals were made.[1]

In 1810 another Republican, Elbridge Gerry, was elected governor. In his first term he made no removals and reappointed those whose commissions expired, although he doubtless found the great majority of office-holders Federalists. His course disappointed his followers; and there is probably some grain of truth in the charge of his enemies, that the Republicans made a change of policy a condition of his renomination, — that is, there was probably some understanding as to what course he would pursue. After his reëlection the Republican legislature proceeded to make the path toward a proscription as smooth as possible.[2] They did this by the trick, so often mentioned, of fixing a definite tenure for certain offices, thus hiding the increase of executive patronage under the guise of a democratic innovation.[3] The most important offices to which this

---

[1] Lowell, *The New-England Patriot,* 132; Bradford, *Massachusetts,* iii. 95; *Massachusetts Spy,* February 12, August 21, 1811.

[2] Austin, *Gerry,* ii. 322; *Massachusetts Spy,* etc., August 7, 14, 21, 1811.

[3] Of the Massachusetts laws passed in June, 1811, ch. xxxiii. provided for the reorganization of the circuit court and the court of common pleas; ch. xlix. forbade county treasurers to serve more than five years continuously; ch. lxxi. gave sheriffs a

limited term was applied were those of the county sheriffs and the clerks of the county courts. Still further to smooth the path of the governor, the appointment to the offices last mentioned was transferred from the court itself to the governor and council,[1] and it was of course arranged that the commissions should expire during the term for which Governor Gerry had been elected.

When the time came for Gerry to declare himself, the respectable old commonwealth was stirred to its depths. The protests of the Federalists were long and caustic and edifying, while on the Republican side a stern puritanic note was raised by a country minister who preached his election sermon from the text, " But if ye will not drive out the inhabitants of the land from before you, then it shall come to pass that those that ye let remain of them shall be pricks in your eyes and thorns in your sides, and shall vex you in the land wherein ye dwell."[2] Governor Gerry fulfilled the wishes of his party,[3] and was bombarded with protests from the public in general,[4] and from dispossessed office-holders. He tried to explain and justify his conduct, arguing that the reappointment of the former discredited office-holders would alarm the Republicans; that Democratic principles demanded that, when the offices fell vacant, equal consideration should be shown to all citizens, no preference being extended to incumbents.[5] His extenuations could not, however, do away with the appearance of sharp practice. It must have been hard for the most discriminating Federalist to believe that the limitation of terms was made simply to hasten the triumph of pure democracy, when he saw that about forty members of the legis-

---

term of five years, adding, " The Governor shall remove from office all Sheriffs now in commission, who shall not be reappointed."

[1] Laws of 1811, ch. viii. This law was repealed in 1814 (see laws of that year, ch. lxxvii.).

[2] *Massachusetts Spy*, December 11, 1811.

[3] Austin says that he placed one Federalist and two Democrats in every circuit, and retained some of the most highly paid officials. Austin, *Gerry*, ii. 343.

[4] *Columbian Centinel*, January 22, 27, February 15, 19, 1812 ; *Massachusetts Spy*, October, December, 1811, *passim ;* February 12, 1812.

[5] Austin, *Gerry*, ii. Appendix B. See also *Massachusetts Spy*, etc., December 11, 1811 ; *Columbian Centinel*, January 15, 1812.

lature received offices which they had helped to make vacant,
not to mention the number given to relatives of members.   As
the *Massachusetts Spy* expressed it : —

> " 'Tis a mighty fine thing, Sir, to be son-in-law
> To a very magnificent three-tailed Bashaw." [1]

The Republican administration of Massachusetts was thoroughly discredited by this affair of the patronage combined
with that of the gerrymander, and it seems no exaggeration,
as the election was so close, to attribute to these scandals the
defeat of Gerry, although he personally erred rather in weakness than by desire.[2]   Governor Strong, who succeeded him,
had his conduct marked out by public opinion.   By one order
he removed all the Gerry appointees whose predecessors had
been removed, and reinstated the old officers.[3]

After the defeat of Gerry no more is heard of the misuse of the
patronage in Massachusetts for many years.   The Federalist
party gradually disappeared, but its exit was marked by no great
proscription.   The soil of the state was not kind to the spoils
system, a majority of the population disapproved of it and did
not intend to allow it.   We note, however, that a minority
were ready and willing to introduce the practice, and were
longing after the plums now out of their reach.   If they could
not command the state, they might, by allying themselves with
a national party, obtain control of the federal patronage ; and
this is just what happened when Jackson was elected.

In the old South, between the Potomac, the Alleghanies,
and the ocean, there is less evidence of discontent and new
methods.   Of South Carolina, Calhoun said in 1849, " Party
organization, party discipline, party proscription, — and their
offspring, *the spoils principle*, have been unknown " ; [4] and this
seems to have been generally true, although Grayson says that
during the nullification contest men were bribed " with money,
with promises of office." [5]   In Georgia there is a faint evidence

[1] *Massachusetts Spy*, etc., July 26, October 23, 1811.

[2] Barry, *Massachusetts*, iii. 346, 364–369 ; *Columbian Centinel*, June 6, 1812.

[3] *Columbian Centinel*, June 24, 1812 ; Bradford, *Massachusetts*, iii. 129.

[4] Calhoun, *Discourse on the Constitution and Government of the United States* in
his *Works*, i. 405.   [5] Grayson, *J. L. Petigru*, 129.

of a desire for the spoils system in 1829, when George R. Gilmer, a representative of the Troup faction, was elected governor through the assistance of the Clarke faction ; and the Clarke leaders wished him to divide the patronage between the two bodies of his supporters.[1] He refused, and for a long time there is no mention of the spoils.

The frontier democracy of the West shared the characteristics of both North and South. During this period the people were divided according to personal sympathy and special issues, and consequently party lines were fluctuating. Hence there was no persistent and studied use of patronage to maintain party organization ; but offices were none the less used by the leaders to promote the ends of the moment, while the people demanded that all public servants, appointive as well as elective, should be in sympathy with the majority. The conditions of this section are best illustrated by a study of Illinois,[2] for which the career of Ninian Edwards serves as a convenient nucleus, if for no other reason than because the Chicago Historical Society has preserved and published his wide and candid correspondence. It will, moreover, be profitable to discuss the national civil service in Illinois rather than the trifling and disorganized service of the state itself.

Ninian Edwards was a Kentuckian of wealth and ability, belonging to the class of Western politicians who relied more on the impression caused by gentlemanly bearing and eloquence than on a democratic aping of the manners of their constituents. While he made no pretence of being one of the people, he was a close and successful student of their desires. When he went to Washington in 1818 as senator, he was thrown into close contact with William Wirt, a friend of his boyhood, representative of the best traditions of Republican purity. One could not be long in Washington at that time without being drawn into the presidential campaign,

---

[1] Gilmer, *The Georgians*, 316 ; Phillips, *Georgia and State Rights* (American Historical Association, *Reports*, 1901, ii.), 110–111.

[2] The struggle in Kentucky over the reorganization of the supreme court brought about by the bank issue is also a good illustration. See Shaler, *Kentucky*, 180–185 ; Little, *Hardin*, 155 ; *National Republican and Ohio Political Register*, December 30, 1825 ; *Jackson Gazette*, February 7, 1829.

and Edwards soon became an ardent supporter and close friend of Calhoun.[1] In 1823 he had the pleasure of introducing to his leader his brother-in-law, General Duff Green, a Western editor, who afterwards became connected with Calhoun by the marriage of their children.[2] These bonds of friendship and marriage formed the basis of Edwards's political affiliations.

In 1820 Edwards became interested in the appointments to land offices in Illinois. The other senator from the state was Thomas, a political rival, and a supporter of Crawford's candidacy for the presidency. Edwards did not hope to secure all the new positions for his supporters or friends, but he made a vigorous effort to obtain an equal share of the patronage. December 22, 1820, he wrote to President Monroe advising that at least one appointment be made from eastern Illinois, recommending several available candidates, and condemning one of the men who had been already nominated, but whose nomination had not yet been acted on. In conversation with Crawford, the secretary of the treasury, he was more explicit, suggesting that all the nominations be left to the senators to divide equally between their respective parties. This proposition was considered as an attack on the prerogatives of the president, and was vigorously condemned by William Wirt in a long though friendly letter. Wirt said the president thought it wrong that a president of the United States "should permit himself to be influenced by considerations of local parties in a state, and that he should nominate with reference to the local effect on the respective senators in their states. For my own part," he adds, "I should consider it a species of bribery." Wirt in another letter made perhaps the first suggestion of "senatorial courtesy." "There is, indeed, another course which he may take and I think he ought to take; which is, to nominate no person whom either senator declares unworthy of an office, if he can find a deserving man in the state

---

[1] Calhoun thinks that Edwards should be one of the ministers to our "southern neighbors" (Calhoun to Edwards, June 12, 1822, Edwards, *Illinois*, 489–491).

[2] Calhoun to Edwards, September 23, 1823: "I have been much pleased with Gen'l Green. He is intelligent and decisive; and must in time become important in the West" (*Edwards Papers*, 210).

free from such objection, — unless, indeed, the objection itself
is destroyed by being discovered to proceed from a personal
feeling, or weakened by flowing from the animosity of local
faction." [1]

Edwards disclaimed all intention of weakening the executive
power,[2] but continued to urge that appointments be made on
a political basis. He was supported in this last position by his
other friend, Calhoun, who wrote to him August 20, 1822:
"Since the return of the President to the city, I have urged on
his attention the subject of making appointments to the offices
to which you referred, and brought before him the names
which you mentioned. . . . I do trust that he begins to feel
the necessity of taking a decided stand. I agree with you that
it is much easier to put down the opposition, where its existence
is once acknowledged, than to prove, to the satisfaction of the
people, its existence. Until the President shall uniformly
make the distinction between friends and foes, in his appointments, this cannot be done. If he will not see the
opposition . . . the country will be incredulous as to its
existence." [3]

This episode either caused or intensified that enmity to
Crawford which blighted Edwards's future career. In 1823 he
published in the *Republican*,[4] the Calhoun organ at Washington,
over the signature "A. B.," a series of attacks on Crawford's
management of the treasury department. Then he gave weight
to these letters by acknowledging the authorship, but too late,
as it seemed, for the charges to be investigated before the
presidential election of 1824, or till after he himself had left
Washington on a foreign mission. Crawford's friends acted
with promptness, recalled Edwards to give testimony, and
secured a report which found the charges unsubstantiated. Edwards felt compelled to resign his appointment as minister to
Mexico, and was visited with a general popular condemnation,
which most historians have considered just. He did not, however, lose the friendship of Calhoun, received a mild support

---

[1] *Edwards Papers*, 168, 176, 181–185.
[2] Edwards to Crawford, January 11, 1821; *Ibid.* 183–185.
[3] Edwards, *Illinois*, 491–492.   [4] Benton, *Thirty Years' View*, i. ch. xiv.

from John Quincy Adams, and was elected governor of Illinois in 1826.[1]

As governor of Illinois, with intimate friends at Washington, he continued his attempt to influence the distribution of the national patronage within the state. September 21, 1826, he wrote to Clay, now secretary of state, that his election as governor had been opposed by the Jackson men, that his success had given him full control of the situation, and that he could dictate the political allegiance of Illinois. " In regard to the Presidential election," he adds, " I am entirely uncommitted, and it is my candid opinion that I shall remain so. So long as some of the Jackson papers continue to assail me, as they have done, and are now doing, my pride would never suffer me to be led into any kind of coöperation with them. And so long as Mr. Adams' officers are permitted imprudently to use his own declarations, and conduct to my disadvantage in my own State, as is done in the accompanying handbill, though it may not drive me from neutrality, I never will enlist under his banners. Some of his warmest friends however have more cause of complaint against the author of this handbill. And I am persuaded that the time is at hand, when the wisdom of Mr. Jefferson's course in regard to the patronage of the administration must become too obvious to be any longer neglected." [2]

Governor Edwards must have felt that he had indeed correctly gauged popular sentiment when but a few days after writing this letter he received one in exactly the same tone from a friend in Philadelphia : " Mr. Adams's magnanimity and forbearance, in regard to non-removals from office, excites my astonishment. . . . I marvel that Mr. Clay is not more on the *qui vive*, in this respect. . . . This policy not only places weapons in the hands of Mr. Adams's foes, but it takes

---

[1] D. P. Cook to Edwards, April 17, 1824: "I shall give the papers to Mr. Clay to-morrow. I want first to show them to some of my friends, who will aid me. Mr. Calhoun, and so do I, think it will be best not to publish them in the *Republican* until after they are printed by the House. . . . Mr. Adams' friends will aid, and stand by you. If Clay acts fairly, I think there will be no danger" (*Edwards Papers,* 223–224). J. Q. Adams, *Memoirs,* vi. 387, 389.

[2] *Edwards Papers,* 259–263.

weapons out of the hands of his friends." [1] The administration was obdurate, though courteous. The president wrote to Edwards, August 22, 1827: "Your recommendation for the appointment of a sub-agent at Peoria will, in the event of a vacancy in that office, receive the deliberate consideration to which it is entitled, and a disposition altogether friendly to him as recommended by you. And your opinion in regard to any appointment of the General Government, in the state of Illinois, will be always acceptable to me." [2]

The desire of the Jackson men in Washington to favor this political trickster was not restrained by the cool temperament and old-fashioned political ideas of John Quincy Adams. John McLean, the postmaster-general, but a supporter of Jackson, wrote to Edwards, November 1, 1826, "Had your letter been received before I re-appointed ——, I should, as I have always done, have appointed the person you named." [3] September 1, 1826, Duff Green, who was now established in Washington, wrote: "I hear that Anderson is dead. Let Cook [Edwards's most important political friend in Illinois] write immediately to Mr. Adams and demand as matter of right that he be appointed his successor. Mr. Adams will scarce deny him and if nominated I will rely upon Calhoun and my friends in the Senate to get him through without opposition." Consequently, when Governor Edwards, after a long hesitation,[4] was forced at length to abandon his neutral position, the policy of the two parties with regard to the patronage was one of the reasons which caused him to take his followers to the Jackson camp.

By the year 1828, then, in every state throughout the North and West the spoils system either was established or there existed an element eager to introduce it. The movement was a growing one, and it was but a question of time and circumstance when the custom would become national. The leaders of the Albany Regency, confident by reason of their success at home, looked for widespread influence through the control of

[1] S. Simpson to Edwards, September 22, 1826 ; *Ibid.* 263-264.
[2] Edwards, *Illinois,* 147. [3] *Ibid.* 484.
[4] *Edwards Papers,* 253-254. Wirt, writing to Edwards, March 22, 1828, still hoped that he would support the administration. Edwards, *Illinois,* 455.

the national patronage. Less powerful state leaders hoped to make secure their local position; while petty politicians the country over longed to see the federal offices change hands as often as did those of the states — at least until they fell into *their* hands. The people in general, as was pointed out in the last chapter, disliked the life tenure and the aristocratic manners of the officials of the existing régime; those who enjoyed the national salaries should, they thought, be of the people. In the frontier states particularly, the superb self-confidence born of the pioneer's single-handed victory over nature balked not at the full measure of democracy, but boldly asserted that all men were created equally able to fulfil the duties of government offices.

It was an age of lotteries, and the prospect of a complete change in the administration offered to all prizes more dazzling than had ever before been presented to the public. The positive, virile virtue of loyalty to one's friends ranked higher in the moral code of most Americans of that day than the more complex one of justice to one's enemies. To reward his friends and to punish his enemies was the proper conduct of a victor. The Jackson managers, therefore, were wise in emphasizing the demand for a reform in the conduct of the civil service. They proposed to forbid the appointment of congressmen to office, and to introduce rotation in office;[1] but the first measure of reform, and for many the culminating one, was to be the turning out, as one New Yorker expressed it, of the "damned rascals" who supported Adams, and the substitution of original Jackson men in their places. Thus the attack on the civil service appealed alike to the people and to their leaders, to the democracy of the East and of the West. It was a phase, and a most important one, of the great revolution which brought Andrew Jackson into the presidency; and John Quincy Adams's attempt to preserve the ancient decorum of office but hastened its overthrow.

[1] *Political Mirror*, 65.

CHAPTER V.

THE ESTABLISHMENT OF THE SPOILS SYSTEM.

1829–1837.

THE election of Jackson threw both his friends and his foes into a fever of expectancy. There was enough of the Delphic element in his utterances to give color to every story as to his intentions; and rumor followed hot upon rumor through the streets of Washington, out into the country presses, and back again in new fantastic guise. The office-holding class and their friends put on a bold face. Webster wrote in January, 1829, "Great efforts are making to put him up to a general sweep, as to all offices; springing from great doubt whether he is disposed to go it." The inaugural did not cast Webster down; he wrote of it March 4, 1829, "What it says about reform in office may be either a prelude to a general change in office, or a mere sop to soothe the hunger, without satisfying it, of the thousand expectants for office who throng the city, and clamor all over the country. I expect some changes, but not a great many at present."[1]

This blindness of the administrative class, whose views Webster voiced, is not without excuse. Impregnated with tradition, they felt themselves indispensable, and could not believe that the new president would attempt to run the government without them: it very often happens that a revolution surprises no one so much as its victims. Their sense of security was doubtless fostered by those letters of Jackson to Monroe which have been already cited;[2] though if they could have interpreted these in

---

[1] Webster, *Private Correspondence*, i. 467, 473.

[2] See also Jackson to Kremer, May, 1824, *Political Mirror*, 68.

the light of an intimate knowledge of Jackson's character, they would have realized that his lenity toward Federalists arose, not from a disregard of party lines, but from a conviction that the old alignment of parties should be replaced by a new one depending on personal allegiance to himself;[1] that while he would not proscribe a man for being a Federalist or a Republican, he would do so for a failure to support the candidacy of Andrew Jackson. While this air of confidence was sufficiently widespread to deceive most historians who have treated of the period into a belief that the cataclysm of 1829 was wholly unexpected,[2] assurance was not universal even among Jackson's opponents; and doubtless many hearts beat fearsomely when, on the Sunday before inauguration, Robert Little preached from the text, "When Christ drew near the city he wept over it."[3]

The supporters of Jackson were boastfully confident that he would interpret reform as they desired. The *Richmond Enquirer*, the most powerful newspaper of the South, prophesied January 1, 1829, " A salutary reform will be attempted under the coming Republican administration . . .; in perfecting it friends will be preferred to opponents — coöperatives to assailants." On the same day it said : " Some have been pleased to speak of reform in this case as synonymous with proscription. This is a designed perversion of the word. The *National Journal* is loquacious as a parrot — in its denunciations of the anticipated ' proscription.' If that pensioned press can torture a salutary change in the administration of the general government, more or less applicable to all departments, and to official agents generally, into a proscription for opinion's sake, its powers are considerably greater than we or the public have hitherto given it credit for. As well may the people be charged with proscription for having removed an unfaithful executive and elected another. They began the work, they conferred the power to effect it." The official organ of the new party at Washington was the *Daily Telegraph*, edited by General Duff

---

[1] *Niles's Register*, xl. 113 ; Derby, *Political Reminiscences*, 65.
[2] See, for example, Parton, *Jackson*, iii. 209 ; McMaster, *United States*, v. 525.
[3] *William Winston Seaton*, 210.

Green.[1] Certainly no one who read its pages could plead igno-
rance as to the intentions of the Jackson managers. As early
as November 2, 1828, it announced, "We know not what line
of policy General Jackson will adopt; we take it for granted,
however, that he will reward his friends and punish his
enemies."
These and numerous other editorials of similar import expressed not only a popular expectation, but also a popular
demand. The editors and politicians did not think that Jackson
would falter; but if he should, they were prepared to teach him
a lesson. The proscription was delayed at first, in order to
avoid friction with the Senate. This check caused the *Telegraph* to "hint it for the benefit of those of our party who are
styled leading men, that every attempt to sustain in office, by
their influence, those who *should be removed*, whether the feeling proceed from mistaken sympathy or from a wish to propiti-
ate, it must prove alike injudicious, and it will necessarily have
a tendency to lessen the regard of the Republican party of
the nation, and ultimately overthrow ties which bind the great
majority to their political interest."[2] The *Telegraph* was right;
the politicians demanded the spoils, and they had the support
of the people. Jesse Hoyt wrote to Van Buren at this time,
"I have said from the commencement of the contest that I
would not support any administration who would support men
in power that had contributed to overthrow the democratic
party in this State. I have preached this doctrine too long,
and it has taken too [blank] a footing here, to be easily got rid
of. This is not only the doctrine in theory, but we require it
to be reduced to practice."[3] The time had come when the
spoils system was to be made national, and Jackson must assume
the task or cease to be the leader of the people.
There does not seem to be room for doubt that the president
was ready to gratify the wishes of his supporters, and yet considerable interest attaches to the steps by which the new policy
was adopted. Something had been done toward committing

[1] *Senate Journal,* 20 Cong. 2 sess. 133 ; *House Journal,* 20 Cong. 2 sess. 271.
[2] *Daily Telegraph,* March 23, 1829, from *Madisonian,* March 28, 1841.
[3] March 21, 1829, Mackenzie, *Van Buren,* 211.

the president even before his arrival at Washington. The pro-scription was by some dated from 1827,[1] when the printing of the Senate was taken from the *National Intelligencer*. The majority which enabled the Jackson managers to take this action also allowed them to postpone the confirmation of nominations sent in by President Adams in the last months of his term, and thus to prevent a recurrence of " midnight appointments." The committee to which certain judicial nominations were referred reported : " Because there are several propositions for a change of the judicial system now depending, and *because the adminis-tration of the government is about to change hands*, it is inexpedient to advise and consent to the nominations now."[2]

Those politicians therefore, who wished the administration to "go the whole hog," as Webster said, had certain accomplished facts to which they could point; but they had also strong oppo-sition to overcome. Major Lewis warned the general that if he adopted the principle of rotation and fully carried it out, the days of the republic would be numbered.[3] The foremost advo-cate of moderation, however, was John McLean, the postmas-ter-general under Monroe and Adams. He fully believed in making appointments for political reasons, and apparently was not vigorously opposed to removals in general; but he was unwilling personally to conduct a general slaughter of the post-masters, as he had appointed very many of them himself and was very popular among them. This situation caused much difficulty to the cabinet-makers. At first it was announced that he would be continued in his old position. Later an exchange was arranged with Major Eaton, who had been selected for the war department; but this proved unsatisfactory; and finally McLean asked for, and obtained, the nomination for associate justice of the Supreme Court; Barry, who was to have had that position, consenting to take the post-office.[4]

[1] Mrs. Seaton to her mother, March 1, 1827, *William Winston Seaton.*

[2] John Chambers to Crittenden, 1829, Coleman, *Crittenden*, 79–80.

[3] Parton, *Jackson*, iii. 224.

[4] McLean's selection was commented on favorably by men of all parties : *Richmond Enquirer*, March 3, 10, 1829 ; *Daily National Journal*, March 7, 1829, J. Q. Adams, *Memoirs*, viii. 112. J. A. Hamilton, *Reminiscences*, 99–100. On the formation of the cabinet, see also Duff Green's letters to Edwards, *Edwards Papers.*

This change astonished the Senate, and was at once perceived to be an omen of evil. The opinion got abroad that the change was made because McLean, though willing to remove officers for officious partisanship in the last election, refused to discriminate in so doing between the followers of Jackson and those of Adams.[1] The *National Journal*, March 7, 1829, said, " The President is to lose the valuable services of the able and independent officer, who, in the discharge of his important duties, has given universal satisfaction, for the purpose of increasing the power and patronage of the President."

If Jackson had really hesitated as to the advisability of adopting a proscriptive policy, the demonstration at Washington on the occasion of his inauguration must have been a convincing argument in favor of it. In the first administrations the personal solicitation of office-seekers was discouraged.[2] When Jefferson took his seat, the newness of the Capitol and conditions of transportation forbade the assembling of a large crowd. Of the second Adams's inauguration, Mrs. Seaton wrote, " The city is thronged with strangers, and *Yankees* swarm like the locusts of Egypt in our houses, our beds, and our kneading-troughs."[3]

This visitation, however, was utterly forgotten in the horror and vexation with which old residents beheld the Jacksonian invasion, the first appearance of a species of four-year locusts that has never since failed to devastate our capital city. The difference was not in numbers of candidates alone, though that was marked, but still more decidedly in character. The trimly dressed gentlemen of the old régime, with their high stocks and good breeding, were jostled by hack politicians from New York and country editors and farmers from the West. " After the ceremony was over," wrote Story, " the President went to the palace to receive company, and there he was visited by immense crowds of all sorts of people, from the highest and most polished down to the most vulgar and gross in the nation. I never saw such a mixture. The reign of King Mob seemed trium-

---

[1] Sargent, *Public Men and Events*, i. 116 ; Poore, *Perley's Reminiscences*, i. 98.
[2] See Washington, *Writings* (Sparks ed.), x. 6.
[3] February 24, 1825, *William Winston Seaton*, 176.

phant." What happened at the executive mansion was so dramatic that it has been described at length by all the writers on the period. The wild stampede to the White House; the crowding round and crushing of the president, indicative of a new familiarity between the people and the government, to the immediate detriment of both; the mad scramble for the good things, — the cakes and ices and orange punch served out in lavish style, but wasted through careless distribution: all these scenes are not picturesque only, but are also emblematic.[1]

Webster wrote to his sister on that day: "A monstrous crowd of people is in the city. I never saw any thing like it before. Persons have come five hundred miles to see General Jackson, and they really seem to think that the country is rescued from some dreadful danger."[2]   It was evident, however, that they did not come solely to rejoice in this salvation. An office-seeking friend of Amos Kendall's said, "I am ashamed of myself, for I feel as if every man I meet knew what I came for." "Don't distress yourself," replied Kendall, "for every man you meet is on the same business." Reports were rife that the office-hunters pressed their claims in a manner which was "the reverse of courteous," that they intruded upon the president's private hours, and "perforated" all the rooms of his mansion "to get a peep at him." These rumors were denied, and the organization of the presidential household was described as rendering such persecution impossible; but the accounts of members of the government confirm the story, — Hamilton, Ingham, and Van Buren all bear witness to the number and pertinacity of the applicants.[3]   Van Buren formulated a scheme to rid the streets of the mob before making removals;[4] but it was not tried, and the disorder, though modified as time went on, seems to have continued until the most desirable places

---

[1] Parton, *Jackson*, iii. 170.   Poore, *Perley's Reminiscences*, i. 93–94 ; Sargent, *Public Men and Events*, i. 163.

[2] Webster, *Private Correspondence*, i. 473.

[3] Kendall, *Autobiography*, 307–308 ; *Niles's Register*, xxxvi. 152 ; *New York Evening Post*, April 17, 1829 ; J. A. Hamilton, *Reminiscences*, 98 ; Shepard, *Van Buren*, 178–179.

[4] Van Buren to Hamilton, March, 1829, J. A. Hamilton, *Reminiscences*, 129.

had been disposed of. This crowd was in effect a monster petition in favor of removals. The administration did not see fit to make a definite pronouncement of its policy. Retrenchment, rather than proscription, was hinted at in the inaugural, " In the performance of a task thus generally delineated, I shall endeavor to select men whose diligence and talents will insure in their respective stations able and effective coöperation, depending for the advancement of the public service more on the integrity and zeal of the public officers than on their number."[1] The editor of the *Nashville Gazette* went to Washington, and after he returned announced, " In all cases where the official influence was prostituted in the last contest, to subserve the electioneering purposes of the coalition, the incumbents will be removed "; others, however, even Adams men, were to be allowed to retain office "provided no other objection existed." The *Richmond Enquirer*, in commenting on this, naïvely remarked, "After this wholesome purgation, what portion of the original executive functionaries will be found worthy to be retained in the service, is not as yet foreseen."[2] After the acts of the administration had revealed its policy, Jackson, in his first annual message, December, 1829, formulated the principles which had guided him : —

"There are, perhaps, few men who can for any great length of time enjoy office and power without being more or less under the influence of feelings unfavorable to the faithful discharge of their public duties. Their integrity may be proof against improper considerations immediately addressed to themselves, but they are apt to acquire a habit of looking with indifference upon the public interests and of tolerating conduct from which an unpracticed man would revolt. Office is considered as a species of property, and government rather as a means of promoting individual interests than as an instrument created solely for the service of the people. Corruption in some and in others a perversion of correct feelings and principles divert government from its legitimate ends, and make it an engine for the

---

[1] Richardson, *Messages and Papers of the Presidents,* ii. 438.
[2] Kendall, *Autobiography,* 433 ; *Richmond Enquirer,* April 7, 14, 1829.

support of the few at the expense of the many.   The duties of
all public offices are, or at least admit of being made, so plain
and simple that men of intelligence may readily qualify themselves for their performance; and I can not but believe that
more is lost by the long continuance of men in office than is
generally to be gained by their experience.   I submit, therefore,
to your consideration whether the efficiency of the government
would not be promoted, and official industry and integrity better
secured, by a general extension of the law which limits appointments to four years.

" In a country where offices are created solely for the benefit
of the people no one man has any more intrinsic right to official
station than another.   Offices were not established to give support to particular men at the public expense.   No individual
wrong is, therefore, done by removal, since neither appointment
to nor continuance in office is matter of right.   The incumbent
became an officer with a view to public benefits, and when these
require his removal they are not to be sacrificed to private interests.   It is the people, and they alone, who have a right to
complain when a bad officer is substituted for a good one.   He
who is removed has the same means of obtaining a living that
are enjoyed by the millions who never held office.   The proposed limitation would destroy the idea of property now so
generally connected with official station, and although individual distress may be sometimes produced, it would, by promoting that rotation which constitutes a leading principle in the
republican creed, give healthful action to the system." [1]

The policy thus enunciated threw every office in the civil
service open to competition.   The vague charge of misusing
office to support Adams was one that could be brought, and
proved *ex parte*, against any office-holder.   The contrast of this
policy with Jefferson's practice of opening up first one set of
offices and then another is striking.   This possibility of a simul-
taneous change of the entire civil list meant that the appointing
power must deal at once with a great number and a great
variety of cases; and the complexity of its task was increased
by the other principle, that the duties of the various offices were

---

[1] Richardson, *Messages and Papers of the Presidents*, ii. 448-449.

so plain and simple that any men of intelligence could perform them. It was A B C democracy: any applicant could aspire to any office. When it is remembered in addition that the offices were hundreds and the office-beggars were thousands, the difficulties of distribution are apparent.

Necessity is sure to evolve any machine that is really essential, but time is required for the process. Thus, although means were finally found for systematically dividing the spoils, they were not discovered early enough to save the Jackson administration from embarrassment. As of old, congressmen were active and anxious to relieve the president by assuming the whole task themselves ; delegations arranged slates, and it was reported that Congress dictated the appointment of Ingham as secretary of the treasury. On the whole, however, congressional influence seems to have been less than usual, and each member exerted influence according to his individuality.[1] Much stress seems to have been placed on petitions. Duff Green urged on Governor Edwards the importance of "signatures"; and a marshalship in Pennsylvania is said to have been awarded to that candidate whose petition was largest. A man who desired the register's office at Crawfordsville brought a petition from the Republican members of the state legislature, with private letters. Probably petitions carried more weight than had been usual, though letters of influential men almost equalled them in importance.[2]

Occasionally testimonials were brought proving the unfitness of the incumbents of the positions applied for. Some notes of this character have been published by a Mr. Derby, who claimed that he carried them with him to Washington. "I certify that I heard Major —— [Melville?] say that he believed Jackson to be a damned rascal": "I certify that many times, in conversation, Major —— said, that he was a public officer under Adams, and thought it his duty to stick by his superior officer, and believed he had more knowledge

---

[1] J. A. Hamilton, *Reminiscences*, 102, 170 ; *Richmond Enquirer*, April 3, 1829 ; *Niles's Register*, xl. 375.

[2] *Edwards Papers*, 427 ; J. A. Hamilton, *Reminiscences*, 98 ; Derby, *Political Reminiscences*, 52–53.

in his little finger, than old Jackson had in his whole body."[1]
Few applicants, however, had sufficiently definite ideas of what
they wanted to enable them to bring charges against a specific
officer. Samuel Swartwout, in a letter to Jesse Hoyt, expresses
the general attitude: "*I hold to your doctrine fully, that* NO
D——D RASCAL WHO MADE USE OF HIS OFFICE OR ITS PROFITS for
the purpose of keeping Mr. Adams in, and Gen. Jackson out of
power, *is entitled to the least lenity or mercy, save that of hanging.*
So we think both alike on that head. Whether or not, I shall
get anything in the general scramble for plunder, remains to be
proven; but I rather *guess* I shall. What it will be is not yet
so certain; perhaps Keeper of the Bergen lighthouse. I rather
think Massa Pomp stands a smart chance of going somewhere,
perhaps to the place you have named or *to the devil.*"[2]

Jackson's two most important advisers with regard to the
distribution of the patronage were Martin Van Buren, secretary of state, and General Duff Green, administration editor
and political manager of the Calhoun faction. Van Buren
tried to avoid the turmoil of the conflict; he did not reach
Washington until March 22; and he wrote to James Hamilton,
his representative with the president, that he was anxious that
his preferences for the cabinet should not be pressed in his
name,[3] though he was glad enough to have Hamilton urge
them. The most important New York appointment, that of
Swartwout as collector, was made against his wishes, and some
of his New York supporters were restive at this unexpected
passivity;[4] but he was none the less a power. His was the
velvet glove; his influence with Jackson lay in the very fact
that he knew when to give way; his followers he rather managed than commanded, letting them fight out their family
quarrels among themselves; but in the end the person who
could serve him was rewarded. He was aptly called the
"Little Magician." As head of the Albany Regency he was

[1] Derby, *Political Reminiscences,* 40.

[2] Mackenzie, *Benjamin F. Butler and Jesse Hoyt,* 50–51. Swartwout got the
great prize of the collectorship of New York.

[3] J. A. Hamilton, *Reminiscences,* 92.

[4] *Ibid.* 123; Mackenzie, *Van Buren,* 210.

looked upon by many Northern politicians as the best man on whom to rely for support when asking for office, and many delegations were sent to Washington to assure him of support in his candidacy for the succession and to request his aid in pushing through a slate of appointments. It mattered not how few Jackson's supporters might be in any district — they were sure to be divided as to the sharing of the spoils. When, therefore, one faction had declared for Van Buren, the other was swift to enroll under the banner of the only other prominent candidate for the presidency, Vice-president Calhoun. The latter interfered in the politics of the patronage much less than Van Buren did, much less than he had done himself at an earlier period; but was ably represented by that typical office-monger, General Green,[1] and so the Calhoun followers were as well taken care of as those of Van Buren.

One of these factional contests took place in Boston, and was described in an elaborate political pamphlet written by one of the participants after he had deserted to the Whig party, and corroborated by the Boston press of the period. The regular state organization declared for Calhoun, and sent Nathaniel Greene, editor of the *Statesman*, to the capital to press upon the administration a list of appointments. Another faction, represented by the *Bulletin*, cried "Stop thief," hastily rallied in support of the Van Buren plan of a second term for Jackson, and sent a counter embassy to make plain to the president their services in the past and their influence for the future. Both delegations were well received, and the offices were divided between them.[2]

A similar conflict in Illinois may be studied in the letters of Duff Green himself to Governor Edwards. The latter expected to profit by the adoption of a policy which he had so long advocated, and his friends supposed that he would have "as much influence over General Jackson as any other man in this state." He evidently desired to declare openly for Calhoun, and to rely upon General Green's influence at Washington; but Green

---

[1] Sargent, *Public Men and Events*, i. 157; *Niles's Register*, xxxvii. 103; Amos Kendall, *Autobiography*, 306.

[2] Van Tyne, *Webster*, 141; Derby, *Political Reminiscences*.

wrote : " It is particularly desirable that the conflicting interests of our party be made to harmonize and to prevent a premature collision. It is agreed on all hands that Gen'l Jackson shall hold a position for re-election if necessary or expedient. Perhaps he may desire it, and if so, no one can prevent his re-election. You will therefore plainly see the impropriety of getting up at this time any new organization of parties based upon any speculation as to a competition between Van Buren and your personal friend." [1]

The inevitable conflict came, however ; and Kinney, an ancient political foe of Edwards, went to Washington, declared for Van Buren, and secured all the Illinois appointments. As early as July, 1829, one of the governor's friends wrote, " I have seen that your expectations have not been realized with regard to the *reforming* system." Green wrote to him explaining the unfavorable nominations, blaming Edwards for not securing enough signatures in favor of his candidates, promising him better luck in the future, and urging him to stand by Jackson ; but through all the letters there is a tone of nervousness and apprehension. By the spring of 1830 Green gave up his hope of defeating Van Buren by secret manœuvre, and acknowledged that his plans and those of his opponents must come into early conflict. He was not ready to break with Jackson, but he wrote : " My own individual opinion is that Gen. Jackson will not be a candidate, and that Mr. Calhoun will be the candidate of the South and West, and that he will also obtain the Democracy of New England. Pennsylvania, New York, and Ohio are more doubtful " ; and he added that the Van Buren plan was to have Jackson reëlected.[2] It is clear from the oscillation of his policy that Duff Green felt that he was losing ground, but not until October, 1830, did he confess to Edwards that his power was waning. " The appointments in your State," he wrote, " have been the source of much anxiety to me. I could not control them." In November he gave up all hope of reconciling the two factions or of keeping on good terms with both, but wrote to Edwards declaring for Calhoun, and adding,

[1] *Edwards Papers*, 379–381, 389–391.
[2] *Ibid.* 204, 427–430, 450–456, 488.

"I feel strong enough for the crisis." In January, 1832, he again wrote to Edwards, "Instead of using the patronage upon the high principle on which it was given to him of promoting the public good, he [Jackson] uses it as a personal chattel, to be administered to advance his own re-election and to advance the private interests of a few dependants."[1] The fact that his mortification over appointments rankled so long after the actual break with Jackson took place would seem to point to that as one reason for his following Calhoun to the tents of the Myrmidons.

Duff Green was not the only political leader who had cause to complain that his recommendations were slighted. In regard to appointments, as in all other matters, Jackson was independent, and would willingly sacrifice party welfare to the calls of friendship or of personal whim. Private considerations alone seem to have led to the choice of Major Eaton to be secretary of war, and of Swartwout as collector at New York.[2] Parton, in his life of Jackson, gives as authentic the autobiographical account of a "Successful Politician"; it is at any rate characteristic. A young man, belonging to one of the prominent political families of New York, but himself of no prominence, obtains a small clerkship at Washington through the influence of Van Buren, and his duties bring him into close contact with the president. One day he asked Jackson if he is not lonesome. "Why should I be lonesome, with the house filled with people?" said the president. "Yes," said the young clerk, "there are plenty here, but they all have axes to grind." The general confessed that he was lonesome, and as it developed that this young man had no axe to grind, he became the president's friend. Subsequently one of the very fat offices in New York became vacant, and he applied for it on his own responsibility, obtained it, and later received a reappointment. Of course Van Buren did not like to see such an office wasted on a political nonentity, but he was too wise to interfere with his chief.

[1] *Edwards Papers,* 548, 553, 578–579. Green's letters to Edwards were not intended for the public eye, contain no cant, and exhibit his true feeling, though not all his feelings.
[2] J. A. Hamilton, *Reminiscences,* 97, 102; Poore, *Perley's Reminiscences,* i. 128.

When, however, he became president, he appointed another man to the post.[1]

The position of postmaster at Albany was an important one for the New York democracy. In 1829 it was still held by that General Solomon Van Rensselaer whose appointment, it will be remembered, had been vigorously opposed by Van Buren, who now felt sure of his revenge, and arranged for a new appointment. General Van Rensselaer, however, went to Washington, gained access to the president, and prepared to tear open his shirt and show the wounds which he had received in fighting for his country. He was instantly confirmed in his post.[2] Men might flatter themselves that they guided Old Hickory, but they needed to drive with a very loose rein, and must be ready to yield the direction on any show of resistance.

The plans of the party leaders were still further disturbed by the Senate. We have seen that friction between the two branches of the appointing power was by no means unusual, but never before 1829 had it assumed any considerable degree of political importance. Now trouble was anticipated from the first, as the Senate would be controlled by the opposition and would be sure to oppose the proscriptive policy. For some days after the 4th of March, Branch, Eaton, and Berrien, although nominated as members of the cabinet, retained their seats in the Senate, in order to facilitate the starting of the administration. So eager were the Jackson managers to secure a quiet launching for their new experiment in government that they deferred some nominations likely to be resisted; and such men as Amos Kendall and William B. Lewis were appointed to office the day after the Senate adjourned. Thus the special session passed off peacefully,[3] and no difficulty was to be feared for eight months.

With the first regular session in December, 1829, began an obstinate struggle. During the summer Jackson had, to a great extent, accomplished his proscription : the full issue was before

[1] Parton, *Jackson*, iii. 255.

[2] Poore, *Perley's Reminiscences*, i. 110, 173 ; Forney, *Anecdotes*, 281–282.

[3] *Columbian Centinel*, March 14, 1829 ; *Massachusetts Spy*, April 8, 1829 ; *Niles's Register*, xxxvi. 34.

the country, and the opposition prepared to make the most of
the popular outcry which, voiced by the anti-Jackson press,
seemed to offer a chance for successful attack. They could
not, of course, take the stand of rejecting all nominations;
public opinion would not have endured a course so factious.
Amos Kendall says that they did "reject on frivolous grounds
many of his [Jackson's] best nominations"; and Louis
McLane wrote to Hamilton, "It is impossible that some evil
spirit is not at work in that body, otherwise the *reckless course*
of the *opposition* must have united the majority in spite of all
men's dislike; but I confess I want the clue to some of the
rejections."[1]

The fact is that the Senate refused to confirm some of the
most prominent Jackson politicians, men of great ability but
particularly obnoxious to the opposition, — men like Isaac Hill
and Mordecai M. Noah.[2] Amos Kendall himself, one of the
most efficient public officers that Jackson appointed, was confirmed only by the casting vote of Vice-president Calhoun.
Some of the men rejected would seem to have deserved their
fate; but whether rejected for good reasons or bad, they became sure of the good-will of the president, who was moved to
inexpressible wrath at this unprecedented opposition to his will.
Sometimes he would give the victim a new position; generally
he would renominate him, even a third time. This bootless
contest went on as long as the opposition controlled the Senate,
the most conspicuous rejection being that of Van Buren when
nominated as minister to England.[3]

The opposition soon saw the futility of thus cutting off nominations in detail, and sought to devise some general bulwark
to protect such of their friends as still remained in office, and to
put a limit to the power of the executive. The Senate adopted
a resolution in 1831, declaring "that it is inexpedient to appoint
a citizen of any one State to an office which may be vacated or

[1] Kendall, *Autobiography*, 301 ; J. A. Hamilton, *Reminiscences*, 166.
[2] *Niles's Register*, xxxviii. 142, 216, 229.
[3] J. Q. Adams, *Memoirs*, vi. 252 ; Calhoun's speech in the Senate, February, 1835
(Calhoun), *Works*, ii. 445 ; *Executive Journal*, iv. 181, 255, 315, 333, 397, 447,
448 ; *Niles's Register*, xl. 249 ; Richardson, *Messages and Papers of the Presidents*,
ii. 574.

become vacant in any other State . . . without some evident necessity for such appointment." Jackson replied by a message, March 2, 1833, in which he claimed that this was an attempt unconstitutionally to restrain the president's appointing power, and said that he felt it to be his duty to abstain from any further efforts to fill the offices nominations to which had called out the resolution.[1] In January, 1832, a more sweeping resolution was introduced by Senator Ewing: "That it is inexpedient for the Senate to advise and consent to the appointment of any person, to fill a supposed vacancy in any office, occasioned by the removal of a prior incumbent, unless such prior incumbent shall appear to have been removed for a sufficient cause."

These resolutions were intended simply to guide the Senate in the execution of its constitutional function of advising and consenting to appointments; but there were many anti-Jackson men who wished to go farther, and to revive the old claim of the Senate to share in the removing power.[2] A very good case might be made out for such a construction of the constitutional clauses governing the subject; but from the point of view of expediency such a course was most undesirable, and the more moderate of the opposition discountenanced it. John Quincy Adams saw the danger of tampering with constitutional principles to further the ends of the hour, and his son wrote an able pamphlet against the proposed action; while the venerable Madison, in almost his last letter, urged adherence to the accepted interpretation, which he had done so much to establish.[3]

Nevertheless, in 1835 a committee to investigate the patronage proposed that the president submit to the Senate the reasons for each removal, a suggestion which had little practical significance, as there was no chance of making it a law, owing to the attitude of the House of Representatives. Jackson was sure to disregard a mere resolution of the Senate. In fact, when the reasons for the removal of Gideon Fitz were requested

---

[1] Clay to J. S. Johnston, April 6, 1830, Clay, *Works*, iv. 257; *Executive Journal*, iv. 150; Richardson, *Messages and Papers of the Presidents*, ii. 636.

[2] *Senate Journal*, 22 Cong. 1 sess. 108; *Niles's Register*, xxxviii. 100.

[3] J. Q. Adams, *Memoirs*, ix. 127, 218–234; C. F. Adams, *C. F. Adams*, ix. 385; Madison, *Letters and Other Writings*, iv. 385.

on the ground that such information was necessary to enable the Senate to act wisely on the nomination of his successor, the president refused to comply, arguing that the power of removal belonged to him exclusively, and that, should the Senate in executive session consider the causes of removal, the officer would thus be subjected to trial by a secret tribunal.[1]

Such crude machinery as did exist for distribution of offices was thus subjected to the double strain of Jackson's independence and the opposition of the Senate, which made it impossible for the leaders of the party to use the patronage with the best possible political effect. The spoils system was introduced, but the spoils were rather enjoyed as the fruit of the victory of 1828 than employed in the manner best calculated to secure victory anew in 1832. An illustration of the utter confusion prevailing in Washington early in the administration is found in the case of the Hartford post-office. One Norton was appointed to the position in place of Low removed. He transferred his family from Washington to Hartford, entered upon the duties of his office, and the next day found himself superseded by John M. Niles. Petitions in favor of Mr. Norton's retention received many signatures, but he was unable to regain the post.[2]

In spite of this confusion and clash of interests, it is possible to distinguish some guiding principles which controlled appointments when Jackson was tractable and the Senate tired of opposition. Samuel Swartwout wrote to Jesse Hoyt (March 14, 1829), " The great goers are the new men ; the old troopers being all spavined and ringboned from previous hard travel."[3] A new generation, or rather the Democratic half of a new generation, came to the front with Jackson, bringing fresh blood and strange manners into the civil service. Moreover, old party distinction disappeared, and men of Federalist antecedents received recognition, though the prejudice against them had by no means died out.[4]

---

[1] Jackson to the Senate, February 10, 1835 (Richardson), *Messages and Papers of the Presidents,* iii. 132–134.

[2] *Niles's Register,* xxxvi. 149, 244 ; *Massachusetts Spy,* June 10, 1829.

[3] Mackenzie, *Benjamin F. Butler and Jesse Hoyt,* 51.

[4] J. A. Hamilton, *Reminiscences, passim ; Massachusetts Spy,* April 15, 1829; *United States Telegraph,* March 10, 1829 ; *Niles's Register,* xl. 113.

It is the general opinion that fitness for the duties of office was scarcely considered by Jackson. James A. Hamilton, who was present at cabinet discussions and was in constant correspondence with Van Buren, tells us that it was never mentioned. Hamilton's memory, however, was very poor, and his statement is contradicted by letters which he himself made public. Thus, Van Buren wrote to him in March, 1829: " I cannot, from my total want of knowledge as to Barry's professional talents, speak as to the propriety of his appointment. Politically it would be well." February 15, 1829, Van Buren wrote to Major Eaton: " You want for the other concern [evidently the cabinet] practical, intelligent, and efficient men, who are conversant with the affairs of the nation, and in whom the people have confidence, — men whose capacities are adapted to the discharge of the public business, whether they might, or might not, shine in the composition of essays on abstract and abstruse subjects." [1] It is evident that efficiency was considered, though it was made of less importance than in previous administrations and was differently defined.

One class of appointments has brought to Jackson, as to other presidents, perhaps undeserved credit, — that of literary men to diplomatic posts. Such appointments are generally non-political and are therefore lauded; but poets and novelists are seldom better diplomats than are politicians, and it is almost as mischievous to use the civil service as a pension fund for literary celebrities as for disabled soldiers or defeated congressmen. The few appointments of this character made by Jackson brought in a flood of applications from budding geniuses all over the country. Livingston, when secretary of state, wrote to an incoming senator who had recommended such a young man for appointment that he had seen the latter and could not make him a consul, — that the selection of Cooper and Irving did not mean that all novelists were good diplomats. [2]

In the majority of cases the most important reasons for appointment were political. Some of the fortunate had been "original Jackson men"; others had made sacrifices by join-

[1] J. A. Hamilton, *Reminiscences*, 93, 97, 129, 139.
[2] Hunt, *Livingston*, 364, 368–369.

ing the party at the last moment; some, like Henry Lee and William B. Lewis, had done Jackson's writing for him. John Randolph, who spent ten days in Russia as minister, and drew $21,407 on his return, contributed the support of his name.[1] As a class, the editors fared the best. The newspapers had been very influential in the campaign of 1828, spreading broadcast charges of dishonesty in Adams's civil service, and of bargain and corruption. The day of the great newspapers, moreover, had not come : the local sheet was the powerful factor; and as the list of subscribers was small, advertisements cheap, and the cost of distribution heavy, such papers were seldom very profitable, and often ruined their owners.[2] It was for this reason particularly that men like Nathaniel Greene of Boston, Dabney F. Carr of Baltimore, Mordecai M. Noah of New York, Amos Kendall, Duff Green, and many others were acknowledged to deserve office. Such appointments were very generally attacked, but Niles pointed out that they were not objectionable if the editors resigned from their papers ; otherwise he said, the franking privilege gave them an undue advantage over their competitors.[3]

It was not proposed that editors resign, or that appointees generally relax their political exertions on receiving office ; office was not merely a reward for past service, but an incitement to further activity. Amos Kendall wrote for the Washington press;[4] and Mr. Noah, in an editorial concerning his appointment as naval officer at New York, said that since his new duties did not interfere with the duties and obligations he owed to the Republican party, he would not abate the attention hitherto paid to the columns of the *Enquirer*, which he hoped to improve in every department.[5] Duff Green, in return for the government printing, made his journal the official mouthpiece of the administration. When the break between the president and vice-president took place, a new paper was estab-

[1] J. A. Hamilton, *Reminiscences*, 98 ; Derby, *Political Reminiscences*, 27. Jackson allowed much more freedom of action to his supporters than one might suppose. Livingston voted against the confirmation of Henry Lee (Hunt, *Livingston*, 354). Adams, *John Randolph*, 296.

[2] Derby, *Political Reminiscences*, 43.   [4] Kendall, *Autobiography*, 372.
[3] *Niles's Register*, xxxvi. 221, 250.   [5] *Niles's Register*, xxxvi. 221.

lished, the *Globe*, and to its editors, Blair and Rives, was given what government printing the Democrats could control.[1] Service was expected of other officers as well. March 30, 1834, William B. Lewis wrote to Hamilton : "Tell Swartwout to peel off his coat and roll up his sleeves also; but, perhaps, as he has to go through the 'glorious Senate,' it would not be prudent for him to do so. Price, as his nomination will be certainly confirmed before the 8th, must do his own and Swartwout's part too."[2] Charles T. Congdon, in his *Reminiscences of a Journalist*,[3] says that in 1840 he saw a circular from Kendall to the deputy postmasters, asking them to work for Van Buren, and adding, "I shall take care that the high-minded and patriotic men who do this service shall have no cause to regret their exertions." Political assessments also appear promptly on the incoming of the spoils system ; Derby describes, apparently truthfully, an early instance of such practice in Boston.[4] The significant fact in regard to the making of appointments is the prominence, hitherto unusual, which was given to partisan activity past and future : the Federalists demanded fitness and harmony of opinion ; Jefferson in addition considered past usefulness to the party; under Jackson the promise of future activity became of paramount importance. To faith must be added good works.

We have discussed the machinery by which the spoils were divided, and the principles by which this machinery was controlled ; the question now arises as to how complete a change was made in the public offices. The impression is very general that the sweep was, proportionally, the largest in our history ; but doubtless the novelty of the proceeding, and the consequent effect it made upon contemporaries, is largely responsible for this view, which is decidedly a mistaken one. The very haphazard manner in which the matter was handled was as favorable to the retention of some officers as to the removal of others. There were Jackson men at Washington who worked to retain

---

[1] *House Journal*, 24 Cong. 1 sess. 10 (December 7, 1835).
[2] J. A. Hamilton, *Reminiscences*, 282.
[3] p. 66.
[4] Derby, *Political Reminiscences*, 85, 97.

some old public servants, either for personal reasons or because of their merit. Hamilton claims that he saved, among others, Henry Wheaton; and Van Buren felt that only with the greatest delicacy could he remove "old Mr. Maury — who, having been appointed by General Washington, has, on that account, some sanctity attached to his commission."[1]

Of an approximate total of 612 presidential officers, only 252 were removed. The number of removals would be more imposing if the deputy postmasters were included; but they were not made presidential officers until 1836. Niles, April 3, 1830, gives a list of 400 removals in this department, and Benton places the number at 600.[2] As there were about 8000 deputy postmasters in the country,[3] the proportion removed was not large; but in many cases the emoluments were so very small as to discourage competition. Moreover, Jackson did not find the civil service entirely hostile to him. Adams's postmaster-general, McLean, was one of Jackson's most conspicuous supporters; and, though he was a moderate man and the charges that he had actively used his appointing power to further his political views are probably untrue, it is not to be supposed that he rigidly excluded Jackson men from office previous to Jackson's election.[4] It is to be presumed, therefore, that a rather large portion of the appointees of the post-office department were Jackson men. Adams estimated, doubtless with some exaggeration, that more than four-fifths of the customs officials were opposed to his election in 1825; and as he made no removals, many would naturally oppose him in 1829. Some of these Jackson men found in office were doubtless removed as a result of the clashing of various interests at Washington;[5] still many must have retained their places. A third explanatory consideration

---

[1] J. A. Hamilton, *Reminiscences*, 98; Van Buren to Jackson, April 14, 1892; *Ibid.* 131.

[2] Fish, in American Historical Association, *Reports*, 1899, i. 74; *Statutes at Large*, v. 80; *Niles's Register*, xxxviii. 105; Benton, *Thirty Years' View*, i. 160.

[3] 8115 (*Official Register*, 1829).

[4] J. Q. Adams, *Memoirs*, vii. 275, 343, 351-356, viii. 8-9; Livingston, *Eminent Americans*, ii. 794.

[5] J. Q. Adams, *Memoirs*, vi. 547; viii. 193.

is that comparatively few removals were made in the South, particularly the sea-board South.[1]   From these states came few office-beggars, that is, beggars for the smaller offices; for positions of dignity they were as eager as any section, and Virginia undoubtedly felt slighted at being left out of the cabinet.[2]   With these facts in mind, we may conclude, therefore, that Jackson's opponents were almost completely swept out of the paying presidential offices in the North and West.

The fate of subordinates in local offices and in the departments at Washington is obscure.   The Blue Books or Official Registers give the changes every two years, but no indication as to cause.   The policy varied, too, with each appointing official, who seems to have been allowed a very large measure of discretion.   Van Buren wrote to Hamilton in March, 1829: "As to the publication in the newspapers I have more to say.

---

[1] Niles (*Register*, xxxviii. 105) gives a list of removals of postmasters by states as follows: —

Maine	15	Maryland	14
New Hampshire	55	Delaware	16
Vermont	22	Virginia	8
Massachusetts	28	North Carolina	4
Rhode Island	3	South Carolina	0
Connecticut	20	Alabama	2
New York	131	Georgia	2
New Jersey	14	Mississippi	5
Pennsylvania	35	Louisiana	4
Ohio	51	Tennessee	12
Indiana	19	Kentucky	16
Illinois	3	Missouri	7
	396		90

If the seaboard South — the Jeffersonian South — be taken by itself, the disproportion is still more striking: —

Virginia	8	Northern States	396
North Carolina	4	Delaware	16
South Carolina	0	Maryland	14
Alabama	2	Kentucky	16
Georgia	2	Tennessee	12
Mississippi	5	Missouri	7
Louisiana	4		461
	25		

There were five for the territories, making 491 in all.

[2] *Richmond Enquirer*, March 10, 1829.

So far as depends on me, my course will be to restore by a single order every one who has been turned out by Mr. Clay for political reasons, unless circumstances of a personal character have since arisen which would make the reappointment in any case improper. To ascertain that, will take a little time. There I would pause."[1] In 1825 there were twelve clerks in the office of the secretary of state; by September 30, 1829, the number had grown to fifteen, but only four of the original twelve were still there; in 1833 but two of these four remained. Amos Kendall, on becoming fourth auditor, insisted that he should control the appointment of his clerks.[2] In 1829 there were sixteen in his office, one more than there had been in 1825; eight of those serving in 1825 were still employed, but one was at a reduced salary. In 1833 two of these eight survivors had disappeared, but their places had not been filled.

The *Globe*, November 4, 1841, stated that there were employed in Washington 220 Democrats receiving $277,115, and 281 Whigs with salaries amounting to $336,308; and Benton says that a majority of the employees there were opposed to Jackson.[3] Such estimates are totally unreliable, for parties during the period were in too chaotic a condition to allow an accurate computation; but it is evident that many subordinates were retained, some because they were indispensable, and some because they imitated the Vicar of Bray. In the local offices a similar diversity of practice is observable. In Baltimore, Philadelphia, New York, and Boston notable changes were made,[4] while in many places there was no abnormal break whatever.

In the discussion of Jefferson's administration, it was pointed out that the attack on the judiciary should be connected with the general policy toward the patronage. The Jackson managers were not greatly disturbed by a hostile judiciary, — they ignored it when it interfered with their plans; but there was another bit of patronage, not officially belonging to the public

---

[1] J. A. Hamilton, *Reminiscences*, 129.
[2] Kendall, *Autobiography*, 308.
[3] Benton, *Thirty Years' View*, i. 160.
[4] *Niles's Register*, xxxvi. 119, 149, 163; *Columbian Centinel*, April 22, 29, 1829; Derby, *Political Reminiscences*, 70–78.

service, which they were unwilling to let slip through their fingers, — the United States Bank. Jefferson wrote to Gallatin, July 12, 1803: "As to the patronage of the Republican Bank at Providence, I am decidedly in favor of making all the banks Republican, by sharing deposits among them in proportion to the disposition they show; if the law now forbids it, we should not permit another session of Congress to pass without amending it."[1] In the days before the free banking system, all banks had the birthmark of politics; and it is not surprising that those in control of the national government demanded a share of the bank patronage. A recent writer has shown that Jackson's attitude was not determined by the Portsmouth episode, but has pointed out on the other hand that Biddle endeavored to conciliate Jackson by favorable appointments, turning the Nashville branch into a Democratic institution and corresponding continually with Major Lewis on this subject. Soon the break between the government and the bank became irreconcilable and the exchange of favors ceased.[2]

Jackson promised more than the removal of unpopular officers; he announced that he would reform the administration, and made efforts to carry out this pledge. His first step, like Jefferson's when he became president, was thoroughly to investigate the accounts of the preceding administration, in hope that facts to its discredit might be discovered. Amos Kendall says: "Among the custom-house officers and other receivers of public moneys, numerous peculators were discovered and hurled from office. The depredations of those who were removed within the first eighteen months of General Jackson's administration, in this department of the public service, were at least $280,000."[3] The real result, however, was to show the substantial honesty of the service under Adams. In some instances it was found that the government was the debtor. The unfavorable balance against Tobias Watkins, whose case was most commented on by the Jackson press,[4] was apparently only technical.

[1] Jefferson, *Writings* (Ford ed.), viii. 252.

[2] Catterall, *The Second Bank of the United States,* 187–189.

[3] Kendall, *Autobiography,* 298, 309–322.

[4] *Niles's Register,* xxxvi. 235–240, 276–280, 285, 298, 315, 332, 341–344, 358–360, 374–376, 389, 421, xxxvii. 399, 411; *Massachusetts Spy,* June 17, 1829.

Various administrative reforms were attempted. To quote again from Kendall: "The unrestrained power of the treasurer over the public funds, by which they could be drawn upon his individual check, was taken away by a new regulation. Frauds in payment of fishing bounties were stopped, and two collectors, believed to have been engaged in them, removed from office; in consequence of which there was a saving, in the first year of the administration in that branch of expenditure, of $51,271.41."[1]

As for retrenchment, Niles asserted that the only action taken had been the abolition of the office of draughtsman in the House of Representatives.[2] This is somewhat unfair. The Democrats had larger plans; in 1830 a House committee brought in an elaborate scheme, if not to reduce expenditures, at least to control them;[3] and in 1833 the president sent to Congress a report from the secretary of state, proposing a reformation of the consular service. This latter plan, while not extensive, was wholesome; consuls were to be discouraged from entering into trade, adequate salaries were to be provided, and fees were to be curtailed and regulated.[4] That more was not accomplished was not solely the fault of the Jackson leaders, for they did not have complete control of Congress. Even with this hindrance, some good was done. For example, the roll of salaries (there were some duplications of officers) at the Norfolk custom-house was reduced from forty-one in 1825 to thirty-three in 1829 and seventeen in 1833; the reduction in the amount paid, however, was only from $15,991.86 in 1825 to $13,164.50 in 1833. Nevertheless, it needs no accumulation of evidence to show that the whole method of appointment told against effective administration. The interest in reform lay in finding opponents wrong, rather than in watching friends carefully. Hamilton says that the president told him, "Go to the duties of your office, and make as much money as you can." Kendall was an efficient officer; but the "close devotion" for six hours each day which he exacted from his clerks,[5] he would

---

[1] Kendall, *Autobiography*, 298.   [2] *Niles's Register*, xxxviii. 25.
[3] *House Reports*, 21 Cong. 1 sess. i. No. 150.
[4] *Senate Documents*, 22 Cong. 2 sess. i. No. 83.
[5] J. A. Hamilton, *Reminiscences*, 140; Kendall, *Autobiography*, 317-320.

probably have dubbed aristocratic leisure before he came into office.

Political reform fared worse than administrative. The appointment of numerous members of Congress to office by the party which had long been denouncing such practice delighted Jackson's opponents,[1] and grieved many of his friends. In Tennessee, Mr. Miller, who intended to run for Congress in support of Jackson, withdrew, ostensibly at least, because the latter had seduced one governor and three senators into his cabinet.[2] Jackson felt such criticism, and in his first annual message said, "While members of Congress can be constitutionally appointed to offices of trust and profit it will be the practice, even under the most conscientious adherence to duty, to select them for such stations as they are believed to be better qualified to fill than other citizens," and he advised Congress to prepare an amendment prohibiting such appointments,[3] but it took no action on the recommendation, and interest in this issue gradually died out after the overthrow of the congressional caucus.

Early in Jackson's term, Philip Hone visited Washington and conversed with many persons prominent in society and in politics. He records: "The proscriptive course which has been pursued in relation to removals and appointments has served to cool their friends and to exasperate their enemies. . . . If Jackson succeeds for another term, it will be owing to the difficulty of agreeing upon his successor, rather than to the popularity of his administration." An intense gloom hung over the city in the spring of 1829;[4] and when, shortly after the proscription began, John Henshaw, a clerk in the treasury department, committed suicide, Adams attributed his act to fear of removal.[5] There can be no doubt that the public opinion of Washington condemned the administration, especially because

---

[1] Sargent, *Public Men and Events*, i. 167.

[2] *Jackson Gazette*, April 4, 1829.

[3] December 8, 1829, Richardson, *Messages and Papers of the Presidents*, ii. 448.

[4] Hone, *Diary*, i. 15 (March 26, 1831); *William Winston Seaton*, 210.

[5] *Niles's Register*, xxxvi. 149; J. Q. Adams, *Memoirs*, viii. 144. Henshaw was a Jackson man, and his act was most credibly attributed either to insanity or to melancholy. *Niles's Register*, xxxvi. 181; *Richmond Enquirer*, May 2, 1829.

of its policy of removals. The capital was thirty years old, with a stable population and an established society. Its solitary industry was government, and when its respected citizens were thrown out of office there was little for them to do but to go back and try to reëstablish their connection with the home communities from which they had long been severed. The alteration of political methods affected Washington more nearly than any other part of the country, and it took time to make the adjustment. July 13, 1829, Van Buren wrote to Hamilton, " Mr. Calvert . . . damns us up hill and down for reducing the value of real estate." [1] When it is recalled that in 1801 very few, even of the higher officers, had brought their families to the wilderness town on the Potomac,[2] and that consequently few homes were broken up by Jefferson's removals, it will seem less strange that this proscription has not lived in the popular memory, while that of Jackson is a well-established tradition.

In the country at large the feeling was not so intense ; but the big-letter headings of the *Columbian Centinel* indicate a disposition to make party capital out of the innovation ; while the newspaper correspondence on the subject is voluminous, containing many letters from dismissed officers, which show the evils of rotation and the true aim of the civil service. Particularly the case of the venerable Major Melville, called the "last of the Mohawks," or participators in the Boston Tea-Party, was exhibited to excite sympathy. The character of many of the new appointees was roundly attacked. Yet the contest was not without its amenities : McLean wrote to one man removed, that he had faithfully performed his duties ; and the Adams papers occasionally acknowledged that good appointments were made.[3]

Aside from personal hardships and the more obvious evils of frequent change of officers, the opposition press most deplored the tendency of the new system to create a class of office-seekers. The *Massachusetts Spy* feared that the nature of our

---

[1] J. A. Hamilton, *Reminiscences*, 142.

[2] See, for example, Pickering to Adams, May 12, 1800, John Adams, *Works*, ix. 54.

[3] *Niles's Register*, xxxvi. 242 ; *Ibid.* xxxviii. 112 ; *Massachusetts Spy*, April 1, 1829 ; *Columbian Centinel*, April 29, 1829 ; *Kentucky Reporter*, October 20, 1830.

institutions tempted every man to fit his son for a profession, that the ranks were becoming overcrowded, and that the unsuccessful would be encouraged to seek government support;[1] and even the *Jackson Gazette* voiced similar fears. It is interesting to note that De Tocqueville, in spite of his American experience, believed that office-hunting was characteristic rather of monarchies than of democracies.[2] The true significance of the crowd of applicants we shall discuss later.

The dissatisfaction was not entirely confined to the opponents of Jackson. Hamilton wrote, April 23, 1829, that he was "cruelly disappointed at the manner in which, and to the extent removals and appointments are made"; and he was not alone.[3] Particularly in the Southern press a note of dissent is perceived: removals are defended as necessary under the circumstances, but obviously it was not universally desired that the custom should become established. In contradistinction to Jackson's optimistic observation in regard to the ability of any American to fill any vacancy, the *Jackson Gazette* said that even the subordinate places required several months, or even years of experience.[4]

No doubt or misgiving, however, can be found in the jubilant note of the *Telegraph* and the *Globe:* they foretold, welcomed, and defended every step in the progress of the spoils system. "Reform," said the *Telegraph*, — "the very word acts like an electric shock upon some men."[5] They had no sympathy for men removed, — those who could not get a living otherwise were not worth their salaries to the government, — let them "root, hog, or die." "There are many clerks in the departments," wrote a correspondent to the *Telegraph*, March 27, 1829, "who feel they have a vested right in the premises, based on the proscriptive claims of the term of twenty, thirty, and forty years' actual possession. Secondly, some approximation of equality in the distribution of the government favors among its citizens ought always to be held in the view of the republic."

---

[1] April 8, 1829.

[2] *Democracy in America,* ii. ch. xx.

[3] J. A. Hamilton, *Reminiscences,* 136; Parton, *Jackson,* iii. 212.

[4] April 25, 1826.

[5] *Telegraph,* March 26, 1829, and November, 1828, to November, 1830, *passim.*

The arguments of the *Telegraph* were widely echoed by the press,[1] and were summed up by Marcy in his famous phrase, " To the victors belong the spoils." The elections showed that, if the people did not support Jackson because of his method of reform, they at any rate supported him in spite of it.

[1] *E. g. Boston Statesman*, November 18, 1828, quoted in Derby, *Political Reminiscences*, 37–38.

CHAPTER VI.

IMMEDIATE EFFECTS OF THE NEW POLICY.

1837-1845.

JACKSON had sown the wind, and Van Buren was to reap the whirlwind; nor can there be much doubt that, so far as the civil service is concerned, he deserved the harvest that he garnered. Martin Van Buren is a man with a recently rehabilitated reputation : we find in him now a force and an ability unacknowledged by his contemporaries, and the temptation is to go to the extreme and to sink the politician in the statesman. It is true that in 1829 he did not directly meddle in minor politics to any considerable extent, and that as president he made but eighty removals.[1] His indirect influence under Jackson, however, we have seen to be enormous; and the chief reason for his moderation while at the head of the government was that the personnel of the service was favorable to him, as is shown by the large number of office-holders who supported his candidacy at the Baltimore convention.[2] It is quite true that the spoils system was not the work of Van Buren or of Jackson, or of any one man; it was the result of a gradual development : but evolution cannot relieve an individual of his personal responsibility any more than predestination excuses a man's sin. The fact remains that Van Buren stood before the country as the head of the Albany Regency and the representative supporter of the spoils system; that he associated with politicians who represented what was worse in the politics of the

[1] Fish, in American Historical Association, *Reports*, 1899, i. 75.
[2] *Niles's Register*, xlviii. 248.

time; and that he appointed Jesse Hoyt to succeed Samuel Swartwout as collector at New York.[1]

It is because of the opportunity which it affords for a study of the results of the spoils system on governmental efficiency that Van Buren's administration is chiefly interesting to the student of the civil service. Principles remained as Jackson had enunciated them; qualifications were the same as in 1829; and the machinery was in a state of transition between the confusion which we observed in the last chapter and the definite order of the fifties. While the materials for such a study are unusually abundant, it is peculiarly difficult to arrive at a fair judgment. Conditions, as we have seen, varied greatly in different parts of the country, and Jackson added another element of diversity.

A spoils system does not drive ability from the civil service; it rather attracts many brilliant men who think they can sail best in troubled waters; it appeals to the gambler's instinct. Such men have characteristics different from those of the seekers after the safe monotony of a life position, but their capacities are fully as great. The really deleterious change that the spoils system does make is to throw open the doors of office to a very inferior class of men, and to lower the minimum of capacity required. This fact, by increasing the distance between the extremes, makes the task of generalization more difficult. A special condition must also be given due weight at this time, — the panic of 1837.

Investigation into the efficiency of the civil service under Van Buren is not much aided by popular criticism of the details of administration, for comments on them are almost as rare, during the twelve years from 1829 to 1841, as during the previous period. The department of the national government that most nearly affects the larger part of our population is the post-office. At the beginning of Jackson's administration, when the great change of personnel had disturbed the delicate machinery of the mails, there was some public fault-finding,[2] but after the

---

[1] Mackenzie, *Benjamin F. Butler and Jesse Hoyt* and *Martin Van Buren, passim;* Von Holst, *United States,* ii. 354, note ; *Executive Journal,* v. 66 (January 29, 1838).

[2] *Massachusetts Spy,* May 13, 1829, quoted in *Albany Argus,* July 17, 1829 ; *Richmond Enquirer,* May 18, 1841 ; *Niles's Register,* xxxvi. 315. There are more

first few months it was heard no more; the tolerance of the American public cannot be exaggerated. There was some congressional investigation, but it was hushed by the death of Barry. Our discussion must therefore be based chiefly on official documents, and, in the main, be confined to two departments, — the land office and the customs service.

The land office was peculiarly liable to suffer from all the adverse conditions of the times. The local offices were widely scattered, and often in places difficult of access; the officers were therefore comparatively independent. The majority of them, moreover, were situated along the frontier, or in the newer districts, where it was often impossible to find, except at long intervals, proper means of forwarding to the central government the money received for lands. Local banking institutions were unsound and local currency worthless a hundred miles away. Moreover, the frontier lacks the business knowledge, and consequently the high standard of business honesty, of a long-established community. As Mr. Garesche, a clever agent of the treasury, wrote to Secretary Woodbury, the code of morality in general was lower than that acknowledged in the East. When, in addition to these circumstances, the sudden expansion of land purchases, springing from $5,000,000 in 1834 to nearly $25,000,000 in 1837,[1] is remembered, with the temptations to speculation thus brought to the land officers, it cannot be astonishing that irregularities are to be found.

During these years the treasury department had special agents travelling about the country examining the condition of the offices, the local standing of the officers, and sometimes their political affiliations. Whether the investigations on the latter point were or were not in pursuance of verbal instructions cannot be ascertained, but the fact that the subject is very often not mentioned would seem to indicate that they were not. A characteristic summing up of such an investigation is as follows: "Messrs. Ball and Leiper appear intelligent men, and no doubt will conduct the business with fidelity and impartiality. They

complaints in letters than in the press, and the blame is generally thrown on the difficulties of travel rather than on the government.

[1] Bourne, *Distribution of the Surplus.*

are zealous supporters of the administration, and very popular." [1]
Mr. Garesche, the ablest of these agents, reported that very few
officers understood bookkeeping: [2] there is scarcely an office
reported in which the examiner did not find errors that, on examination, proved careless rather than fraudulent; the different
sets of books hardly ever coincided. In 1836 Garesche was
sent to New Orleans to investigate fraudulent land purchases,
which rumor magnified to such an extent that the governor
mentioned the subject in a message to the legislature; but close
examination by a legislative committee revealed scarcely anything definite, except some looseness in dealing with purchasers. [3]

Such incompetent bookkeepers could not successfully cover
up extensive frauds; but the government was not as particular
as it should have been in enforcing the land laws, and a clever
man could buy as much land as he wished regardless of restrictions. Many of the officers bought land extensively on their
own account, sometimes covering it with the name of a near
relative or partner. [4] Some loaned out for their own advantage
the government balances that they held; and many were in the
habit of exchanging money, a practice which might or might
not be dishonest, but which was certainly improper considering
the monetary conditions of the time. One receiver of public
money was reported as farming out his office. [5] The locating of
purchases upon the plats seems to have been poorly done, a
circumstance from which resulted much confusion; but the only
complaint commonly made to the special agents by the public
was that the land surveying was not done rapidly enough, [6] and
this may have been the result of the voracious demand rather
than of inactivity.

That the crisis of 1837 should under these conditions have

[1] *Senate Documents,* 23 Cong. 1 sess. vi. No. 439, p. 26.

[2] *Ibid.* p. 19.

[3] *House Documents,* 25 Cong. 2 sess. ix. No. 297, p. 297.

[4] *Senate Documents,* 23 Cong. 1 sess. vi. No. 439, p. 2; *House Documents,* 25
Cong. 2 sess. ix. No. 297, pp. 192, 205, 297 ff. Every report contains a list of such
lands.

[5] *Senate Documents,* 23 Cong. 1 sess. vi. No. 439, p. 28; *House Documents,* 25
Cong. 2 sess. ix. No. 297, pp. 192, 292.

[6] *Senate Documents,* 23 Cong. 1 sess. vi. No. 439, p. 18.

staggered the land office can cause no surprise. The statement of Clay, that sixty-four out of sixty-seven of its local officers were defaulters, may have been temporarily true;[1] but owing to the wise leniency and careful nursing of Secretary Woodbury the loss was not so great as might have been anticipated. It is impossible to state, with any near approach to accuracy, what the loss finally amounted to; $750,000 would fairly approximate it.[2]

If we may trust the apparently frank reports of the special agents, it is noticeable that nearly all these men had the confidence of their communities;[3] and often, though they had an unfavorable balance against them, they retained the confidence of the treasury department. An interesting case is that of the receiver of public money at Columbus. He had speculated with government funds and had lost, and he appeared as a defaulter. Mr. Garesche, who examined the case, wrote to Woodbury: "The man seems really penitent; and I am inclined to think, in common with his friends, that he is honest, and has been led away from his duty by the example of his predecessor, and a certain looseness in the code of morality which here does not move in so limited a circle as it does with us at home. Another receiver would probably follow in the footsteps of the two. You will not, therefore, be surprised if I recommend his being retained, in preference to another appointment; for he has his hands full now, and will not be disposed to speculate any more. . . . He has, moreover, pledged his word that, if retained, he will strictly obey the law. . . . Lenity towards him . . . might stimulate him to exertions which severity might perhaps paralyze." He further stated that the deficit amounted to $55,965.54, and that the defaulter owned land that, if sold at

---

[1] Speech at a Harrison convention, August 17, 1840, Clay, *Works*, vi. 218.

[2] *House Documents*, 25 Cong. 3 sess. iv. No. 122, particularly pp. 15–37; *House Reports*, 25 Cong. 3 sess. ii. No. 313 (pp. 143–147 give a list of the unfavorable balances). The amount due from receivers on the list of defaulters, January 15, 1838, was $1,073,837.41, of which $248,159.13 had accrued prior to March, 1829. *Niles's Register*, lvi. 140–141.

[3] What few complaints are found are chiefly made by disappointed land purchasers, and they rarely make out a good case. See *House Documents*, 25 Cong. 2 sess. ix. No. 297.

$1.25 per acre, would amount to $61,549.98.[1] We may disagree
with Mr. Garesche as to the expediency of retaining the officer
under the circumstances, but he was certainly right in his estimate of conditions. It was, in the mind of most frontiersmen
and inhabitants of new places, a very long step between stealing
another's money and speculating with it. The main fault lay in
the general unfamiliarity with business methods; and we may
question whether even Adams could have kept the service entirely above its environment, though he might well have done
better than Jackson and Van Buren.

Somewhat different was the plight of the customs department.
There the defalcations were less widespread; but the individual
cases were more striking, and the losses were due to simon-
pure dishonesty. Educated by thirty years of corrupt politics,
the New York politicians were ready to make the most of the
chance that Jackson gave them. Swartwout proved a "king of
defaulters"; his stealings were estimated, in 1838, at $1,250,000.
So cleverly had his books been falsified that as late as 1836 he
deceived a committee politically hostile to him. He passed the
evening of his days abroad, accompanied in his flight by Price,
the district attorney, who stole a paltry $60,000 on his own ac-
count, but aided Swartwout in his operations.[2]

Jesse Hoyt, who succeeded to the New York collectorship, was
more fortunate rather than essentially better than Swartwout.
He drew the interest on large sums of public money, and left a
temporary deficit of $160,563.31, which would have been much
larger if he had not written off in his own favor, without any
legal justification, $201,580 as a one per cent fee on the duties
collected.[3] The congressional reports make it clear that the

---

[1] *House Documents*, 25 Cong. 2 sess. ix. No. 297, pp. 241–258. Von Holst,
unfamiliar with the American idiom, understood Garesche as saying that the man
had "his hands full" of stolen money, and as advising Woodbury to keep him for
that reason, on the analogy of the fox and the gorged flies; and he uses the case as
a text for a denunciation of the administration. Von Holst, *United States*, ii. 355,
note.

[2] Woodbury's Report, *House Documents*, 25 Cong. 2 sess. v. No. 111; *Ibid.* 25
Cong. 3 sess. ii. No. 13, iii. No. 54, iv. No. 122; Von Holst, *United States*, ii. 350–
354; Poore, *Perley's Reminiscences*, i. 129; *Globe*, May 22, 1839.

[3] *House Documents*, 27 Cong. 2 sess. vi. No. 212, pp. 65–67. The entire report
contains 1720 pages.

custom-house was regarded as the Democratic citadel of New York, and that the collector's chief function was to return a Democratic majority.[1] Some idea of the loss of efficiency is given by the fact that, while the collection of customs under Adams cost one and one-half per cent, it cost under Swartwout two and one-half, and under Hoyt five and one-half;[2] it is impossible to estimate the financial loss of the government, as much of this was the result of fraudulent assessment and connivance at the illegal entry of goods. These evils, unlike those of the land office, were due solely to the spoils system : Jackson alone was responsible for Swartwout; Van Buren alone was responsible for Jesse Hoyt, and neither Swartwout nor Hoyt would have been appointed by any previous administration.

The spoils system was violently attacked from the beginning. The leaders of the opposition were personally affected by it. Clay wrote, "Our poor friends, Cutts, Watkins, and Lee, are among the sufferers."[3] It was easy for those who were being despoiled to see distinctly the evils which the system brought in its train. Clay wrote, May 15, 1829, "Incumbents, feeling the instability of their situation, and knowing their liability to periodic removals, at short terms, without any regard to the manner in which they have executed their trust, will be disposed to make the most of their uncertain offices while they have them, and hence we may expect immediate cases of fraud, predation and corruption." In a debate in 1831, Webster magniloquently elaborated these and other evils ; and in the same year the National Republican convention in New York violently denounced the proscription.[4]

The efforts of the Whig leaders to check Jackson's course were futile, as we have seen, but they served to make both sides think out their principles. The first attempt to define the programme of the opposition was made March 7, 1834, when Clay

---

[1] *House Documents,* 27 Cong. 2 sess. vi. No. 212, pp. 67, 459–462, 479–481, 487–488 ; *Senate Documents,* 23 Cong. 1 sess. v. No. 422, vi. Nos. 435, 442 ; *House Documents,* 27 Cong. 2 sess. ii. No. 77, vi. No. 212.

[2] D. B. Eaton's report, *House Executive Documents,* 46 Cong. 2 sess. No. 94.

[3] Clay, *Private Correspondence,* 226.

[4] Clay, *Works,* v. 376 ; Sargent, *Public Men and Events,* i. 286 ; *Niles's Register,* xl. 278.

introduced into the Senate a series of resolutions embodying some doubtful constitutional interpretations and referring several questions to committees.[1] At the next session of Congress a committee was appointed to consider the whole subject of the reduction of the patronage, and to report to the Senate such measures as seemed advisable. Calhoun was chairman, and Judge White, who had served on the similar committee of 1826, was an active member. Benton, who had been the leading figure in the previous investigation, was now in favor with the administration, and so could take no prominent part in a proceeding which was an implied criticism of Jackson. The report was submitted February 9, 1835, and was at once ordered to be printed for public distribution, together with Benton's report of 1826.[2] The bills which were its logical outcome were not presented with the report itself, but may be combined with it in treatment. The suggestions in brief were: (1) a constitutional amendment to secure the distribution of the surplus; (2) a provision that banks be charged interest on the national money left with them on deposit — measures intended to cut down the patronage. In addition, the following regulations in regard to that part of the civil service which must be retained were proposed: (3) that the Four Years' Bill be repealed; (4) that the accounts of all disbursing officers be periodically laid before the Senate; (5) " that, in all nominations made by the President to the Senate, to fill vacancies occasioned by removal from office, the facts of the removal shall be stated to the Senate at the same time that the nomination is made, with a statement of the reasons for such removal."[3]

The debate brought forth by this report was brilliant. Webster devoted the greater part of his speech to the exposition of his favorite doctrine that the Senate possessed the constitutional right to advise and consent to removals. He was willing to support the bill proposed, because he thought that the restric-

---

[1] *Senate Documents,* 23 Cong. I sess. iii. No. 155.

[2] *Senate Journal,* 23 Cong. 2 sess. 148. In regard to it, see Madison, *Letters and Other Writings,* iv. 34 ; J. Q. Adams, *Memoirs,* ix. 357 ; Tyler, *The Tylers,* i. 524.

[3] *Senate Documents,* 23 Cong. 2 sess. iii. Nos. 108, 109 ; *Congressional Debates,* 23 Cong. 2 sess. 361, 422.

tions, and particularly the regulation that the president should present to the Senate the causes of removals, "mild and gentle" as they were, would have some effect in correcting the evils which beset the progress of the government. Clay took the same general ground, but proposed an amendment resembling the Tenure-of-Office Bill of 1867. Calhoun delivered by far the ablest speech, but he, too, occupied himself chiefly with the constitutional question, taking it up from the point of view of expediency.[1]

These speeches, and others, were eloquent and sincere; they exhibited high ideals of the civil service pleasing to contemplate, and are full of passages suitable for quotation by the civil service reformer. When we turn, however, to the measures proposed, we find a paucity of invention painful to contemplate. If these men, after ten years of discussion of the civil service, could not propose measures better calculated to improve it, their ability has been overrated. The fact is, that what had so long occupied their attention was not primarily the civil service, but the patronage: their first object was not to secure good work, but to reduce the power of the president; it was still political and administrative reform which they felt necessary. The bill passed the Senate by a vote of thirty-one to sixteen,[2] slept for a year, and then was killed by the House in committee of the whole. The Whigs, therefore, were constrained to wait for the adoption of their plans until they should obtain control of all branches of the government.

The interest in these debates evinced in the country at large was great enough to urge the Whig leaders to redoubled efforts;[3] and when the crises of 1837 and 1839 came, they pointed to them as a fulfilment of their predictions. With unremitting zeal they belabored the administration for the fraud and incompetency which infested the service. As far as issues are discernible in the noisy campaign of 1840, reform was the

[1] Webster, *Works*, ii. 88 ff. ; *Congressional Debates*, 23 Cong. 2 sess. 461, 518–524, 553–563.

[2] *Ibid.* 576.

[3] See a petition from the legislature of Connecticut (*House Documents*, 25 Cong. 2 sess. xi. No. 442) and a resolution of the Tennessee legislature, October 12, 1835 (*Good Government*, June 15, 1896).

most prominent. Particularly was this true in the South, where the state-rights men, a little out of sympathy with many of the schemes of their Northern allies, could join unequivocally in the plan to curtail the powers of the chief executive. The Democrats vainly brought countercharges, claiming that all the defaulters had been Federalists and were now at heart Whigs.[1] This was quite too absurd to fool the people, and the result of the election was to place the Whigs in full control of the government and give them an opportunity to put into effect the reform that they had been so long preaching.

How was the reform to begin? Should the Whigs follow the precedent set by Jackson? These questions forced themselves peremptorily forward in the very hour of victory. Though Harrison, in a letter to the people of Tennessee, indicated that he would not make removals· for opinion's sake, the question could not be considered as settled. The cabinet eagerly discussed it, and the opposition papers announced that a proscriptive policy was being forced upon the president by the Whig leaders, especially by Clay. Whatever might be the position of the leaders, the insistent call of the office-seeking mob, numbering from thirty to forty thousand, that travelled to Washington could not be mistaken. We have the testimony of Adams that they were orderly and well-behaved; but their influence on the policy of the administration was precisely the same as that of their predecessors in 1829, and they found a voice in the blatant *Madisonian.* Whatever its repugnance, the cabinet during March, 1841, decided upon an extensive change of personnel throughout the civil service.[2]

Much time might be spent in discussing the chain of events that led up to this decision; but it would be time wasted, for

---

[1] See speech of Mr. Duncan in Congress, *Globe*, May 23, 1839. Lists are given showing money lost to the government by defalcations of Federalists, beginning with the $12,898 hypothecated by John Adams, and including the $1,250,000 taken by Swartwout. It will be remembered that in 1836 Swartwout supported White for the presidency.

[2] Poore, *Perley's Reminiscences*, i. 259, 382; *Globe*, April 27, 1841; J. Q. Adams, *Memoirs*, x. 439; *Richmond Enquirer*, March 6, 11, 1841; Tyler, *The Tylers*, ii. 32. Niles, quoting from the *Madisonian* of April 6, 1841, attributes to the pertinacity of these men the death of Harrison. *Niles's Register*, lx. 83.

the result was practically dictated by circumstances. It was a fundamental weakness of the civil service as established in the United States at that time, that when one party had begun to turn out its opponents, its successors were almost forced to do the same. The long continuance of the Republican party in power after 1801 had put off the evil time, but had not changed the conditions. Ninety-nine out of every hundred Whigs thought that the Democrats deserved punishment for the proscription of 1829, and that the most appropriate penalty would be to turn them out of the offices they had usurped. For many years, moreover, the Whigs had been criticising the civil service as corrupt, and naturally their first step in reform was to put new blood into it: *similia similibus curantur.* When it is remembered, in addition, that the majority of the Whigs were human Americans, who wanted a good office if they could get it, it must be conceded that a proscription was inevitable.

One result of the proscription was an amusing *volte face*, not uncommon in American journalism. The Democratic papers were filled with material that might have been cribbed from their opponents of 1829. They resorted to the old device, that the Federalists used in Jefferson's time, of publishing each day extracts from speeches which had been delivered by the Whig leaders in condemnation of Jackson, and beneath these headings citing specimens of their practice now that they were in power. The more conservative Whig papers barely mentioned offices, and printed appointments only, omitting removals, as Niles claimed that Jackson editors did twelve years earlier. The *Madisonian*, however, boldly took up the gospel of the *Telegraph*, and resorted to all the old arguments of the spoilsmen, — rotation, and the duty of the executive to complete the proscription that the people, by removing the elective officers, had begun. Papers of a middle type did not defend removals in general, but rejoiced in the ejectment of "brawling and unscrupulous public lecturers."[1]

The most effective answer to criticism that the Whigs could

[1] *Richmond Enquirer*, May 7, 10, 1841; April 13, 1841, quoting *Springfield Gazette.*

have given would have been the adoption of the measures which they themselves had proposed in 1835. This obvious course they did not follow, either because they had become convinced that such schemes were impracticable, or because they merely considered that circumstances alter cases. When Mr. Watterson, in June, 1841, introduced a resolution preceded by a long preamble setting forth the sentiments of Webster, Clay, and Crittenden on the question of the patronage, and calling for "the names of all officers dismissed . . . with the reasons for the dismissals in each particular case," the House refused, by a vote of 130 to 57, to suspend the rules to allow the resolution to be considered.[1] Two reports were presented to Congress: one to the House by Garrett Davis in 1842, recommending that the law of 1820 be repealed, and that removals be made for stated cause only; and the other to the Senate by J. T. Morehead in 1844, embodying an argument for the right of the Senate to advise and consent to removals; but no action was taken on either of them.[2]

Instead of carrying out their programme and so justifying their good faith, the Whigs attempted the impossible task of defending their own action by showing how black were their opponents. Commissions were appointed to investigate government offices wherever mismanagement was suspected. One was sent to Norfolk; another headed by Matthew St. Clair spread dismay through Washington; the most important was that of which Poindexter was chairman, and which exposed the rottenness of the national service in the city of New York. These commissions exposed much fraud; but some of them committed the error of sitting behind closed doors, and they were therefore denounced by the Democrats as "espionage commissions,"[3] whereby their findings were greatly discredited, and the excuse which they were expected to furnish for the Whig proscription was deprived of its effect.

---

[1] *House Journal,* 27 Cong. 1 sess. 147–148.

[2] *House Reports,* 27 Cong. 2 sess. iv. No. 945; *Senate Documents,* 28 Cong. 1 sess. vii. No. 399.

[3] *Niles's Register; Richmond Enquirer,* May 2, 1841; Richardson, *Messages and Papers of the Presidents,* iv. 152, 154, 162; *House Documents,* 27 Cong. 2 sess. ii. No. 77, iv. Nos. 213, 230, vi. No. 212; *Richmond Enquirer,* May 21, 28, 1841.

The mere fact that removals were made does not prove that the spoils system was adopted; and it is, therefore, important to study more closely the position of the great Whig statesmen in 1841, and the general policy of the party. Clay was undoubtedly the leader, and he seems to have disdained petty politics. Curtis, the friend of Webster, endeavored to secure Clay's support for the collectorship at New York by promising to work for the latter's nomination for the presidency in 1844 — the matter to be kept secret from Webster. Clay seems to have been shocked at the proposition, to have rejected it, and to have desired to inform Webster. He made it a rule to support no applicants for positions;[1] but this attitude was more a matter of convenience than of probity, and is therefore not particularly commendable, for, when appointments have to be made by personal selection, if the best men refuse to interfere, the choice is thereby left to their inferiors. He evidently found it difficult to maintain his aloofness. March 15, 1841, he wrote to General Harrison that he had not said that Mr. Curtis should not be appointed to the New York collectorship. "I have never," he said, "gone beyond expressing the opinion that he is faithless and perfidious, and, in my judgment, unworthy of the place."[2]

Webster wrote to Everett, February 2, 1841, that he did not know what would be done in regard to the foreign agents. "As to officers out of the cabinet," he said, "little or nothing is yet known. The richer collectorships and attorneyships are subjects of much competition; so are the post-offices in the great cities. I intend to exert my influence to get a snug little place for I. P. Davis, and that is all the purpose, relative to such matters, that I have as yet expressed."[3]   His later official con-

---

[1] Clay, *Private Correspondence*, 448–451.

[2] *Ibid.* 452–453. He asks Harrison whether he has dictated "in the administration of the public patronage? The whole cabinet as well as yourself," he adds, "can say that I have recommended nobody for any office. I have sought none for myself or my friends. I desire none. A thousand times have my feelings been wounded by communicating to those who have applied to me, that I am obliged to abstain inflexibly from all interference in official appointments." See also Tyler to Clay, April 30, 1841, Tyler, *The Tylers*, iii. 94.

[3] Webster, *Private Correspondence*, ii. 100.

nection with the administration forced him to take somewhat more interest in appointments; but all the evidence confirms the impression derived from this letter, that on the whole he considered the selection of civil servants a subject unworthy of his serious attention.[1]

The sudden death of Harrison and the accession of John Tyler spread consternation through the ranks of the Whig office-seekers. It was feared that he might be unwilling to remove Democrats; but, as Greeley says, " he turned out better than had been expected." Tyler felt bound by the hopes that General Harrison had excited, and appointed many to whom the latter had promised places, but whom he did not live long enough to commission. In the end of April he wrote a friendly letter to Clay: " My attention is turned to the removals from office after the manner that you suggest, and I hope that to the recent appointments you have nothing to object. The post-office at Lexington shall be attended to." The proscription was therefore continued in spite of the "accident." [2]

The machinery for distribution was not much in evidence in 1841. Whig congressmen naturally received many requests for the use of their influence; but Adams thought that success depended on whether the congressman was in favor with the cabinet;[3] and this administration seems to have more closely controlled appointments, both general and local, than that of twelve years before.[4] Senator Tallmadge wrote to President Harrison: " The more I reflect on the subject, the more I am surprised at the nomination suggested to you of Mr. —— as Marshal for the Northern district of New York. I do not

---

[1] See Webster to Dutton, May 9, 1830; *Ibid.* i. 500; Harvey, *Reminiscences of Webster,* 178; Poore, *Perley's Reminiscences,* i. 382. Van Tyne (*Webster,* 375-389) discusses his effort to secure a place for his son in 1849, but there is scarcely any reference to general appointments.

[2] Greeley, *Recollections of a Busy Life,* 215, 310; Tyler, *Parties and Patronage,* 68; Tyler, *The Tylers,* ii. 32, 310, iii. 94.

[3] J. Q. Adams, *Memoirs,* x. 436, 441, 460. Of one applicant he said, " I might as well undertake by my influence to obtain for him the office of porter at the gate of heaven" (*Ibid.* 446).

[4] Even the names of men to be appointed inspectors in the custom-houses were sometimes sent from the capital. See *Richmond Enquirer,* May 18, 21, 1841; Tyler, *The Tylers,* iii. 94-96.

know the man and I never heard of him — and I insist upon
it, that it is my right, representing the State of New York, to
be heard in relation to the appointments in the state — no
man knows more about the state than myself — and I repeat
that the appointment of ———— is the best appointment
that can be made. . . . I am willing to take the responsibility
of it." This vigorous protest was heeded, but not until Tallmadge had written several letters and had secured the support
of "a large portion of the Whig senators of New York, the
leading members of the Assembly and all the acting canal
commissioners."[1] The local party organization of New York
City made an effort to control minor appointments there, but
with only fair success ;[2] and the hand of the administration was
everywhere felt. In the country as a whole there would seem
to have been less machinery and less friction than in 1829.

Claims for office were based on a great variety of grounds.
There were charges of nepotism;[3] and the removal of Dr.
Martin, the experienced chief clerk of the state department to
make way for Webster's son, was certainly in questionable taste,
though some excuse for it is afforded by the intimate relations
which exist between that officer and the secretary of state.[4]
As usual, the martyrs of the Jacksonian persecution were considered as having just claims upon the administration ; but the
most convincing argument that the office-seeker could submit
in support of his application was service to the party. Activity
or docility in Congress still commanded recognition, though it
had now come to be regarded as undignified to leave the legislative for the administrative service, and the old opposition to
the appointment of congressmen had not entirely disappeared.
Levi Lincoln endeavored to avoid this latter criticism by resigning his seat before receiving his nomination to the collectorship
at Boston.[5]

Newspaper men were still the most important single class of

[1] From manuscripts not available for reference.
[2] *House Documents*, 27 Cong. 2 sess. vi. No. 212, p. 68.
[3] The *Richmond Enquirer*, May 7, 1841, notes in office two of Clay's relatives,
two of Webster's, and one each of Chittenden's, Ewing's, and Tyler's.
[4] Tyler to Hugh S. Legaré, May 16, 21, 1843, Tyler, *The Tylers*, iii. 112.
[5] J. Q. Adams, *Memoirs*, x. 460; *Richmond Enquirer*, April 2, May 20, 1841.

party workers, and they were given fitting recognition,[1] although the Whigs had criticised the appointment of editors by Jackson. Not so many, however, obtained prominent posts as previously, for the business was becoming more profitable and leading editors did not need office. After a bitter debate which very nearly resulted in a duel between Clay and King of Alabama, Thomas Allen received the printing of the Senate as a reward for his dashing conduct of the *Madisonian.* The *Madisonian* followed Tyler in his quarrel with the Whigs, whereupon the latter returned to the ever loyal *National Intelligencer.*[2]

Politicians of a low grade were occasionally successful, particularly those from Pennsylvania, where the Whigs had a reputation for sharp practice. The appointment of Alexander Ferguson, popularly known as Bela Badger, to the naval office at Philadelphia was considered very discreditable.[3] The qualifications of the man who was appointed collector at New York are described as follows in a letter from Peter B. Porter to Clay: "Although not personally popular, [Curtis] is represented as possessing an extraordinary share of tact or stratagem; and as being able, by his skill in planning and combining, and his untiring industry in executing, to produce the most astonishing political results. That, with the office of Collector (which he [Weed] considers as second only in influence to that of Postmaster-General) he could, on all important occasions, command the vote of the city of New York, and *par conséquence*, of the State. . . . Now I do not doubt that Mr. Curtis is a man of rare address. . . . And I have as little doubt that if he succeeds in obtaining the office, its patronage will be disposed in favors to his particular political friends."[4]

---

[1] The *Richmond Enquirer*, April 6, 1841, quoting from the *New York Herald*, gives half a dozen such cases. The statement that Tyler never made such appointments is disproved by the single case of the editor of the *Statesman*.

[2] *Richmond Enquirer*, May 11, 1841; Blair and Rives secured the Senate's printing in 1841 (*Congressional Globe*, 26 Cong. 2 sess. 197). Clay, however, had the matter reconsidered after March 4, and the establishment of the Whig majority, and Allen was then appointed (*Ibid.* 256; *Senate Journal*, 27 Cong. 1 sess. 25). For the appointment of Gales and Seaton, see *Senate Journal*, 28 Cong. 1 sess. 21.

[3] *Niles's Register*, xxxvii. 132; *Globe*, April 26, 1841; *Richmond Enquirer*, May 14, 1841. He was removed a year later. *Executive Journal*, vi. 153.

[4] January 28, 1841, Clay, *Private Correspondence*, 448–450.

While the methods of selection were thus much the same under the Whigs as under the Democrats, the former drew, in many parts of the country, from the wealthier portion of the population, and so commanded a greater share of business ability. Webster sent an able circular to the heads of departments, instructing them to prevent all interference with elections on the part of public officers and all assessments for political purposes, and to require promptness in rendering accounts.[1] There were more complaints at the appointment of abolitionists than at the conduct of the service.[2] Although the repeal of the subtreasury act left public money at the discretion of the public officers, there were no defalcations and no frauds for the succeeding administration to investigate. The climax of praise is reached when we are able to quote from the diary of John Quincy Adams, for a date some time after the starting of the new government, that " as yet, the appointments have not been absolutely discreditable." [3]

The sweep of 1841 was by no means so nearly complete as that of 1829. The 458 removals made, out of a possible total of 924,[4] would seem to represent a proportionately greater change than at that time; but, for reasons which will appear later, only 304 of these removals should be here considered. Of the usual conditions, three — the number of officers who are indispensable, of offices whose emoluments are too small to attract, and of friends in office — should all be kept in mind; but the exemption of the South is not so marked as formerly, and one new condition must be added. In 1841, for the first time, many officers resigned to escape removal. Among them was George Bancroft, collector at Boston, in commenting on whose resignation the prejudiced *Madisonian* said that he took this

---

[1] *Niles's Register*, lx. 51-52.

[2] The appointment of General Wilson to be surveyor-general of Wisconsin was particularly obnoxious. The influence of Joel Eastman and of Webster was supposed to be responsible for these appointments. *Richmond Enquirer*, January 29, May 14, 1841. The *Globe*, May 28, 1841, makes some complaint of confusion owing to change of personnel. For praise, see *Richmond Enquirer*, May 23, 1841 ; *National Intelligencer*, June 2, 1844.

[3] J. Q. Adams, *Memoirs*, x. 449.

[4] Fish, in American Historical Association, *Reports*, 1899, i. 76.

action because of some technicality of the customs law by which a resigning officer might receive certain fees that would not be paid to one who was removed.[1] The proscription extended, as was customary, beyond the presidential offices into the departmental and local offices. Levi Lincoln, at Boston, is reported to have had, within three or four days, 830 personal applications for the fifty places within his gift.[2]

This study of the conduct of the civil service under the first administration of the Whigs reveals the fact that they adopted all the characteristic practices of the spoils system. Their leaders were indifferent; either willingly or perforce they permitted a repetition of the deeds which they had so violently condemned. The fact that the offices were better executed and the public better served than previously proves, not that the spoils system was non-existent, but that it is not absolutely synonymous with bad service ; that efficiency depends more on the characteristics of the men appointing and appointed to office than on the method of selection.

Special attention should be paid to Tyler's 154 removals, which involved a curious episode after the resignation of Webster, when the break with the Whigs was complete and the president alone was responsible for the policy pursued. Tyler had looked with disgust on the Jacksonian proscription ; and his son, Lyon G. Tyler, asserts that he retained his scruples on becoming president, and countenanced removals only because he felt bound to fulfil many of the promises of Harrison ; and that even this feeling of obligation did not prevent his tearing in pieces whole lists of proposed appointments which involved removals.[3] A minute study of his conduct, however, shows that, as the fight grew fiercer, he found it impossible to forego the use of a weapon so ready to his hand as the patronage.

Tyler considered himself a " Republican " of the old school, and Levi Lincoln argued on this supposition in July, 1841, when he desired the treasurer at Boston, who was not a Whig,

---

[1] *Madisonian*, March 12, 1841.

[2] *Richmond Enquirer*, March 11, April 2, 1841, quoting *Boston Post.*

[3] *Congressional Debates*, 23 Cong. 2 sess. 596 ; Tyler, *Parties and Patronage*, 68; Tyler, *The Tylers*, ii. 310.

to be retained. By the summer of 1842 to be a Democrat became a recommendation to Tyler. W. W. Irwin, one of the " corporal's guard," wrote to Caleb Cushing in regard to the postmaster at Harrisburg, " He is a Democrat and I don't want to see him removed." May 16, 1843, Tyler wrote to Hugh S. Legaré, who was acting as secretary of state, advising him to appoint as chief clerk Dr. Martin, who had been removed by Webster. This appointment, he said, would be equivalent to putting a Democrat at the head of a department. Not only were the Democrats to be placated, but a third party was to be formed, and the president eagerly looked about for places to give to friends and supporters. J. A. Scoville wrote to Calhoun, October 25, 1842, " I wish with all my heart we had the control of Mr. Tyler's appointments, but Mr. Rhett writes me that he thinks Tyler is working for his own nomination." When Calhoun became secretary of state, he wrote to R. M. T. Hunter: " The claims on the part of Mr. Tyler's political and personal friends on him are pressing, . . . many of them have had their expectations excited for a long time. . . . Acting, as I suppose, under the force of the circumstances alluded to, he makes most of his appointments on his own responsibility without consulting the appropriate Department. This, however, is in strict confidence." [1]

Vacancies did not occur often enough to answer the president's needs, and he gradually began a proscription of his own. April 1, 1842, he wrote to N. Beverley Tucker : " Do you know Samuel Merry, the receiver of public money at St. Louis, who and what is he ? And if he is not the proper sort of man, how would Mr. Brown like the place ? " While this sweep was not extensive, it included many valuable posts, among them the ministry to Brazil; the collectorships at Portland, Boston, Savannah, Mobile, Baltimore, and New York; the post of surveyor at New Orleans, Baltimore, and New York; the naval office at New York; the post-offices at Indianapolis, Philadelphia, and Albany; the governorships of Florida and Wisconsin; and many more of salient political importance. The climax was

[1] *Calhoun Correspondence* (American Historical Association, *Reports*, 1899, ii.), 602, 856. Tyler, *The Tylers*, iii. 94–96, 103, 112.

reached in the spring of 1844, when the president was pushing with all his might and main the annexation of Texas. In June the *Tribune*, apropos of the removal of the surveyor at New York, remarked, "All our office-holders who are not of the latest Tyler and Texas stamp, with India rubber consciences and a firm belief in the integrity and disinterestedness of the Accident, will soon go overboard." [1]

It is not surprising that a president without a party encountered difficulty with the Senate, and that scarcely a post was filled without one or two rejections or withdrawals. Particularly unwilling were his opponents to allow him to fill an associate judgeship of the Supreme Court, although he made a very creditable selection for it. The Whigs especially opposed this nomination before the election of 1844, in hopes that the appointment might be deferred until Clay became president. After the election had taken away this hope, the Senate confirmed the nomination of Samuel Nelson, previously chief justice of New York. [2]

Tyler's appointments were, as Calhoun said, made from the ranks of his personal and political friends, with the personal element fully as prominent as the other. [3] His personal friends were men of ability and honesty, and consequently the service suffered no detriment except that which was inevitable from the frequent changes. Among his appointees were Caleb Cushing, Robert Rantoul, Jr., and Henry A. Wise, men of ability; while many others, themselves unfamiliar, had names which indicate local respectability. The only removal of special interest was that of Solomon Van Rensselaer, who was at last deprived of office.

In the summer of 1844 the political status of Tyler and his friends was precarious. Nominally a candidate for reëlection,

[1] Tyler, *The Tylers*, iii. 99–100. *Executive Journal* for the period. See also Appendix D, below.

[2] Tyler nominated John C. Spencer, then Silas Wright, then Chancellor Walworth; after the election he withdrew this name and presented Nelson's. Hammond, *Silas Wright*, 396–401.

[3] On the one hand, he was charged with nepotism (*Daily Atlas*, December 25, 1844), on the other with paying insufficient attention to friendship (Tyler, *The Tylers*, ii. 404, note).

he really had no chance whatever of success. What, then, would be the standing of the men he had placed in office? Most of them were Democrats and could support Polk's nomination. Could not Tyler, by withdrawing in his favor, secure consideration for them? These questions were in everybody's mouth. Robert J. Walker, unwilling to risk Texan annexation by a divided vote, wrote to Polk asking if Jackson would not reinstate Tyler in the Democratic party; while Tyler's friends suggested to Jackson a union of forces, whereby they would be brought "into the support of Polk and Dallas," and would be "received as brethren by them and their friends, all former differences forgotten." Jackson answered these propositions with an emphatic "no"; but Tyler apparently believed that, openly or tacitly, some arrangement had been reached. He withdrew from the race, and on September 13, 1844, wrote to his daughter that if Polk came to power, the new administration would be a continuance of his own.[1]

Polk seems to have been in some danger of committing himself to this policy, as he requested Tyler to give a certain position to his brother. Tyler readily assented to this proposition, which seemed to establish his position in the Democratic party; but if he really thought that an agreement had been made to retain his friends in office, he showed bad faith and an extreme lack of tact by continuing, between the election and the inauguration of Polk, to make removals and appointments, for which at that time there could have been no motive other than a desire to provide for his friends. The result was that Polk, even if he wavered for a time, in the event justified the confidence of Jackson, who wrote to him: "The offices are filling up by Tyler. . . . I have said to my friend Blair that you have sufficient energy to give yourself elbow room, whenever it becomes necessary."[2]

---

[1] Tyler, *Parties and Patronage*, 81–82 ; Tyler, *The Tylers*, iii. 139–146.

[2] Tyler, *The Tylers*, iii. 88, 155. Niles quotes the *Globe* and the *Richmond Whig* to the effect that the "nondescripts" will get nothing from Polk, and advises that Whigs and Democrats combine to exclude Tyler men from office. *Niles's Register,* lxiv. 331. *Executive Journal,* vi. December 16, 23, 30, 1844, January 27, February 21, 1845.

"The revival of the old democracy by the elevation of General Jackson in 1828, and the accession of a new set of men in 1829, presented the first rabid and hungry scenes of office-begging that the government of this country ever experienced. The spirit with which the democratic dynasty of 1829 went into power began to leaven the whole political world in the country. Violence and rancor increased throughout the republic. . . . On Harrison's accession was there reform or change in their exhibitions? Not at all. . . . The torrent of office beggars set over him and the cabinet like the torrent of Niagara over its precipitous cliffs. . . . The principle of rewarding friends and punishing foes, by using the public offices of the country for the purpose, has been recognized and practised for the last twenty years by both parties; but it is a practice and a principle which has existed only in modern times." This editorial from the *New York Herald* of 1849 was in substance perfectly true. Both parties were now thoroughly committed to proscription; and he was indeed a hypocrite, as Marcy said, who did not acknowledge that, as an actual fact, to the victor belonged the spoils. So far as the national service was concerned, this policy was, moreover, an innovation of "modern times": some political removals had indeed been made by Adams, many by Jefferson, and there was from the first some play of factions about the federal offices in various states; but not until 1829 did the genuine spoils system come into existence; and since that date it has flourished without break, though with some recent diminution.

We have found that, by turning our attention from national politics to those of the states, it is possible to discover for the spoils system a pedigree the authenticity of which is vouched for by strong family resemblance. In 1820 it was an institution of New York and Pennsylvania; it found adherents even in staid Massachusetts, and strong pressure was being brought to induce the central government to give it favor. As years passed, adherents increased and pressure grew, until we are surprised, not so much that it received general recognition at last, as that its adoption was delayed so long. This steady progress, advancing with constantly accelerated speed towards universal acceptance, overcoming the repugnance of the Whig leaders, although they were committed against such use of the patronage, and of Tyler, although his father had been one of the first to raise his voice against the evils of political appointments, implies such an impelling force behind the movement as can be roused only by an institution peculiarly adapted to the time and fitted to serve some important function in the body politic. It is not sufficient, therefore, to have traced the rise of the spoils system : we cannot claim to have any adequate understanding of its history until we have discovered the cause of its strength by discovering the need which it fulfilled.

The true cause for the introduction of the spoils system was the triumph of democracy. If the people as a whole are to exert any tangible influence on the conduct of government, they must be organized. Unorganized they may effect a revolution, but they cannot thereby control administration. The division of the people into parties is not sufficient to secure this pervasive influence; it gives them an opportunity to vote on special questions and at stated intervals, but not to select the questions or to vote when the issue is fresh in the public mind. If the majority is to mould the policy of the party, if the *demos* is to be kept constantly awake and brought out to vote after the excitement of the hour has passed away, it is necessary that the party be organized. There must be drilling and training, hard work with the awkward squad, and occasional dress parade.

This work requires the labor of many men : there must be captains of hundreds and the captains of tens, district chiefs and ward heelers. Now, some men labor for love and some for glory; but glory comes only to the leaders of ten thousands, to the very few — it cannot serve as a general inducement, and even those who love must live. It is an essential idea of democracy that these leaders shall be of the people ; they must not be gentlemen of wealth and leisure, but they must — the mass of them at any rate — belong to the class that makes its own living. If, then, they are to devote their time to politics, politics must be made to pay. It is here that the function of the spoils system becomes evident; the civil service becomes the pay-roll of the party leader ; offices are apportioned according to the rank and merits of his subordinates, and, if duties are too heavy or new positions are needed, new offices may be created. To apply these facts to America, the spoils system paid for the party organization which enabled the democracy of Pennsylvania to rule after 1800 and which established "a government of the people" in the United States in 1829.

An interesting illustration of the interrelation of democracy and these, its two concomitants, is to be found in the history of the old South before the war. There democracy did indeed exist, but without party organization or the spoils system, and the aristocracy habitually controlled the government. It is to be noticed, however, that when in a party convention the leaders of the South met the leaders of the North, the latter often had to yield; for they knew that although the platform might be a little distasteful to the rank and file of their supporters, party organization and discipline would prevent the dissatisfaction from reaching the polls — the party would stick together. In the South, on the other hand, very many men formed their own political opinions and acted upon them, while many more followed some particular leader, irrespective of party.

The armor in which democracy won its early victories in this country, and to which it still clings in great part, may now seem crude and heavy and inapt to the wearer; but we should not forget that at the time of its introduction it was the very best that had been devised; that by it, for the first time in history, a numerous and widely scattered people was enabled itself to direct its whole force to its own advancement; and present appreciation of the evils of the spoils system should not blind us to the fact that in the period of its establishment it served a purpose that could probably have been performed in no other way, and that was fully worth the cost.

CHAPTER VII.

THE SPOILS SYSTEM TRIUMPHANT.

1845–1865.

> As it was in the beginning
> Is to-day official sinning,
> And shall be evermore.
> — RUDYARD KIPLING.

THE period from 1845 to 1865 marks the apogee of the spoils system in the United States : the old traditions of respectability had passed away, and the later spirit of reform had not arisen; the victors divided the spoils and were unashamed. The general interest was turned almost completely from attempts to limit the patronage of the executive and to improve the service, to the rival fortunes of the office beggars. These were, perhaps, watched with an interest the more keen because of the lack of sporting contests, of national base-ball leagues, and international yacht races. Horace Greeley paraded a contempt for such petty squabbles, and attributed to his subscribers a like disdain, but nevertheless added that those who wished the correct news in regard to such matters should read the *Tribune*.[1] The presidential election became a quadrennial "event," with the civil service as the prize. Every 4th of March great mobs filled the capital, and the streets and saloons were crowded with men betting heavy expense and vast loss of time on the chance of getting something out of the hurly-burly.[2] This period can

---

[1] *New York Tribune*, March 10, 23, 1853, March 23, 1857.

[2] The *New York Herald*, March 8, 1849, said: "We know something of the scenes exhibited by office beggars at Washington on the change of the dynasty. Any one who saw the sight presented in the month of March, 1829, on the first accession

best be made clear by first giving a brief account of each
administration, and then examining the structure of the spoils
system.

Of no previous president had so little been known before
inauguration as of Polk, and consequently the development of
his policy was closely watched. Whig papers predicted that a
sweep would be made, but for a time it hung fire. March 28,
1845, John Quincy Adams heard that Buchanan, Walker, and
Mason were against a general turnout; Marcy, Bancroft, and
Johnson for it, and that Polk also favored it. By April 2 the
proscription had begun, and Adams talked of it with Joseph
Gales, who said that for the first time rotation was distinctly
avowed as a motive for making removals.[1]

Within the Democratic party there were many men who
thought that they could dictate to this upstart president, but
those who knew him did not share this opinion. Buchanan
wrote to Governor Shunk of Pennsylvania, December 18, 1844 :
" You ask my advice in regard to recommendations from you
to President Polk. I think you ought to be cautious in giving them, if you desire that they shall produce the effect your
recommendations well deserve." Buchanan's impression that
caution would be necessary in dealing with the president must
have been strengthened when, in February, 1845, the latter told
him that he must retire from the cabinet if he became a candidate for the presidency; and that while head of a department he
must not be long absent from Washington.[2] The clearest indication of Polk's independence is given by his treatment of the
various Democratic factions. Calhoun probably expected to
retain his position as secretary of state,[3] for his policy seemed

of General Jackson to the presidency, or the similar exhibition that was displayed in
March, 1841, when General Harrison became chief magistrate, can readily conceive
the crowds of expectants, the hungry and importunate beggars, the miserable scramble
for office, and the terrible annoyance to the president and cabinet, which will be
revived with full energy about these days in Washington." See also *Ibid.* April 6,
1849, March 9, 1853, March 11, 14, 25, 1857; *Boston Daily Advertiser*, March 13,
1849 ; *Republic*, June 14, 1849 ; *New York Tribune*, March 12, 1857.

[1] *Boston Courier*, March 1, 1845 ; J. Q. Adams, *Memoirs*, xii. 187, 190.

[2] Curtis, *Buchanan*, i. 528.

[3] Calhoun to Mrs. F. G. Clemson, March 11, 1845, *Calhoun Correspondence*
(American Historical Association, *Report*, 1899, ii.), 647-648.

to harmonize with that of the president, yet he was allowed to
retire. Tyler, as we have seen, hoped that his friends would
be left in their respective offices, but he was disappointed.
Polk did confirm his own brother in the post of chargé d'affaires
at Naples, to which Tyler had appointed him, and continued
a few others in office. John G. Mason, Tyler's secretary of
the navy, was made attorney-general because he was Polk's personal friend, and some members of the third party were transferred to inferior places; but the majority were removed or
they resigned.[1]

Much more striking was the fate of the *Globe*. Since its
foundation it had been the exponent of the Jacksonian democracy, and the Blairs fully expected that such would continue to
be the case. The fact that they had supported the nomination
of Van Buren and opposed the annexation of Texas was offset
by their acquiescence in accomplished events; while a recognition of their claims would tend to salve the wounds which the
Baltimore convention had caused; moreover, the influence of
the dying Jackson was enlisted on their side. All this availed
not against Polk's desire to be master. The venerable Mr.
Ritchie was called from the *Richmond Enquirer* and established
at Washington as editor of the *Union*, which was destined to
occupy until 1857 the position, now given it of official organ
of the Democratic party.[2] Polk seems to have used the patronage for the purpose of pushing through his own policy, rather
than of cementing alliances with hostile factions.[3]

Three hundred and forty-two removals were made during
Polk's administration; but the country was by this time so
used to the practice that little complaint is heard, save in the
case of one long lingering survivor of the Revolution. The
president was, however, criticised as introducing politics into
the naval service by displacing General McNeil and his assist-

---

[1] *Executive Journal*, vii. 12, 14, 15; *New York Observer*, March 22, 1845; *Boston
Courier*, March 15, 26, 1845; *New York Observer*, March 22, 1845; *Executive Journal*, vi. 348, 377, 433, 441, 443, vii. 12, 14, 15.

[2] Von Holst, *United States*, iii. 6.

[3] The report got abroad that he was determined to appoint none who persever-
ingly annoyed him. See *Connecticut Courant*, March 23, 1845; *Boston Courier*,
March 27, 1845.

ants from the dry dock at Brooklyn,[1] a criticism that grew more general as the Mexican War progressed. Wise men regretted, what we must all now most deeply lament, that the policy of rotation led to the recall of Henry Wheaton, at a time when the perfection of his equipment promised a splendid fruition for American diplomacy.[2] In regard to appointments, Webster wrote to his son Fletcher, March 13, 1845, " I must do him the justice to say, however, that he appears to me to make rather good selections from among his own friends." On the whole, many of his appointments were praised,[3] while none excited any very marked disapproval, except from those immediately interested.

In 1849 the Whigs still had some qualms of conscience about making any extensive sweep; but, as the *Republic* said, " If, forsooth, the administration adopt the construction contended for by the party of the spoils [that the Whigs should make no removals], proscription will be perpetuated and the Whig Republican party proscribed forever."[4] " Thus far on my way to Washington," wrote Seward, " I find myself floating on a strongly increasing tide of people. . . . The world seems almost divided into two classes, both of which are moving in the same direction; those who are going to California in search of gold, and those going to Washington in quest of office. How many adventurers are preparing themselves for disappointment, revenge, and misanthropy!"[5]

The man who was to determine the fate of these eager pilgrims was even less known politically than Polk, and among

---

[1] Fish, in American Historical Association, *Reports*, 1899, i. 77; *New York Observer*, March 29, 1845.

[2] William R. King wrote to Buchanan, March 28, 1846: "I greatly doubt the policy of making removals when the incumbent possesses talent and information, and from a long residence has acquired facilities for obtaining useful information. . . . This I know runs counter to your theory of rotation in office; which may be correct as respects office at home, but should not, I think, apply to those held abroad" (Curtis, *Buchanan*, i. 567). See also W. V. Keller, *Henry Wheaton, on Appreciation* (1902).

[3] Webster, *Private Correspondence*, ii. 206; *Boston Courier* (Whig), March 25, 26, 1845.

[4] June 14, 1849.

[5] Seward, *Seward*, ii. 100; *Boston Daily Advertiser*, March 13, 1849.

his many negative recommendations which were pressed upon public notice was the suggestion that, as he was not a politician, he would have no friends to reward with office, and could therefore proceed with impartiality, but after the election enough "original" Taylor men sprang up to absorb all offices had he yielded to them. Taylor's policy continued for some time problematical. He said in his inaugural that he would make "honesty, capacity and fidelity indispensable prerequisites to the bestowal of office"; but many feared that a fourth prerequisite was intended, though not mentioned; namely, antenomination support of General Taylor. It was thought that he might, acting under the direction of his secretary of state, Clayton, try to build up a new faction. In Massachusetts the division between the Taylor men, of whom Abbott Lawrence was the most prominent, and the supporters of Webster, who could not get over their disappointment at losing the nomination,[1] was very bitter; and it was expected that this and similar feuds would be reflected in the appointments. Taylor did not quite justify these predictions, for, while he held aloof from the old party leaders, he did not refuse them recognition, and appointed friends and relatives of both Webster and Clay to office. Yet Clay was much displeased, and considered the appointments of Taylor both "wrong and impolitic"; he was disappointed at finding a second Whig President intractable, and was incensed at the weight given to Crittenden's advice, which Seward described as being "at once honest, misconceived, and erroneous."[2]

A significant contest took place in regard to the New York appointments. Seward became friendly with the president's brother, and expected, as senator, to control the patronage in that state; but Taylor developed an unusual respect for the vice-president, and when the time came, Mr. Fillmore, an opponent of Seward, was found firmly intrenched in the confidence of the executive. February 27, 1849, Seward, always optimis-

---

[1] *Boston Courier,* March 27, 1845; Richardson, *Messages and Papers of the Presidents,* v. 6; *New York Herald,* March 15, 1849; Curtis, *Webster,* ii. 356-358.

[2] Clay, *Private Correspondence,* 613-614; Clay to Nicholas Dean, June 21, 1849; *Ibid.* 587; Seward to Weed, February 27, 1849; Seward, *Seward,* ii. 101.

tic, wrote to his wife that he and Mr. Fillmore had "begun to agree." Later, when more aware of his difficulties, he wrote to Weed, "I have stipulated for time and inaction concerning Marshals, Postmasters, District Attorneys, and there I leave these matters." At that time he was employed until eleven every morning with applicants for office. March 10 he wrote again to Weed : " Mr. F. cannot now agree to anything but that he and I shall go together to the Secretary and each name a candidate for Marshal. . . . The Cabinet is not unfavorable, but timid in their conduct between F. and myself. General Taylor has got out by casting all responsibility on the Cabinet." Again, March 24 : " Let Governor Fish now write to me when you have any advice to give the Cabinet. Some of the members take *that* point with great respect. It is the State Administration at Albany that is to be strengthened, and the Governor is its acknowledged head. This saves the necessity of deciding between the V. P. and the Senator." This suggestion was acted upon and the affair was settled ; Seward wrote, March 29, that "every member of the Cabinet breathed more freely." In the preliminary encounter as a whole, Fillmore fared rather better than Seward ; but later events brought the latter into the closest intimacy with the president, who came to listen attentively to the seductive voice of Seward's *alter ego*, Thurlow Weed.[1]

Under Taylor 540 of the 929 presidential officers were removed ; and in his first year, out of the total civil service of 17,780, 3406 were removed and 2802 resigned. When Congress met in December, 1849, this record was violently attacked, Senator Bradbury leading the way with a resolution asking the president to lay before the Senate " all charges which have been preferred or filed in any of the departments against individuals who have been removed, . . . with a specification of the cases, if any, in which the officers charged have had opportunity to be heard, and a statement of the number of removals made under each department," a resolution which he amended later by adding, "including subordinates in the customs-houses, and other branches of the public service." The debate was acrimonious,

---

[1] Bancroft, *Seward,* i. 206 ; Seward, *Seward,* ii. 100, 107 ; Weed, *Autobiography,* 587, 590–591.

but purely partisan, the Democrats accusing the president of insincerity, and the Whigs defending his action on the ground that it was made necessary by the previous conduct of the Democrats. No useful suggestions were made in the discussion.[1]

When Fillmore succeeded to the presidency in 1850, there was almost as complete a change of policy as if an opposing party had come into power, and the drooping interest in the patronage revived. July 12, 1850, Seward wrote that Washington was "filling up with strangers"; and letters and newspapers are full of the absorbing topic. Seward, of course, fell from favor. He wrote to Weed, July 15: "I shall not touch, or attempt to touch, an appointment. I shall vote for all appointments." In order to get rid of Weed, Fillmore offered him the Austrian mission. On the other hand, the traditional leaders of the party felt their influence revive. Clay wrote to his son, in August, that his relations with Mr. Fillmore were "perfectly friendly and confidential," which of course meant that his advice was generally followed, and added that he anticipated that his candidate for the Lexington post-office would prevail. Fillmore made eighty-eight removals, indicating that he did not attempt entirely to undo the work of his predecessor, but that he did make use of his power to support his policy by rewarding his friends.[2]

The independent attitude of Polk had been followed by the split in the Democratic party in 1848. Probably in the tangle of motives which drew the adherents of Van Buren to the point of actual separation, resentment at their exclusion from office would be found to be a cord of some strength. When, therefore, all factions came together in 1852, it was expected that all would receive a share of the fruits of victory. President Pierce was not adverse to such a policy: like Polk, in being a dark horse, he differed from him both in distinctly aiming for a second term and in trying to conciliate and patch together the

---

[1] Fish in American Historical Association, *Reports,* 1899, i. 78 ; *Congressional Globe,* 31 Cong. 1 sess. 74, 160 ; Appendix, 480–496 ; also 31 Cong. 2 sess. 36–42.

[2] Seward, *Seward,* ii. 145 ; Weed, *Autobiography,* 596–598 ; Clay, *Private Correspondence,* 611 ; Fish, in American Historical Association, *Reports,* 1899, i. 79 ; *New York Herald,* March 15, 1849 ; Rhodes, *United States,* i. 184.

various factions of the party, rather than in boldly taking the lead.

He settled to his task in a businesslike way; but though he fixed hours for callers, he was pursued by them at all times and in all places. The cabinet officers received applicants, mechanically heard their stories, filed their papers, and then discussed their cases. It had by this time become the custom to put aside all ordinary business for the first month after the inauguration, in order that the administration might devote all its energies to the war of the spoilsmen. Pierce made Marcy secretary of state, a step which, it was feared, indicated a tendency to favor the "Softs" in the New York appointments; but a slate, greatly commended for its cleverness, was arranged for the state, which offset this danger by giving the best local appointments to the faithful "Hards" or "Hunkers," while the "Softs" or "Barnburners," or "Van Buren men," received just enough to keep them quiet.[1]

Through the country at large, office-seekers were divided into "Old Fogies" and "Young Americans." The "Old Fogies" in New York State were the members of the Albany Regency; they had for a long time monopolized appointments, and as early as 1845 were unpopular as habitual office-holders. It was pointed out that an aristocracy was but a group of men enjoying the sole benefit of state emoluments, and that by this definition the Regency had ceased to be democratic.[2] Since 1830 national politics had been controlled by one generation of leaders in both parties, and each proscription meant, to a great extent, simply the return of those exiled by the last. Was this rotation in office? Marcy was an Old Fogy, and seems to have been largely influential in selecting men for foreign posts; the *New York Herald* was led to complain that Young America was exiled to Central America. It advertised white hair-dye for office-seekers.[3] Aside from these family quarrels, Pierce's appointments excited comparatively little comment; the press was apathetic.

[1] *New York Herald*, March 11, 18, 21, 23, 30, 1853; *New York Tribune*, March 21, 1853; McLaughlin, *Cass*, 283.

[2] *New York Tribune*, October 1, 1845; *New York Herald*, March 17, 1853.

[3] March 22, 24, 1853.

For President Buchanan it was left to round out the spoils system. Pierce had made 883 removals,[1] thus practically exorcising all non-Democratic elements from the civil service. Now Buchanan attained the presidency, as the *Herald* said, " with infinite labor, at vast expense, and by the skin of his teeth." Much of this effort had been caused by the office-holders, nearly all of whom had aided Pierce in his struggle for renomination. Should they be spared, though they were Democrats? Were not the supporters of the successful candidate the real victors? Buchanan decided that the civil service should be remanned, and announced that no one should, unless under exceptional circumstances, receive a reappointment after his commission expired. The argument used to defend this innovation was, of course, the long-suffering one of rotation in office, which now was understood as implying that offices were but prizes and should not be enjoyed for more than four years by any good Democrat.[2] The idea was not a new one, for Andrew Johnson, when member of Congress in 1846, had offered a resolution to the effect that subordinate positions should be held for eight years as a maximum.[3]

Much criticism of this new practice was nevertheless aroused. Marcy said that the maxim, " To the victors belong the spoils," was attributed to him, but that he never would have advised pillaging one's own camp. Yet so good was party discipline that no serious trouble resulted, and many faithful partisans even resigned voluntarily in order to maintain their standing in the party. The principle of rotation was not carried to an entirely logical conclusion ; many an officer escaped incidentally through some unusual political influence, and the whole South was exempted. It was said that the North and West demanded change, but not the South ;[4] and Buchanan was enough of a Democrat to execute the will of the people according to local tastes.

[1] Fish, in American Historical Association, *Reports*, 1899, i. 80.

[2] Curtis, *Buchanan*, ii. 185–186 ; *New York Tribune*, March 10, 1857 ; *Connecticut Courant*, March 14, May 9, 1857; *New York Herald*, March 4, 16, 18, 23, 1857.

[3] *Congressional Globe*, 29 Cong. 1 Sess. 192–193.

[4] *Connecticut Courant*, March 21, 1857; *New York Herald*, March 23, 1852; March 16, 18, 28, 1857 ; *New York Tribune*, March 12, 20, 28, 30, 1857. The

Buchanan's interpretation of rotation in office was acted upon steadily until Roosevelt succeeded McKinley in 1901;[1] and another innovation made in 1857 has continued to the present time, and will probably prove permanent, that is, the abolition of the official organ of the administration. He gave to Allen, the editor of the *Union,* the collectorship of Portland, Maine, and announced that no paper would succeed to the intimate relation with the government which it had occupied.[2] Yet the *Union* continued its existence and still enjoyed, to some extent, the confidence of the cabinet.

At the time of the inauguration, the *Herald* expressed the hope that the new president would not attempt, as the last one had done, to coneiliate all factions, but would pursue an independent course. This required more moral courage than Buchanan possessed, and he soon became involved in the usual meshes of intrigue, while endeavoring to arrange all-satisfying slates for Boston, Philadelphia, Baltimore, and New York.[3] The contests for the appointments in these cities throw much light on the politics of the time, and one example is worth giving as an illustration of the influences at work in securing appointments. In New York, the focus of the excitement, the most respected of the factions was the New York Hotel set, consisting of the capitalists of the Democratic party. These men were reported to have a special claim on the president, as they had contributed heavily to carry the Pennsylvania state election, which had such an important bearing on the nominating convention of 1856; and it was whispered besides that, unless they were conciliated, Robert J. Walker would not accept the governorship of Kansas. They secured the collectorship for Augustus Schell, an eminently

---

hold of rotation, in the West, is amply illustrated in the history of Lincoln's attempt to get into Congress. See Tarbell, *Lincoln,* ii. 194–206.

[1] There was at this time the usual flood of applications, but they were not acted upon.

[2] *New York Herald,* March 24, 28, 1857. Some hoped that he would appoint some "Old-Line Whigs" who voted for him. *Connecticut Courant,* March 14, 1857.

[3] *New York Herald,* March 4, 11, 18, 20, 26, 1857; *New York Tribune,* March 17, 18, 1857.

respectable gentleman.[1] At the opposite extreme of the social scale was the unterrified city democracy of the "Bloody Sixth,"[2] headed by the mayor, Fernando Wood. The New York Hotel set furnished money, Wood supplied votes. Isaiah Rynders, as the chief representative of this element, obtained an important office, — the marshalship; he was a notorious politician, with an evil reputation of many years' standing, and his appointment was gleefully derided by the opposition press.[3] Between these extremes were cliques and factions of varying degrees of respectability and rapacity. "Prince John" Van Buren, one of the most accomplished of political anglers, landed the next most important office, the postmastership, for his friend, Isaac Fowler, or rather, he secured for him an exemption from the principle of rotation. The naval office was obtained by General Sickles for his friend, Samuel B. Hart.[4]

In national politics, Buchanan favored the South, and his administration of the patronage reflects this tendency. One of the most notable instances was that of the California appointments. All the patronage for that state was given to Dr. Gwin, of a well-known proslavery expansionist family of Mississippi; while Broderick, the other senator, of more moderate views, was totally excluded from favor. The Kansas appointments afford another example of the same tendency.

Buchanan's removals were scattered through his entire term.[5] The Democratic party was gradually disintegrating under the stress of the slavery contest; the orthodox were becoming steadily fewer, while the recalcitrant needed constant punishment. The most important break was that which occurred when Douglas proved unwilling to support the administration in its Kansas policy; when, in 1858, he was contending with

[1] *New York Tribune,* March 21, 24, 25, 27, 1857; *New York Herald,* March 27, 1857.

[2] *New York Herald,* March 21, 1857.

[3] *New York Tribune,* March 25, 1857; *Connecticut Courant,* March, 22, 1845, March 28, 1857.

[4] *New York Herald,* March 7, March 17, 25, 1857.

[5] Forney, *Anecdotes,* 221; *New York Herald,* March 4, 1853; *New York Tribune,* March 25, 1857; *Connecticut Courant,* April 4, 11, 1857; Brooks, *Lincoln,* 206; Fish, in American Historical Association, *Reports,* 1899, i. 81.

Lincoln for the senatorship from Illinois, he was read out of the party, and the whole executive patronage was turned against him.[1] It was probably because of these feuds that Buchanan's appointments were more severely criticised than those of any previous president except Jackson. In themselves they do not seem to have been noticeably worse.

We are very prone to disentangle the web of the past, pick out the salient features, and then imagine that they, and they alone, absorbed contemporary attention as well as our own. Thus, when we speak of the Republican victory of 1861 and the inauguration of Lincoln, we think of the on-coming Civil War, and picture the men of that date as occupied wholly with the insoluble problems of slavery. Very differently employed, however, was the mind of the average politician: it was a party victory, and the customary scenes of party triumph were to be witnessed in the threatened capital. Lincoln said that he felt like a man who was letting offices in one end of his house while the other was burning down.[2] An interesting illustration of conditions in Washington is given by one of the participants, who says that a large number of enthusiastic Republicans who desired post-offices formed a guard to protect the president from assassination, thinking that thereby they might obtain easy access to him and so press their claims to the best advantage.[3]

Contemporaries complained that Lincoln devoted too much time to such matters;[4] and now that criticism of him has become somewhat akin to treason, lamentation is made that these petty affairs were so much forced upon him. The fact is, it was part of Lincoln's God-given fitness for his time and place that he was a politican as well as a statesman. The Republican party was new; it was composed of diverse, hostile elements; it was full of petty jealousies, and its discipline was not good: if it was to be kept together, much depended on a proper disposition of the favors the president could bestow. If he had had no patronage,

[1] See speech of Forney on this occasion, October 28, 1858, Forney, *Anecdotes*, 363-365.

[2] Lamon, *Recollections of Abraham Lincoln*, 212.

[3] Address of Mr. Keyes of Madison, Wisconsin, at a convocation at the University of Wisconsin, February, 1902.

[4] Dana to Adams, March 9, 1863, Adams, *Dana*, ii. 264.

if the spoils system had not been in vogue, all might have been well; but, as conditions were, the appointment to a petty post-office might be fraught with much import to the safety of the Union.

Lincoln made 1457 removals, there being 1639 places within his gift.[1] When it is remembered that to many posts in the South no appointments could be made, and that consequently no removals are noted, it will be seen that the sweep was the most thoroughgoing that had ever been made; indeed, it was almost complete. This fact is partly to be explained by the long years during which Southern influence had been predominant at Washington, a circumstance which had made loyal men keenly suspicious of all who had obtained government favors. The stress and confusion of the time, and the rapid changes of the political kaleidoscope, are indicated by the fact that the occupants of some offices were changed two and three times between 1861 and 1865.

In making appointments, Lincoln pursued a middle course between Polk's independence and Pierce's attempt to please all factions. He took pains to consult every one who had any right to be heard, but controlled everything with a loose yet powerful rein.[2] He had the faculty of pleasing men by asking their advice even if he did not take it. He let everything that would settle itself do so, provided certain general conditions were complied with. He made no attempt to obtain the men best fitted to perform the functions of the various offices, except in case of the very highest; for minor places he did not even insist that a man be fit. When a man was once appointed, Lincoln would neither remove him until he was thoroughly discredited, nor promote him; for in either case there would be a new office to fill.[3]

Among the things considered in conferring office, geography

---

[1] Fish, in American Historical Association, *Reports*, 1899, i. 82.

[2] See the correspondence of prominent men of the period, *passim*. He regularly consulted senators, delegations, governors. He pleased Hamlin very much by asking him to name the New England member of the cabinet, but in the end merely inquired which of four men the New England delegation preferred. See Weed, *Autobiography*, 614; Lincoln to Hamlin, December 24, 1860, Hamlin, *Hamlin*, 374.

[3] Tarbell, *Lincoln*, ii. 66, 418.

was very prominent throughout the administration; but the early attempt to procure a balance between the various elements — Whig, Democratic, Abolitionist, and Know-Nothing — that had combined to make up the Republican party was abandoned as time went on. The new division that grew up between the Radicals and the Conservatives was treated with an even hand, a policy which of course seemed unequal to some of those most interested. One of Secretary Chase's correspondents wrote that there was "war from the White House" upon Chase's friends. There was no such war. Lincoln wrote to an over-zealous postmaster the best letter ever written on the subject of the participation of government officials in party politics.[1] While offices in general were used to prevent, and not to encourage, faction fights, and so skilfully used that the end was often obtained, minor places were often employed to please powerful individuals; and Lincoln did not forget himself in this connection, but appointed relatives and friends to places which might profit them and not harm the country.[2] In general, Lincoln used his patronage — which, it must be remembered, was enormously increased by the war — for the purpose of serving the country by solidifying the Republican party. While he did not attempt any personal aggrandizement, he yet balked at nothing when the greater object was in view. Charles A. Dana gives an incident that seems authentic. He says that Lincoln, in order to secure the admission of Nevada as a state, — upon which, as he thought, hung the fate of the thirteenth amendment, — authorized the offer of several good offices to some doubtful congressmen to secure their votes.[3]

Military appointments were treated, as they have been nearly always in time of war, as standing somewhat apart. The selection of volunteer officers was largely the work of the governors,

---

[1] Tarbell, *Lincoln*, ii. 400; Welles, *Lincoln and Seward*, 34; —— to Chase, October 30, 1863, *Chase Manuscripts;* Lincoln to M. McMichael, April 5, 1864, Lincoln, *Complete Works*, ii. 558.

[2] Lincoln to A. J. Hamilton, August 20, 1863, Tarbell, *Lincoln*, ii. 378; *Ibid.* 17, 105–106, 340; Lincoln to Chase, October 26, 1863, and to Seward, March 6, 1865, Lincoln, *Complete Works*, ii. 430, 658.

[3] C. A. Dana, *Reminiscences of Men and Events of the Civil War*, in *McClure's Magazine*, x. 564–565.

but Lincoln took care that they should not appoint Republicans only.[1] It is, of course, unnecessary to point out that this separation was not by any means complete, and that politics interfered often and seriously with the good conduct of the war. If Lincoln had made appointments for merit only, the war might have been shortened; on the other hand, he might not have preserved a united North to carry on the war.

Lincoln showed to what use the spoils system could be put by a statesman, but he nipped in the bud a further development of the system, which was threatened. Politicans began to ask why, if rotation were correct doctrine, and a man should hold office only four years, a general sweep should not follow the beginning of every new term, even if a president succeeded himself. A demand gained ground that Lincoln should entirely re-allot the offices after March 4, 1865; and Washington was, as usual, filled with office-seekers on that day. Lincoln, however, was unwilling to go through the worry and labor of the task, and made a conclusive announcement that the administration would remain unchanged throughout.[2] From that time the popularity of rotation declined. The tide had turned.[3]

[1] A. T. Rice, *Reminiscences of Abraham Lincoln by Distinguished Men of his Time,* 140–141.

[2] F. B. Carpenter, *The Inner Life of Abraham Lincoln,* 276; *New York Tribune,* March 4, 7, 1865.

[3] For fuller treatment of Lincoln and the patronage, see Tarbell, *Lincoln,* i. 423, ii. 23; also an article by C. R. Fish in *American Historical Review,* viii. 53–69.

CHAPTER VIII.

MACHINERY OF THE SPOILS SYSTEM.

THE civil service had by the middle of the nineteenth century become so extensive that the careful supervision which the earlier presidents exercised became impossible; and, as appointments continued to be made by personal selection, organization and division of labor became more and more necessary. Naturally, this organization was built upon such foundations as existed, and the change was not so much in the system as in the shifting of the balance of work and responsibility from the cabinet to outside forces.

Members of Congress had from the beginning been influential in suggesting names; but as appointments came to have greater political significance, they came to speak with greater authority — that is, if they belonged to the party in power. During the period in question, minor positions in the various congressional districts were practically in the gift of the members, as they are to-day.[1] If some city of more than usual importance

[1] Riddle, *Recollections of War Times*, 24. March 9, 1849, Lincoln wrote to the secretary of the treasury: "Colonel E. D. Baker and myself are the only Whig members of Congress from Illinois — I of the Thirtieth, and he of the Thirty-first. We have reason to think the Whigs of that State hold us responsible, to some extent, for the appointments which may be made of our citizens." He asked to be heard when such a one was to be appointed or when an office was to be filled in that state. He sent various recommendations for offices which were in his district; but he did not consider that he held them in absolute gift, for he made himself the medium for recommendations which he did not favor. When the functions of the office vacant or to be vacated were restricted, or almost restricted, to his district, he claimed the right to be heard independently of Colonel Baker. When this was not the case, he recognized that the whole delegation — in this case only two in all — should be consulted. In regard to the pension agency, he wrote that, as it pertained

was included within the district, the advice of the senators from the state would be sought, or, at least, of the senator particularly interested in the section in question.[1]

It was a natural practice for the various members from one state, belonging to the same party, to get together and talk over the situation; instances have been cited in the Continental Congress, and in the administrations of Washington and Jefferson and of most subsequent presidents. Between 1845 and 1865 the practice hardened into a custom, and the power of the delegation became almost absolute. At the beginning of Pierce's term, the *Herald* said that Congress showed itself willing to relieve the president of all trouble in regard to the patronage, as it had divided up into committees to portion it out. Lincoln said that he could not overrule the Rhode Island delegation in regard to the Providence post-office; and he probably made very few nominations to important local positions without the previous consent of the delegation, or at least of the senators.[2] The influence of the delegation extended beyond the local offices. Owing to the importance of geographical considerations in this country, each state is quite sure to have a share of the general offices. In 1853 the *Herald* announced that a state having

to the whole state, Colonel Baker had an equal right with himself to be heard concerning it; but that, as the office was located in his district, he did not think it probable that any one would wish to remove from a distance to take it, and therefore his influence should be greatest. Lincoln, *Complete Works*, i. 151–154. On the whole, his correspondence indicates that a peculiar weight was at that time attached to names suggested by members of Congress, but that the latter did not dictate. See *New York Herald*, March 6, 11, 1853; *New York Tribune*, March 16, 1861.

[1] Riddle, *Recollections of War Times*, 24; Lincoln to the postmaster-general, March 12, 1861, Tarbell, *Lincoln*, ii. 340. Postmaster-general Blair (under Lincoln) said that he accepted the recommendation of a majority of the responsible patrons of the district served by the office; that in case of doubt the representative, if an administration man, was consulted; and that the senators controlled their home offices. United States Civil Service Commission, *15th Report*, 1897–1898, p. 472.

[2] "They have resolved themselves into committees to parcel out the patronage of the several states, and avow openly that the president must make the nominations which they dictate" (*New York Herald*, March 11, 1853). See also the issues of March 8 and 9, and the *Tribune* of March 10; Lincoln to Governor Sprague, May 10, 1861, Lincoln, *Complete Works*, ii. 45. On his policy, see also *Ibid.* 23, 200; to Chase, April 11, 1861, *Chase Manuscripts*.

a cabinet officer would not be given a foreign minister.[1] It became customary to assign an office to a state, and allow the delegation to select the particular recipient who should be chosen for the honor;[2] but this custom was not as firmly fixed as that by which the local patronage was dispensed.

Often no member of Congress from the state belonged to the administration party, or there might be local factions within the party hostile to the congressional delegation; and in such cases other means of information had to be sought. The older method of Washington and Jefferson, who were accustomed to write to some man of family or local standing, had, with the growth and the democratization of the country, come to be less practised; but to some extent the want was supplied by the rise of the boss. Thurlow Weed, for instance, was always ready to advise about New York appointments, and generally advised well.[3] Bosses, however, were as yet rare, and were at this period usually in Congress. The various New York factions sent delegates to Washington, if they had no official prolocutor;[4] and this example was often followed by other localities, even though the prize was less valuable. The governors sometimes proffered, and were sometimes asked for, advice; but the weight attached to it varied greatly with the different presidents. Taylor considered it decisive in case of a struggle at Washington, while Lincoln treated it rather curtly when offered gratuitously, and when he asked for it he made it plain that it was advice and not dictation that he desired.[5]

One really important new tendency is to be noted. In 1841 the ward caucuses of Whigs in New York City assumed the

---

[1] *New York Herald*, March 17, 1853.

[2] Lincoln to Gillespie, May 19, 1849, Tarbell, *Lincoln*, ii. 299 ; *American Historical Review*, iii. 290.

[3] Weed, *Autobiography*, 473. He describes with great satisfaction his relation with various presidents. Among the men having especial influence over appointments may be mentioned Duff Green, Corwin, Dix, Crittenden, Clay, and Benton.

[4] *New York Herald*, March 9, 1853. These appointments were so important that men from all over the country claimed a voice in them.

[5] Seward to Weed, March 24, 1849, Seward, *Seward*, ii. 107 ; Lincoln to Governor Sprague, May 10, 1861, Lincoln, *Complete Works*, ii. 45 ; to Governor Morton, June 28, 1862, to Governor Pierpont, October 16, 1862, and to Governor Tod, March 9, 1863, Tarbell, *Lincoln*, ii. 347, 352, 361.

right to dictate minor appointments, and in 1861 it was urged that friction and bitterness would be spared if postmasters were to be elected by vote of the Republicans in their respective districts. Lincoln favored this latter plan in at least one particular instance, and several such elections were held and their returns duly honored by the appointing powers.[1] This scheme illustrates how far the distinction between elective and administrative offices had been lost. The germ of it is to be found as far back as Jefferson's administration, when it was argued that he should carry out the proscription which the people had begun, and should extend it to the offices which they could not directly reach. What the result of such an arrangement would have been may be conjectured from the experience of New York, where it was given extensive application in the constitutions of 1821 and 1846, and where it led, not to the extinction of the spoils system, but to the solidification of party organization.

The president and cabinet could not abdicate all their responsibilities; the decision, the final word, rested with them. Then, as now, the fourth assistant postmaster-general was patronage officer and distributed the numerous local offices in that large department. Even if he did usually follow the advice of others, he was a man of power. When, as so often happened, the delegations were not unanimous,[2] and when the local powers were not satisfied with the selections of congressmen, the administration had to award judgment. Few members of the cabinet, moreover, were content to be absolute nonentities: they were responsible for the conduct of their subordinates, and thought it was but fair that they should have some share in picking them out. Many of them were men of political ambition, and desired to build up in the various states bodies of supporters. In consequence, there was often friction between the head of a department under which an officer was to serve, and the representatives of the state from which he

[1] *New York Tribune*, March 13, 1861; Lincoln to Stuart Brown, March 30, 1861, Tarbell, *Lincoln*, ii. 340–341 ; Hollister, *Schuyler Colfax*, 173 ; United States Civil Service Commission, *15th Report*, 1897–1898, 472.

[2] Instances are numerous. One of particular interest was the struggle of ex-Senator and then Representative Benton with the majority of the Missouri delegation. See *New York Tribune*, March 8, 1853.

was to be chosen and in which he was to exercise his functions. To govern such cases, President Pierce laid down the general rule, that every nomination must be approved by the secretary of the proper department;[1] but the difficulty was inherent in the system and could not be settled by rule. No minor question vexed Lincoln more than that of the adjustment of these rival claims. Secretary Chase was insistent on his rights, while Seward and Weed argued that they were best acquainted with the needs of the Republican party in New York State, and that, if they agreed with the senators, further consultation was unnecessary. Lincoln adopted the same rule as Pierce; but the disagreement was never adjusted, and finally a contest of this kind was the immediate cause of the withdrawal of Chase from the cabinet.[2]

The president himself had great potentialities of power; he determined the relative influences that each of these forces should be allowed to exercise, and if he was a strong man, like Lincoln, he could lay down the general qualifications for appointment. The number of men actually selected by him was usually small, yet each separate appointee owed to him his position. In the end, the power went to the strong man.

To take our history as a whole, Washington probably controlled appointments more fully than any other president; under Monroe the members of the cabinet possessed their greatest power, and under Pierce the congressional delegations were most dictatorial. It was not until after the close of the period covered by this chapter that senatorial courtesy acquired its preëminence.

That this system tended to bring many politicians into office is obvious. Military service ceased to be so often rewarded with civil position as formerly. Pierce, during his campaign, had laid much emphasis upon his career in the Mexican War, and after his election was deluged with applications from his old companions in arms;[3] but, in general, veterans were fewer than

[1] *New York Herald*, March 12, 1853. At this time the machinery of distribution excited much interest and was much commented on. See the *Herald* and the *Tribune* of March and April, 1853.

[2] Welles, *Lincoln and Seward*, 71; Hart, *Chase*, 315-317.

[3] *New York Herald*, March 8, 18, 1853.

at any other period of our history, and consequently played a smaller part in politics. Among those who had rendered political service, the newspaper men seem to have received fewer rewards than previously. In 1845 the franking privilege was restricted, and minor post-offices were thereby rendered less profitable to local editors; while the men who controlled great national organs could not afford to take office. In fact, after 1861, Horace Greeley was rather a dictator of appointments than a seeker after them; and though Lincoln once offered James Gordon Bennett a foreign mission to keep him in good humor, he knew beforehand that the offer would not be accepted.[1] It was the rise of these great metropolitan journals that caused the discontinuance of the official organ at Washington. No pensioned press at the capital could compete with the *Tribune* and the *Herald*, whose able correspondents gave pictures of the daily working of the government, generally as accurate and always more intimate than the *National Intelligencer* or the *Union* had ever vouchsafed.

The pay of congressmen continued small until 1856, when it was raised from the eight dollars a day and mileage, that had held for so long, to three thousand dollars per annum, also with mileage. It is not surprising that before 1856 members made many applications for office. The *Herald* said in 1853: "The Louisiana applicants are in a melancholy way. Their members are so busy, rumor says, in grinding their own axes, that their constituents are little better than orphans." It was, moreover, quite the customary thing for members defeated for reëlection to receive, *sans reproche*, some offer of substantial consolation. Thus Lincoln was offered the governorship of Oregon by Taylor.[2]

Men whose only occupation was politics were not, even in this period, very numerous; still a class of professional politicians existed and received many posts. Some of these men

---

[1] *Statutes at Large*, v. 734; *New York Observer*, April 26, 1845; *New York Tribune*, March 11, 1853; *Connecticut Courant*, March 21, 1857; Lincoln, *Complete Works*, ii. 44, 653.

[2] *New York Herald*, March 16, 21, 1853; *Boston Daily Advertiser*, March 17, 1849; Lincoln, *Works*, i. 159.

were notorious, and their appointments were received with great disapprobation. An amusing example of their claims is found in 1857, when it was proposed to appoint Count Gurowski, master of many languages, as translator to the state department; but strong opposition developed because the place was demanded for a Tammany man who knew several Indian languages.[1] The politician received his office, not only as a reward, but as a retaining fee.

From the beginning of our government there has been complaint of the activity of office-holders; and such complaint will probably never cease, as it is practically impossible to draw a working distinction between the proper interest of the citizen and the obligations of the servant of the government. The *Herald* (March 16, 1853) said, "The Hard-Shells repudiate with scorn the doctrine that quiet men are entitled to office, for they say this would be a premium for inactivity, desertion, and hypocrisy, which would strike a heavy blow and a sore disappointment at men of principle and action, and they contend, would prove ruinous to the party." The system of appointment brought into the leading positions men prominent in local politics, and it is not surprising to find them attending national conventions in the interest of the leaders who secured their preferment.

Much more laborious service than this was required, however. Thus the struggle for the New York collectorship was always severe, not only because of the emoluments, but because the post was considered to carry with it the dictatorship of New York City. After Pierce's inauguration the *Herald* remarked, "Now let the seven or eight hundred Whigs in office here turn their attention to sweets of private life." These men had worked under the direction of the collector for the Whig party, and their successors were expected to work for the Democratic organization. The investigation of Poindexter in New York brought out the fact that these minor officers felt at liberty to leave their duties for several days, without permission, to attend to party work.[2] What was true of the great

[1] *New York Herald*, March 5, 1857. This may have been a joke.
[2] *Ibid.* March 30, 1853, March 14, 1857; Clay, *Private Correspondence,* 448-

cities was true, in varying degree, of smaller ones. Lincoln wrote in 1849 that the postmaster at Springfield, Illinois, had served on the Democratic central committee during his entire term, and had identified himself with local politics the more effectively because he enjoyed a not very burdensome office, located at the seat of the state government.[1]

Assessment of official salaries for party purposes appeared in national politics simultaneously with the spoils system. In 1830 the men appointed by Jackson to offices in Boston were asked to contribute, not indeed to a campaign fund, but to pay, for the editor of the *Statesman*, the debts which the latter had contracted during the campaign. The attempt was not entirely successful, but by 1840 a regular system of assessments existed in some places. In New York, officials in the custom-house were all assessed, just previous to the various elections, for sums differing according to their salaries. No distinct threats seem to have been made; but most men paid, and it was noticed that those who did not generally lost favor. A clumsy witticism of the *Boston Courier*, March 26, 1845, illustrates the prevalence of the practice : "A strange case of Hypochondria! A disappointed office-seeker of our acquaintance fancies himself a salary of $2000 a year, and has locked himself up in an iron safe, for fear of being used up by assessments for party purposes." Throughout the forties, fifties, and sixties this unofficial taxation was an accepted rule.[2]

Although corruption may have been widespread, actual instances of it are rarely brought to light. Lincoln bought votes with offices, and Buchanan was accused of doing so; but such bargains are seldom capable of proof. Fiscal dishonesty is more tangible; but here again the thieving was covered by a garment, though a scant one, of legality, and since the investiga-

---

450. In 1857 Schell removed 389 out of 690 employees. *House Documents*, 27 Cong. 2 sess. vi. No. 212 ; *House Executive Documents*, 46 Cong. 3 sess. No. 94, p. 11.

[1] To the postmaster-general, April 7, 1849, Lincoln, *Complete Works*, i. 153.

[2] Derby, *Political Reminiscences*, 85, 97 ; *House Documents*, 27 Cong. 2 sess. vi. No. 212. A San Francisco official, as the story goes, was assessed, but refused to pay. Lincoln wrote to him asking for his reasons ; he gave them and was no more bothered.

tions which were made during this period were purely partisan,[1] it is impossible to distinguish fraud from maladministration. Both existed and both cost the government heavily, but the popular interest in the threatening political dangers of the patronage and in the suspected dishonesty of the service, which had characterized the period from 1811 to 1840, had died away, and had not yet been succeeded by a demand for efficiency. Every one knew that money was lost, but no one of sufficient influence troubled himself to get behind the mutual recriminations of the politicians and find out who was really at fault.

While this apathy accounts in part for the lack of expressed dissatisfaction at the conduct of the government, it is extremely probable that public business was administered, though expensively, yet much better than one would imagine from a description of the spoils system. Jackson was partly right when he said that the duties of most public officers were not hard : the party leaders were only too glad to multiply the offices until the duties of none of the inferior positions would overtax the energy or the ability of the most commonplace citizen. Moreover, the argument of American adaptability is true, though hackneyed. Particularly in this very period the life history of the average citizen showed a great variety of occupations pursued with fair success, and an amazing capacity for acquiring a simple rule of thumb and applying it with ingenuity. The study of Van Buren's administration showed us that high ability was not lacking when required : a man who could organize a party for victory could administer a large body of officials with vigor. The recent success of Mr. Hanna in politics, taken in conjunction with the fortunes honestly accumulated by politicians like Amos Kendall, illustrates the similarity of talent required by a party organizer and the manager of a great administrative enterprise.

Another fact that should not be lost sight of is that rotation in office was never actually practised. First, many men secured a long intermittent term of service by coming into office when-

---

[1] There was an investigation of Fillmore's conduct of the patronage (*House Reports*, 36 Cong. 1 sess. v. No. 648, p. 5). See also the Galphin investigation, *Ibid.* 1–835 ; Curtis, *Buchanan*, ii. ch. xii. ; *New York Herald*, March 9, 1853.

ever their party came to power, even though they were removed by the other party; secondly, a large residuum, often composed of those performing the most technical duties, were always left in their places, by whom the continuity of departmental tradition was preserved;[1] and thirdly, instances of promotion, even from staff to presidential positions, are found.[2] It would be tedious to mention even the more conspicuous of these men. The most prominent was William Hunter, who served in the state department from 1829 to 1886. The well-known case of the Fox family, which has held the consulship at Falmouth, England, from the time of Washington to the present year (1903), is interesting rather than important.[3] John Randolph Clay occupied with honor various positions in the diplomatic service continuously from 1830 to 1861.[4] It often happened that when a politician was appointed to an office, as a collectorship, he found an efficient and trained deputy, whom he retained in office under him, and who bore on his shoulders the weight of service. The result was a double-headed system, — a working director, representing the public service side of office-holding, and a political director, who was paid for being a good servant of his party.[5]

Some few attempts at improvement are to be noted. Between 1851 and 1853 the question of efficiency was discussed in two reports to the Senate. It was discovered that examinations for

[1] See Appendix B. See above, pp. 49, 90, 148; for other cases, *National Intelligencer*, April 16, 1849, and *New York Herald*, March 4, 16, 1853.

[2] See *New York Herald*, March 9, 1853. The *New York Tribune*, March 11, 1853, says: "The appointment of Peter G. Washington to be the Assistant Secretary of the Treasury, is an excellent one. . . . He has served a long lifetime in office here, having by dint of excellent sense and a faithful and laborious discharge of duties devolved on him, raised himself step by step from a clerkship of a lowest grade, to his late position." Elisha Whittlesey retained his position of first comptroller of the treasury from 1850 till 1857, and was again appointed by Lincoln (*Executive Journal*, viii. 109, x. 293, xi. 376). See also Davis, *Rise and Fall of the Confederate Government*, i. 24–25.

[3] *New York Evening Post*, March 3, 1902. Charles Forrester, his father and his son, together served over one hundred years in the New York post-office (D. B. Eaton, *The " Spoils" System*, 76, note).

[4] Livingston, *Portraits of Eminent Americans*, i. 133; also Blue Books for the period.

[5] *New York Herald*, March 20, 1853.

candidates had been tried in the treasury department, and that they were approved by all the members of the cabinet except Webster. It was recommended that pass examinations be held for the lowest grades of clerkships, and that all vacancies above these, except the chief clerkships, be filled by promotion. In 1853 pass examinations were prescribed by law, and a few years later the system was reported as working well.[1] The character of the examinations, however, depended entirely on the discretion of the department head, who was also the appointing officer; and consequently they amounted to little. In 1857 Howell Cobb, secretary of the treasury, announced that his examinations would be strict, and that he would remove no one except for cause. It is perhaps unjust to suggest that when he added to the customary causes of removal, the buying of lottery tickets and the frequenting of gaming houses, he had anything in mind other than the establishment of moral decorum at Washington.[2] Salmon P. Chase also announced his intention of making these examinations something more than a name; but the very fact of these special announcements shows that as a rule the examinations were a farce.

In 1856 a bill was enacted providing for the improvement of the consular service by the appointment of twenty-five consular pupils. They were to pass a qualifying examination, and those "possessing the requisite qualifications, and exhibiting an aptitude for the consular service, who have been faithful in the performance of their consular duties, will, from time to time, be recommended to the president for promotion"; in 1857 this bill was repealed. In 1864, on recommendation of the secretary of state and the finance committee of the Senate, Mr. Fessenden urged that the repealing clause be repealed; and after a debate in which the proposed law was attacked as undemocratic, as not making adequate provision for promotion, and as unwise on the ground that the consuls were not fit to educate pupils, a poor fragment of the former act was finally

[1] *Senate Executive Documents,* 32 Cong. 1 sess. ix. No. 69; 32 Cong. 1 sess. No. 95; *Statutes at Large,* x. 211; *New York Herald,* April 2, 1853; *House Executive Documents,* 33 Cong. 2 sess. ii. No. 3, pp. 97–98.

[2] *New York Tribune,* March 10, 1857.

passed. This provided that consular clerks should be appointed, — not more than thirteen to be in service at any one time, — and that they should be over eighteen years of age and should receive not more than a thousand dollars a year. A new provision was added, that they should not be removed except for cause stated in writing and submitted to Congress at the session next following.[1]

These petty improvements could not be supposed to touch the great evils of the spoils system, as the most noxious of its effects were social. The government service, which should have set the example of stability to the country at large, was conducted on principles radically wrong. Besides this, the subtle attraction that public offices have always had for the average American brought into the ranks of office-hunters many times the number that could find places. As the *Herald* said: "If loss of time be taken into consideration, and loss of money, it costs him [the office-seeker] probably his first year's salary to obtain office. . . . The consequence is, that many of these officials cheat the public by various frauds and impositions, in order to indemnify themselves for their losses. At the end of four years they are, perhaps, set adrift upon the world, without any calling or business connection."[2]

The result was that a large class of persons led a fluctuating existence. Many were, at times, reduced to such an extremity that they would do practically anything in return for the most trifling recognition, and hence constantly tempted the not unwilling party leader to go deeper and deeper into questionable practices by offering themselves as fit instruments. The effect on the general public was twofold : people were led to regard the agents of the government with contempt even while the offices proved alluring, and the political sense became somewhat blunted. The very intelligent Washington correspondent of the *Tribune* complained: "The 'spoils' doctrine is . . . at the bottom of the Galphanizing which has of late come to be so fashionable as to permit each current instance thereof brought to light, to pass

---

[1] *Statutes at Large*, xi. 55, 160 ; *Congressional Globe*, 38 Cong. 1 sess. 1115 ff. ; and Appendix, 181–182.

[2] *New York Herald*, March 9, 1853, also March 11, 1857.

out of popular recollection almost without receiving a second thought. And, further, . . . it threatens to bring more evils upon us than any dozen others of the many elements conspiring, as it were, to entirely change the character of the Government of the United States." [1] During the fifties no practicable method of reform was suggested, and during the Civil War the very depths of the spoils system were sounded in the conduct of the national service in the Southern states. Yet in 1865 the attention turned toward England, the Sumner and Jenckes bills, and the check given to rotation promised a new and better era.

[1] *New York Tribune,* March 15, 1853; see also *Niles's Register,* lxiv. 351 (July 29, 1813).

CHAPTER IX.

A STRUGGLE FOR THE PATRONAGE.

1865–1887.

THE more effective for party warfare the patronage became, the more bitter grew the struggle for its control, and the more persistently did the contestants resort to the constitution for support. That the administration of the civil service was an executive function could scarcely be denied; but the constitution left open the question how this power was to be divided between the two branches of the executive, the president and the Senate. Instances of constant minor friction, occasioned by the rejection of nominations, have been given; and the comprehensive plans of 1826 and 1836 for limiting the president, while due primarily to partisan opposition, illustrate the continued jealousy of the Senate. Nor, in spite of the defeat of these proposals, had the president's prerogative remained entirely unscathed. Madison regarded the Four Years' Law of 1820 as an unconstitutional encroachment: if Congress could limit the term to four years, it could make it one day, and tenure would be at the pleasure of Congress and not of the president. As a matter of fact, however, the result of the limited term had been to increase the power of the executive, and to all intents and purposes Lincoln found his legal relation to the civil service little different from that of Washington.

The immense expansion of presidential power during the Civil War naturally tended to heighten the Senate's distrust, and under this stress it put its views more effectually upon record than during the eighty years preceding. The first act creating the national banking system in 1862 gave the comptroller of the currency a term of five years, during which he could be removed only by and with the advice and consent of the Senate. How far this was an intentional reversal of the practice urged by Madison in the famous debate of 1789 and accepted since that time, it is impossible to say ; but evidently the significance of the change was not realized by the majority in Congress, for in the amendatory bank bill of 1864 the provision was modified, and the president was merely called upon to state to the Senate the causes of the removal.[1] In 1863, again, a clause was added to the military appropriation bill forbidding the payment of money to men appointed during the recess of the Senate " to fill a vacancy in any existing office, which vacancy existed while the Senate was in session and is by law required to be filled by and with the advice and consent of the Senate, until such appointee shall have been confirmed by the Senate." [2] In the light of these provisions, it seems not improbable that the clause of the act of 1864 requiring the president to submit reasons for the removal of consular clerks[3] was inserted rather from a desire to limit the power of the former than to protect the latter, particularly as it was not part of the original bill of 1856. This manifest jealousy of the overgrown power of the president suggests that, even if Lincoln had lived, a contest would. have been inevitable ; but where there would have been discussion, mutual concessions, and final agreement under Lincoln, there was war under Andrew Johnson.

The inauguration of the new president in 1865 seemed fairly

[1] *Congressional Globe*, 37 Cong. 3 sess. Appendix, 189 ; 38 Cong. 1 sess. Appendix, 169.

[2] *Ibid.* 37 Cong. 3 sess. Appendix, 183–184. The following provisions point in the same direction. In 1843 it was provided that one cadet for West Point should be taken from each congressional district, thus suggesting by inference that each member should have the appointment of one. In 1862 the intention was made plainer, — that the "number allowed at the Academy" (Annapolis) should be "two for every member," while the president was to have two for the District of Columbia and ten "at large" and three to be selected from enlisted boys. It was not, however, until 1875 that it was distinctly stated that the nomination should be made "on the recommendation of the member" (Eaton, *Civil Service in Great Britain,* 285).

[3] *Congressional Globe*, 38 Cong. 1 sess. 1115, and Appendix, 182.

propitious.   As a result of Lincoln's wise decision to make no
changes at the beginning of his second term, the administrative
machine had settled down with the prospect of running on
quietly for four years. Johnson seemed prepared to follow
out Lincoln's policy. The calm was, however, delusive. It is
unnecessary even to enumerate the causes that brought about
the divergence of the president and a majority of the Republicans in Congress; for our purpose it is sufficient to note that,
at a time when the relations between the two branches of
the executive were particularly strained, the man who became
president was utterly devoid of tact, opinionated and somewhat
obstinate, a good fighter but a poor leader.

When it became evident that a struggle for supremacy was
to ensue, Johnson began to strengthen his position.   Three
resignations allowed him to reconstruct his cabinet to his satisfaction, except that Stanton remained in the war department.
A. W. Randall, the new postmaster-general, became the organizer of the president's forces;[1] and through the year 1866
various conventions were held in which the presidential programme was enunciated. The most important was that at Philadelphia, in August, where an address was adopted which was
intended to appeal to all the elements opposed to the congressional scheme of reconstruction, and which invoked the watch-
word " Union," so potent before 1860.   The statement that
this convention was composed almost wholly of office-holders
and office-seekers does not seem quite justified : no greater
proportion of its members is found in the Blue Books of 1867
and 1869 than is usual in such conventions ; but after adjourn-
ment many individuals and whole delegations visited the president, and doubtless the patronage was one of the topics discussed
at these conferences.[2] Shortly afterward, the laying of the
corner-stone of the Douglas monument in Chicago gave Johnson
the opportunity to "swing round the circle."   In his speeches
during this journey he freely declared his intention of not allowing his enemies to enjoy government positions, epitomizing

---

[1] Gorham, *Stanton*, ii. 311.

[2] *Nation*, August 3, 27, 1866; a list of members is to be found in the *New York
Tribune*, August 14, 1866; see also August 21, 1866.

his views at St. Louis in the vigorous assertion that he would "kick 'em out" of office.[1]

The president intended then to use the patronage in his struggle with Congress, and he found it an apt and powerful instrument. Fear of removal might be counted on to keep some Republicans loyal to their official chief, while the Democrats, who constituted the bulk of his supporters, would be especially pleased to get back to the pastures from which they had been driven five years previous. Moreover, no president except Lincoln had had such numerous rewards to distribute. The most important additions to the list of presidential officers were the 364 internal revenue collectors and assessors; but the subordinate service was swelled in almost every department. Although the army was immediately reduced, its reorganization necessitated the appointment of about two thousand officers for the regular establishment.[2]

The actual proscription began shortly after the Philadelphia convention, when the postmaster-general, Randall, is said to have sent out a "bread and butter" circular, demanding that office-holders support the policy there outlined.[3] Resignations and removals were daily noted in the press from this time on. Owing to the chaotic conditions of Johnson's presidency, it is impossible to get a clear idea of the amount of change. The executive journal of the Senate records 903 removals; but some senators accused the president of sending in many nominations without stating that the cause of the vacancy was removal, and sometimes from the same place two or three removals were made. Moreover, the proscription continued throughout the administration, and the initial sweep was not particularly severe; an official report gave the total number of removals during 1866 at only 466 out of a possible 2934.[4] There were great local differences: of twelve internal revenue officers in

---

[1] See Sumner in *Congressional Globe*, 39 Cong. 2 sess. 542.

[2] *Executive Journal*, xiii. 11–19 (December 22, 1862); Blue Books, 1861, 1863, 1865; Blaine, *Twenty Years of Congress*, ii. 124.

[3] *New York Tribune*, August 21, 22, 1866; *Congressional Globe*, 39 Cong. 2 sess. 493.

[4] Fish, in American Historical Association, *Reports*, 1899, i. 83; *Congressional Globe*, 39 Cong. 2 sess. 492, 1517.

Wisconsin, ten were changed; in Ohio, nearly all; in Indiana, only about one-half; and in California, only one. Removals could not, of course, be made very rapidly at first, as time was necessary to discover who were the friends and who the enemies of the president. The intention, however, was clear.

It was natural that this sweep, although not so extensive as several that had gone before, should arouse more bitterness than any other; and the anger of the Republicans was seven times heated by the appointment of some hated Copperheads to take the place of the martyrs who had been decapitated. The fact that the important military appointments in the South were made with discretion could not serve to mitigate their wrath; and, arrogant in the strength of their majorities in Congress, they were not content to sit idly by and allow the president to go on in this course unchecked; it would be dangerous to permit him to build up a party of his own, and the Republicans felt bound in honor to protect such of their friends as were still in office.[1]

The position of the president was, however, firmly based on long-established constitutional interpretations, while the part that congressmen played in allotting appointments rested on custom alone; probably no one had ever realized how independent the former really was in theory, for practice had always been based on mutual concession. Never before had a strong, determined president faced two houses of Congress opposed to him in so momentous a crisis; and for the first time the question of their respective constitutional powers over the patronage became one of widespread interest. In order to make the succeeding events intelligible, it is necessary to discuss briefly the constitutional provisions on this subject, and the questions that were left open.[2]

---

[1] *New York Tribune*, August 14, 23, 25, 27, September 27, 1866. It was the report at Washington that two thousand removals were made. *Congressional Globe*, 39 Cong. 2 sess. 1041 ; *Nation*, May 1, August 16, September 1, 1866 ; August 22, November 2, 1867 ; January 2, 1868.

[2] This brief discussion is almost entirely from Miss Salmon's *Appointing Power of the President*, and the debate on the Tenure-of-Office Act of 1867 as found in the *Congressional Globe*.

Two clauses of the constitution relate to the president's authority on this subject : —

" He shall nominate, and, by and with the advice and consent of the Senate, shall appoint ambassadors, other public ministers and consuls, judges of the Supreme Court, and all other officers of the United States, whose appointments are not herein otherwise provided for, and which shall be established by law. But Congress may by law vest the appointment of such inferior officers as they think proper in the president alone, in the courts of law, or in the heads of departments.

" The president shall have power to fill up all vacancies that may happen during the recess of the Senate, by granting commissions which shall expire at the end of their next session."

Both these provisions were incomplete. The first contained no mention of removals, an omission which the first Congress, under the lead of Madison, interpreted as meaning that the power of removal was one of the general executive functions belonging to the president *ex officio*. This construction was maintained to the time of Johnson, but not without severe criticism from those who believed that the power of appointment carried with it that of removal, and that consequently the consent of the Senate was necessary for both alike. This opinion was most conspicuously put forward in the great debate of 1836; but it was held both before and after, and was supported by many distinguished thinkers on constitutional law, by a statement of Hamilton in the *Federalist*, by a closely analogous decision of the Supreme Court, and, on the testimony of Justice McLean, by the opinion of Chief-justice Marshall and the court when he was at its head.[1] It might, then, fairly be considered a moot point in 1866, although seventy-seven years of practice should have counted heavily in favor of the established interpretation.

The significance of the other clause depends upon the meaning of the word " happen." The alternatives were most clearly set forth by Reverdy Johnson, who described the sentence as involving an ellipsis, it being possible to make it read

---

[1] *Congressional Globe*, 39 Cong. 2 sess. 434, 438, 440. Federalist (Ford ed.), 511. The case is that of ex-parte Hennen, 13 *Peters*, 259.

either "happen to exist" or "happen to occur." If "occur" were taken, the provision obviously referred merely to cases in which the vacancy was one newly arising during the recess for which the appointment was to be made. As an actual fact, the official practice had been to take the other interpretation, and this had the support of a number of attorneys-general.[1]

The deductions from the "happen to exist" reading were far-reaching. If the president issued a commission to a man for a certain post, the appointee would under any circumstances be secure therein until the end of the next session of Congress; but unless the president had sent in his name to the Senate and that body had confirmed it, his tenure would cease at that date. There was, however, no reason why the president should not at once reappoint him, for, when his commission expired, a vacancy happened "to exist." There was no easily assignable legal reason, therefore, why the president might not neglect to send in the name at all, and with a little trouble completely obviate the necessity of consulting the Senate. This extreme possibility was a theoretical rather than a practical danger, for not even Johnson showed an inclination to push his power to such an extreme;[2] but it furnished a good argument for alarmist orators.

The Republican counter attack was first directed against the president's control of the army and navy. In July, 1866, a statute provided that no officer in the military or naval service should "in time of peace be dismissed from service except upon and in pursuance of the sentence of a court-martial."[3] In the first session of the thirty-ninth Congress, a bill was introduced into the House for the purpose of reversing the current interpretations of the constitutional clauses and of establishing those favorable to the Senate. It did not, however, become a law. On the first day of the next session, Mr. Williams of Oregon asked leave to bring into the Senate a similar bill, denominated a bill "to regulate the tenure of offices." It was read twice,

---

[1] *Congressional Globe,* 39 Cong. 2 sess. 409, 410.

[2] *Ibid.* 39 Cong. 2 sess. 492. He did, however, frequently reappoint men rejected by the Senate. *Ibid.* 390; also 39 Cong. 3 sess. 436.

[3] *Ibid.* 39 Cong. 1 sess. Appendix, 338.

and two days later referred to the joint select committee on retrenchment.[1]

The bill, which became the Tenure-of-Office Act of 1867 as reported by Mr. Edmunds from this committee, was designed emphatically to assert the share of the Senate in the removing power. The first clause provided that all officers except members of the cabinet, duly appointed with the advice and consent of the Senate, should be entitled to hold their offices until a successor had in like manner been appointed. The second contained a provision that, for causes which should seem to him to be sufficient, the president might suspend any officer and appoint a temporary successor; such cases should be reported to the Senate within twenty days after the meeting of Congress next following; if the Senate agreed that the causes warranted removal, the office was to be vacant, and a nomination could be made; if not, the old incumbent was to resume his functions. The third clause represented an attempt to define the word " happen " by the addition of the words " by death, resignation, expiration of terms of office, or other lawful cause "; that is, the president was not to have power to fill vacancies caused by removal; if the Senate should not, in its next session, confirm a successor to the officer who died or resigned or lost his office by the expiration of his commission, the office was to remain in abeyance, and its functions were to be performed by whatever officer could lawfully execute them in case of accidental vacancy. The fourth section provided that the act should not be construed to extend the term of any officer which was already limited by law.[2]

There was no doubt that this bill, at any rate in its main provisions, would pass both houses of Congress; yet the debate was long and acrimonious, and requires review. The primary constitutional question as to the exercise of the removing power, which was involved in the first section, was discussed with great learning by Reverdy Johnson and Williams of Oregon.[3] The same champions led the discussion of the second and third clauses of the bill in a debate which was more animated and less

---

[1] *Congressional Globe*, 39 Cong. 2 sess. 17.

[2] *Ibid.* 30 Cong. 2 sess. 382.   [3] *Ibid.* 39 Cong. 2 sess. 438, 440, 460, 461.

hackneyed. Johnson defended the existing practice, and showed the inconvenience that would arise if the president could fill only vacancies "occurring," and not all those "existing," during the recess; and Hendricks illustrated this point by showing that the bill establishing the Freedmen's Bureau was passed early enough to prevent the vacancies which it created from occurring in the recess of the Senate, but too late to be filled before the Senate adjourned. He disapproved of the recommissioning of men rejected by the Senate, and was inclined to believe it unconstitutional; but he did not explain how the contingency was to be avoided.[1] Williams based his constitutional interpretation on two leading ideas: "One is that this filling up is to be temporary; and the other that it is to be exercised within a given time. . . . I understand this clause as to vacancies . . . to be intended simply to bridge over that space of time which may intervene between different sessions of the Senate."

The debate naturally wandered from constitutional questions to those of expediency. Williams of Pennsylvania said of the bill in the House, "It proposes to improve the rare advantage of the dissociation between the party in power here and the President of its own choice, for the correction of a great evil, by a surrender and dedication of the spoil which that party may be supposed to have won, upon the public altar, and for the nation's benefit through all coming time." It would have been somewhat difficult to explain the precise nature of this sacrifice, but the idea that an exceptional occasion was to be used for permanent gain was a common one in the Republican press.[2]

It was Senator Sumner, in fact, who was the first to admit the real cause of the proposed act. "At last," said he, "the country is opening its eyes to the actual condition of things. Already it sees that Andrew Johnson, who came to supreme power by a bloody accident, has become the successor of Jefferson Davis in the spirit by which he is governed and in the mischief he is inflicting on his country. . . . He is a usurper, who promising to be a Moses, has become a Pharaoh. Do you ask

---

[1] *Congressional Globe,* 39 Cong. 2 sess. 386–387, 409–410, 441. See also report of the judiciary committee of the Senate, 1888. *Executive Journal,* xxvi. 196–202.

[2] *Congressional Globe,* 39 Cong. 2 sess. 18; *Nation,* February 7, July 12, 1866.

for evidence? It is found in public acts which are beyond question. It is already written in the history of our country. And now in the maintainance of his usurpation he has employed the power of removal from office. Some, who would not become the partisans of his tyranny he has, according to his own language, 'kicked out.' Others are left, but silenced by this menace. . . . Wherever any vacancy occurs, whether in the loyal or the rebel States, it is filled by the partisans of his usurpation. Other vacancies are created to provide for these partisans. I need not add that just in proportion as we sanction such nominations or fail to arrest them, according to the measure of our power, we become parties to his usurpation."[1] Up to this time the debate had been conducted with decorum, but from now on speeches became more and more violent and partisan.

Amendments were offered from time to time. Some were merely with intent to clarify and improve the bill, as that of Sherman, which added an enforcement clause. He pointed out that the bill passed in Lincoln's time, against the payment of salaries to officers appointed in certain defined ways, had not been observed; and, at his suggestion, very heavy penalties were created for those paying or receiving salaries for services rendered contrary to the Tenure-of-Office Bill.[2] A more important amendment was that introduced by Mr. Van Winkle, fixing a definite term of four years for all presidential offices not heretofore limited by law. This roused Mr. Johnson, who remembered the issues of the almost forgotten past. "I do not know," said he, "that any statute ever passed has created more trouble and done more mischief than that fixing a short term of office for these several appointees." His protest did not strike a responsive chord, and the amendment seems to have failed merely because the managers were unwilling to encumber the bill with miscellaneous matter.[3]

Sumner, who, throughout the debate acted as chief toreador in baiting the presidential bull, skilfully escaping by just the

---

[1] *Congressional Globe*, 39 Cong. 2 sess. 542.

[2] *Ibid.* 39 Cong. 2 sess. 390, 404, 405.

[3] *Ibid.* 39 Cong. 2 sess. 406.

breadth of a hair from being caught in a breach of senatorial privilege, proposed to make the appointment of all officers receiving over one thousand dollars annual salary subject to the confirmation of the Senate. This led to a fierce onslaught of radical oratory. Sumner acknowledged that it would increase the labors of the Senate; but he would not have them shirk their duty, and the duty of the hour was "protection to the loyal and patriotic citizen. . . . You may ask," he added, "protection against whom? I answer plainly, protection against the President of the United States. . . . There was no such duty on our fathers . . . because there was no President of the United States who had become the enemy of his country." Nevertheless, Fessenden and Edmunds succeeded in convincing the majority that the Senate's time could be more profitably spent than in protecting the night watchmen of New York and Boston.[1]

By far the most important amendment, however, was that introduced by Mr. Howe when the bill was first brought in by the committee, by which it was proposed to strike out the clause excepting the cabinet officers. This, like Mr. Sumner's amendment, received its support from the Republican radicals, who entirely reprobated the theory of Edmunds and Reverdy Johnson that these officers should be the confidential advisers of the president. So little conception was shown of the nature of our government, that Mr. Howe compared the relations of the heads of departments and the president to those between the king and the ministers in England. The more moderate Republicans, voting with the Democrats, defeated the proposition in the Senate. In the House it was again put forward, and was more ably supported; the report of Mr. Jenckes, setting forth the patronage which the various secretaries dispensed, was used with much effect; and this, combined with the desire to protect Stanton in his place at the head of the war department, secured the passage of the amendment, though by a narrow majority. A conference committee was then appointed to adjust the differences between the Senate and the House, and a compromise was agreed upon, to the effect that the heads of

[1] *Congressional Globe,* 39 Cong. 2 sess. 470, 525–528, 543, 547.

departments should hold for the term of the president by whom they were appointed, and one month thereafter, subject to removal by and with the advice and consent of the Senate. The bill with this amendment was vetoed by the president, was passed over his veto, and became a law on March 2, 1867.[1]

The debate as a whole is disappointing, because so little desire was shown to improve the opportunity presented to accomplish a real reform. Few senators seemed to sympathize with Mr. Howe's statement that he found no special fault with the doctrine, " which," he added, " I believe has been preached only for thirty or forty years, that to the victor belong the spoils; but the victory which entitles a man or a party to the spoils is a victory which is achieved by the assent of the American people; it is not a victory which is attained by desertion." Yet, although few of the Republicans defended the existing system, and although they occasionally mentioned reform as a desirable object, the only senator whose remarks indicated intelligent consideration of it was Mr. Doolittle, who called attention to the success of British-American administration of Indian affairs, and drew lessons therefrom. Some senators were, of course, conversant with Mr. Jenckes's reform bill; but they seem to have been little influenced by its principles. The only object in mind, other than the immediate one of restraining Andrew Johnson, was the assertion of the dignity of the Senate[2] and the general lessening of executive powers. Reverdy Johnson, whose speeches and discussions were by far the ablest throughout the debate, called attention to the fact that power might be abused by the Senate as well as by the president; but this argument did not appeal to the senators in general. The Tenure-of-Office Bill of 1867 marked the first definite success that the Senate had obtained in its contest with the president for the control of the patronage; it was a partisan measure, directed against a particular president.

The attitude of the president toward the new act was a question of the utmost interest. He had vetoed it in an able message,

---

[1] *Nation*, February 7, 1867; *Congressional Globe*, 39 Cong. 2 sess. 382–388, 938, 969, 1514, 1964, 1977; E. C. Mason, *Veto Power*, § 28.

[2] *Congressional Globe*, 39 Cong. 2 sess. 460, 524, 1040.

in which he claimed that it was unconstitutional; and, now that it had been passed over his veto,[1] the question remained whether he would accept the restrictions imposed or would disregard the action of Congress.[2]   On March 7 a long list of nominations was sent to the Senate, among which was one that might have precipitated the crisis if either side had so desired.   A certain man was nominated in place of another "to be removed"; the name was referred to a committee, but was withdrawn by the president before a report had been made.   Soon after a man was nominated in the place of another "to be removed for inefficiency," and the Senate evinced its satisfaction with the cause expressed by confirming the nomination.[3]   Still, the president could not be said to have committed himself to the policy of always stating a cause.

In December, 1867, the judiciary committee reported a series of resolutions intended to regulate the activity of the Senate under the new law.   It was provided that the president and Senate could remove an officer by the nomination and confirmation of a successor; that, in case an officer were suspended, the Senate might consent to his removal by confirming the nomination of another to his position, without specifically approving or disapproving the cause of suspension; and that cases of suspension be referred to the committee most interested in the offices involved.[4]

While the Senate was thus carefully avoiding the issue, but was exercising liberally its undoubted power of rejecting nominations, the president was preparing to force the question into the courts.   He struck directly at Stanton, the foremost of the men whom the law was designed to protect, asking for his resignation on May 5, 1867, and, on his refusal to resign, suspending him one week later.   Johnson, in his notification to Stanton,

---

[1] C. E. Chadsey, *Struggle between President Johnson and Congress over Reconstruction* (Columbia University, *Studies in History*, viii. No. 1), 135.

[2] *Nation*, October 17, 1867.

[3] *Executive Journal*, xv. 349, 366, 376 (March 7, 8, 1867); 465, 572 (March 18, 28, 1867).

[4] *Ibid.* xvi. 105 (December 13, 1867).   This account of the events leading up to the trial of President Johnson is drawn from Professor Dunning's chapter on the trial of President Johnson.   W. A. Dunning, *Essays on Reconstruction*, 253–303.

made no reference to the Tenure-of-Office Act, but gave as his authority the power vested in him as "president by the Constitution and laws of the United States." Stanton protested that no legal cause of removal, or of suspension, was given; but he yielded, and Grant consented to act in his place. On December 12, 1867, Johnson, strictly in accord with the provisions of the new law, but still with no reference to it, reported the suspension to the Senate.[1] His plan seems to have been that, if the Senate refused to concur in removing Stanton, Grant should refuse to give up his office, and Stanton would thus be forced to appeal to the courts. This plan was submitted to the commander-in-chief, who approved of it provisionally, but after an examination of the law refused to perform his part of it. Consequently Grant remained at his post until January 13, 1868, when the Senate formally refused to agree to the removal of Stanton; whereupon Grant wrote to the latter that, by virtue of the Tenure-of-Office Act, the suspension was at an end, and that he was ready to hand over the office.[2]

On February 21, Johnson announced to the Senate that he had removed Stanton and appointed General Lorenzo Thomas in his place "*ad interim*."[3] This was the first definite announcement on his part that he did not recognize the validity of the law passed nearly a year before, and the House at once proceeded to impeach him. It does not fall within the purpose of this work to follow the progress of that trial. The chief point of dispute rested on the interpretation of that ambiguous clause which was the result of the compromise between the Senate and the House on the question whether the provisions of the bill should or should not apply to cabinet officers; and the defence held that Stanton had not been appointed by Johnson, that the latter was serving a term of his own, not a remnant of the term of Lincoln, and that consequently the removal was not in violation of the law. This position was held by just enough Republican senators to prevent the accusers of the president from securing the two-thirds majority necessary for conviction in an

---

[1] *Executive Journal*, xvi. 95.
[2] *Ibid.* 130; C. M. De Witt, *Impeachment of Andrew Johnson*, chs. iii. and iv.
[3] *Executive Journal*, xvi. 170.

impeachment trial, and, to the disgust of most of the Republicans, the outcome was an acquittal.

The crucial vote was taken on May 26, and Stanton at once tendered his resignation to the president. The latter had already, on April 23, sent in the nomination of General Schofield as secretary of war, "in place of E. M. Stanton, removed." The Republican majority could not overlook this assertion of the president's right to remove, nor could they, now that they lacked the two-thirds vote, profitably continue the contest; they, therefore, on May 28, confirmed the appointment, but expressed their opinion that the secretary of war had not been "legally removed," but had voluntarily relinquished his post.[1]

All efforts to bring the matter to a determination had now failed. In December, 1868, the president recognized the law sufficiently to recommend its repeal; but practically until the end of his term the president administered the civil service under one interpretation of the constitution and the Senate under another. Technically the president fared the best, for the Senate had to recognize his nominations if it wished to take any share whatever in the appointments, and in practice it often assented to a nomination in which the last occupant was mentioned as "removed" or "to be removed."[2] In fact, the executive journal does not read differently from the journals of previous administrations. The Senate's power of rejection, however, was not in question, and consequently it could throw out nominations to its heart's content, and the obstinate pertinacity of the two branches of the appointing power led to many prolonged contests.[3]

Congress indulged, too, in many petty annoyances. Already, in 1867, it had cut down the contingent fund for the state depart-

[1] *Executive Journal*, xvi. 236, 239.

[2] Richardson, *Messages and Papers of the Presidents*, vi. 673; *Executive Journal*, xvi. 303, 306 (July 13, 1868); 319 (July 18, 1868).

[3] The case of the postmastership at Newburgh, New Jersey, is an illustration. Johnson renominated J. H. Reeve, whose term had expired; Reeve was rejected, again renominated, and again rejected (*Executive Journal* xv. 249, 328, 429, 451). Benjamin H. Mace was next named and rejected (*Ibid.* 699, 710). A Mr. Lomas was put up and defeated (*Ibid.* 714, 741). The president once more brought forward Mr. Reeve, who, according to the journal, was confirmed (*Ibid.* 743, 758); but

ment from $60,000 to $30,000, and now it proposed to limit the number of special agents who could be appointed by the several departments. Sumner, who realized the needs of the state department, vigorously opposed this action; Seward furnished him with a letter showing how moderately the power had been used during the existing administration, and the bill failed. The irritation was carried so far that the Senate's confirmation of the nomination of Reverdy Johnson as minister to England could be referred to as an act of gracious courtesy.[1]

The battle was over. Both sides had spent their ammunition, and the administration went out amid desultory firing along the outposts.

It was generally considered that the Tenure-of-Office Act was passed as an emergency measure, and would be repealed as soon as the Republicans elected a president of their own faith. President Grant, in his first annual message, earnestly recommended its repeal. Already in April, 1869, however, the new Congress had expressed its approval of the act by amending it. The first two sections were so remodelled as to allow suspension at the discretion of the president, for he was no longer required to report to the Senate "the evidence and reasons" for his acts; and cabinet members were placed on the same footing as other officers.[2] On the other hand, in order to prevent the president from keeping in office men commissioned during the recess, he was ordered to nominate persons for all vacancies within thirty days after the commencement of each session, and, in case of rejection, to send in another name as soon as possible. The enforcement clauses were retained. The House had desired a total repeal, but the Senate had stiffly refused to yield what it had gained, and its subsequent action showed that it had no intention to yield up a power which it had so long desired.

either the record is defective or the president imagined that there must have been a rejection, for he nominated William A. Boyce "in place of J. H. Reeve, rejected" (*Ibid.* 763). Boyce was thrown out (*Ibid.* 766); Lomas was now tried again, and he at last was confirmed (*Ibid.* 847).

[1] *Congressional Globe*, 40 Cong. 2 sess. 845, 952, 1769; *Nation*, February 21, 1867; *Nation*, June 18, 1868.

[2] December 6, 1869, Richardson, *Messages and Papers of the Presidents*, vii. 38; *Statutes at Large*, xvi. 6–7 (ch. x.).

The executive journal reflects this increased interest in appoint-ments, and the tenacity with which the Senate maintained its position.

In March, 1869, Senator Edmunds introduced a resolution to the effect that "the term of office of all officers affected by the act regulating the tenure of certain civil offices is limited by that act upon the pleasure of the President of the United States in the appointment of others to said offices by and with the advice and consent of the Senate," and that "the President of the United States may rightfully, under and in the spirit of existing laws, nominate to the Senate persons for office accord-ing to his discretion and independent of any question respecting the conduct or capacity of any incumbent." This failed of approval, as did also a resolution of contrary intent offered by Senator Trumbull the following December, "That in case of a nomination sent to the Senate in place of an officer suspended by the President, it is the duty of the committee having the nomination in charge to inquire into the propriety of the change proposed." December 17, 1869, a resolution was proposed "that in the consideration of nominations and other subjects submitted to it [the Senate] by the President, . . . it is its right to be furnished with all papers and documents relating to such matter belonging to the files of the Executive branch of the Government or any Department thereof." This resolu-tion also failed, and for it was substituted a respectful request for information in the particular case then under discussion.[1]

As no fixed rules were adopted, the practice of the Senate varied. Usually, nominations in the place of officers suspended were confirmed without comment. Sometimes there was investi-gation, and occasionally evidence was printed for the use of the Senate. Often this was in answer to a protest on the part of the officer suspended.[2] The result was nearly always an ulti-mate approval of the action of the president. So regular was this action that in 1886 Senator Hoar said that no suspended officer had ever been reappointed. This is not quite correct: December 6, 1869, President Grant sent in a list of officers of

---

[1] *Executive Journal*, xvii. 22, 313, 320, 323.

[2] *Ibid*. xvii. 323, 365, 403; xix. 250, 297; xxi. 319, 439.

the Indian department "suspended during the recess of the Senate, pursuant to the provisions of the second section of 'An act to amend an act regulating the tenure of certain civil offices,' approved, April 5, 1869," and requesting the Senate to consent to their removal. In the case of seven, consent was refused, and when they had served out their terms one of these seven was nominated for reappointment and was confirmed.[1] There was constant pressure to make public the results of these investigations, and often the injunction of secrecy was removed.[2] The main motive for this was that it was found impossible to preserve absolute secrecy, and that as a result garbled reports got abroad. In 1871 it was voted that the executive journal be printed to the end of the fortieth Congress (1869), and in 1901 it was published to the end of the fifty-first (1891). In 1885 it was voted that nominations and confirmations be daily printed in the *Record*.[3]

There was constant friction between the Senate and the successive presidents over minor questions of form. In December, 1870, the Senate felt it necessary to declare that the president could restore a suspended officer without consulting it. In 1873 it returned as not "regular" the nomination of Richard Busteed to a judicial position, "to take effect on the resignation of David C. Humphreys"; and in 1874 it returned other nominations, "it being the judgment of the Senate that commissions ought not to antedate the time of actual appointment."[4] A very annoying practice of the Senate was to request the return of its resolutions confirming or rejecting nominations, in order that it might reconsider them. December 19, 1872, the chair ruled that such motion was out of order, as the Senate had completed its function, and could not reopen the question without the initiative of the president. The latter, however, usually complied with such requests, or sent a mes-

---

[1] *Congressional Record*, 49 Cong. 2 sess. 140–141; *Executive Journal*, xvii. 289–290, 545–546, 622, 682.

[2] *Ibid.* xvii. 311 ; xxv. 340.

[3] *Ibid.* xxvii. 434, 461–462, 475–477, 487–488, 501–504, 507, 516–517, 588, 590, 598 ; xviii. 110 ; xxv. 197. See also back of title-page of each volume.

[4] *Ibid.* xvii. 594 ; xviii. 396 ; xix. 437.

sage stating that the commissions had been signed, and were therefore beyond his power of recall. In some cases Grant ignored the requests,[1] and the officers in question continued to serve.

Under Hayes the Senate was more aggressive than under Grant, and December 11, 1877, resolved "that the President be respectfully requested to inform the Senate, with a view to the transaction of its executive business, whether in any of the instances of nominations hitherto sent to the Senate, stated to be for appointment in place of officers removed, such removals had been made at the time of sending such nominations to the Senate." The president was able to reply, January 14, 1878, "that in the instances referred to removals had not been made at the time the nominations were sent to the Senate. The form used for such nominations was one found to have been in existence and heretofore used in some of the departments, and was intended to inform the Senate that if the nominations proposed were approved it would operate to remove an incumbent whose name was indicated."[2] Such nominations were nearly always approved by the Senate simply by the confirmation of successors to the persons removed.[3]

In addition to this constant manifestation of interest and assertion of minor rights, the Senate used vigorously throughout this period its power of rejecting nominations. Under Grant there were 58 contested cases, of which 9 resulted in rejection; under Hayes 92 contests, 51 being decided against the president; in Garfield's short administration there were 7 contests with 2 rejections; 37 of Arthur's nominations were contested, 8 successfully; Cleveland suffered 8 defeats in 30 contests.[4] The Senate had always possessed the power of rejection, and had at times used it freely, but never before so continuously in the case of nominations by presidents with whom the majority were on friendly terms. To be sure, some

---

[1] *Executive Journal,* xviii. 352, 386, 400; xix. 460; xx. 178; xxi. 353; xxii. 97.

[2] *Ibid.* xxi. 169, 199.

[3] Exceptions, see p. 202 above; also *Executive Journal,* xx. 375. The latter was the case of a military officer.

[4] *Executive Journal,* session for the periods mentioned.

of these rejections reflect special hostility to Grant and Hayes; but on the whole they were scattered pretty evenly, and indicate a fixed policy of aggression rather than a temporary expedient. In the same way, the Senate had presumably always had the power to ask for information concerning nominations, but it had never before exercised it so freely. Particularly it interested itself in ascertaining whether appointments were divided evenly among the several states. A characteristic resolution is that of April 8, 1878, "That the annexed messages be respectfully returned to the President with the request that the Senate be informed of the residence of the nominee, where that fact is omitted, and whether the nomination is to remove an incumbent where that statement is omitted." [1]

These are outward and visible signs of the inward political growth of a new power of the Senate — the attempt of the senators by combination to make the president a mere clerk to transmit to the Senate as a constitutional body nominations handed to him unofficially by the individual senators. A crisis was brought about in the spring of 1881, when President Garfield attempted to reward some of his New York supporters at the expense of the friends of Senator Conkling. The latter protested; the other senator, Platt, joined him, as did Vice-president Arthur, Postmaster-general James, and sixty out of eighty-one Republican assemblymen of New York. Garfield persisted in sending the most offensive of the nominations — that of Mr. Robertson to be collector — to the Senate, whereupon Conkling and Platt resigned. In a letter to Governor Cornell they stated the facts, and added that they were forced to choose between "plain and sworn duty" and "disloyalty to the administration which they had helped to bring in." The letter continued, "Although party service may be fairly considered in making selections of public officers, it can hardly be maintained that the Senate is bound to remove, without cause, incumbents, merely to make places for those whom any individual, even the President or a member of the Cabinet, wishes to repay for being recreant to others and serviceable to him." [2]

[1] *Executive Journal*, xxi. 287 ; see also xvii. 187, 383, and xxi. 55.
[2] *Nation*, May 19, 1881.

This action on the part of the New York senators must be regarded as an attempt to enforce the doctrine that not only could the Senate control appointments, but that the senators should severally control those for their respective states — a doctrine which may be considered as the high-water mark of the Senate's claims. Fortunately, the New York legislature did not support this theory, and Conkling and Platt were defeated for reëlection. Nor can the subsequent election of the latter be regarded as in any way a vindication of the principle here set forth; it was due rather to changed circumstances, and to his own great skill. The Senate itself rejected the doctrine put forward by unanimously confirming Robertson.[1]

The notoriety of this incident did much to promote interest in the repeal of the Tenure-of-Office Act. This had been urged by Grant and Hayes, and a bill for the purpose had been passed in the House of Representatives.[2] In April, 1884, President Arthur asked the Senate to consent to the removal of a certain officer, whereupon Senator Hoar proposed a resolution, " That in the judgment of the Senate it is within the constitutional power of the President to remove the officer named in his message if, in his judgment, the public interests require." This was too radical a departure, and Senator Edmunds's resolution, that " in view of the foregoing message the Senate advise and consent to the removal," was passed; but Senator Hoar succeeded in affixing to it the clause, " and that the Senate does not hereby express an opinion as to the constitutional relations of the President and the Senate in the matter of removal from office." [3]

Senator Hoar did not lose interest in the matter, and did not let others lose it. He was assisted by the agitation in favor of civil service reform and by a vigorously worded message of President Cleveland in 1886. December 14, 1885, he introduced a bill to repeal the Tenure-of-Office Law, which was referred to the judiciary committee; but it is significant that in the House a

---

[1] *Nation*, June 23; July 28, 1881.

[2] Richardson, *Messages and Papers of the Presidents*, vii. 38, 605; *Congressional Record*, 49 Cong. 2 sess. 113.

[3] *Executive Journal*, xxiv. 249, 254.

corresponding bill was given to the committee on the reform of the civil service. The debate in the House was unimportant, and the bill passed by a vote of 172 to 67.[1] In the Senate the discussion was more keen. Hoar, in his introductory remarks, said that he did not suppose there were ten men in the Senate who objected to the repeal. The next day, however, Senator Edmunds vigorously defended the original act. He ably reviewed the constitutional arguments, and dwelt at some length on the danger of giving the patronage into the hands of the president alone; he dwelt upon the removals then being so rapidly made by the existing administration, and on the necessity of some regulation to restrain the president; the repeal of the Tenure-of-Office Act, he declared, would be a step backward in civil service reform, by facilitating removals.[2] Hoar replied in a speech longer than his first, in which he maintained the unconstitutionality of the act of 1867, pointed out (incorrectly) that no suspended officer had ever been reappointed, that in all encounters with the executive the Senate had been worsted, and that the prestige of the latter could not fail to suffer from the attempt to control the president. He added, that the first step in civil service reform was to impose the responsibility of it on the president.[3]

The repealing bill finally passed the Senate by a vote of 32 to 22; perhaps the speech of Senator Edmunds had given the question a partisan cast, for the negative vote was composed of Republicans, while Hoar and Ingalls were the only prominent members of that party to vote in the affirmative. As the Senate bill was not amended in the House, it was forwarded to the president as soon as passed by the latter body, and on the same day he approved it.[4] Thus the original interpretation of Madison was allowed to revive, and responsibility was once more

---

[1] Richardson, *Messages*, viii. 380–381 ; *Senate Journal*, 49 Cong. 1 sess. i. No. 83 ; *House Reports*, 49 Cong. 2 sess. i. No. 3539 ; *House Journal*, 49 Cong. 2 sess. 834 (March 3, 1887); *Congressional Record*, 49 Cong. 2 sess. 2700. The figures are taken from the *Record*, which is evidently corrected. Eighty did not vote.

[2] *Congressional Record*, 49 Cong. 2 sess. 113, 136–140.

[3] *Ibid.* 140–141.

[4] *Senate Journal*, 49 Cong. 2 sess. 84, 569, 603 (December 17, 1886). *Statutes at Large*, xxiv. 500.

concentrated. Yet, while the Senate resumed the legal position it had held previous to 1867, the history of the intervening years could not be forgotten; its prestige was too firmly fixed to depend on a single act, and the senators unofficially and by "courtesy" have continued to this day the main dispensers of the patronage.

CHAPTER X.

PERIOD OF CIVIL SERVICE REFORM.

1865–1901.

Two fundamental errors had characterized all important plans devised in the United States for the reform of the civil service prior to 1860: first, they aimed rather to hinder removals than to control appointments; and, secondly, they tended to shift the power from the shoulders of the president to the Senate, and by dividing the burden to do away with all sense of personal responsibility. There had been, to be sure, some suggestions that did not share these errors, — Noah Webster, for example, had suggested to Jefferson that he make local appointments according to the advice of the judges and selectmen of the neighborhood,[1] and pass-examinations were introduced in 1853; but Webster's scheme was not adopted, and pass-examinations proved but the merest palliative, so that the history of effective reform begins after the Civil War.

In taking up this history, moreover, we have to break the continuous course of development, the steady progress from cause to effect, which we have been studying; for the first practicable plan of improvement was not the result of internal evolution, but was an instance of what Professor Lamprecht would call "reception." A really comprehensive story of the civil service reform movement should be, not national, but international; it was not so much a local peculiarity as a manifestation of a stage of national growth.[2] England was ready for the

---

[1] Webster to Jefferson, February 20, 1809, *Good Government*, October 15, 1894.

[2] Note the introduction of appointment by competitive examination into Canada in 1882, Victoria 1883, United States 1883, New York 1883, Massachusetts 1884.

change before the United States, and attacked and solved the problem, while we profited by her experience. A good illustration of the non-American origin of the system finally adopted is the fact that its expansion has been from the national government to the states, and not, as is the case of nearly all native reforms, from state experiment to national application. Yet, though the progress of reform was accelerated and its form in part determined by the English movement, it would not have obtained so sudden and so substantial a victory in America if conditions had not been ripe for its success.

The bloated civil list, and the unusual irregularities produced by the Civil War, for the first time attracted serious attention to the problems of administration; and though the majority of congressmen still held to the plans of 1826 and 1836, and multiplied restrictions upon the power of the president, some men of influence began to cast about for new remedies. It was natural at this time, when foreign travel had so greatly increased, and so many Americans were acquainted with the excellences of the public service in many countries of Europe, that the systems which had succeeded there should be investigated for our behoof; and in 1863 Secretary of State Seward requested John Bigelow, consul-general at Paris, to report on French methods of collecting the customs. Mr. Bigelow's reply described and warmly recommended a system of appointment by competitive examinations; but it led to no immediate result, unless it be that it stirred Charles Sumner to introduce, in 1864, his bill, "to provide for the greater efficiency of the civil service." It is more probable, however, that Sumner's action was taken independently, and was based upon knowledge of English conditions and correspondence with his many English friends. His bill provided for a board of examiners, appointment by competitive examination, promotion by seniority, and removal for good cause only; it received some favorable comment from the press, but was dropped without action.[1]

The first man to grapple with the question of administrative reform in a thoroughly practical manner, and to give to it the continued and single-minded devotion that so complex and vital a

[1] Jenckes, *Report*, Appendix K, p. 176; Sumner, *Works*, viii. 452–457.

problem demanded, was Thomas Allen Jenckes of Rhode Island. A lawyer of marked ability, a man of wealth and belonging to a family of much local consideration, he assumed a position of importance from his first entrance into the House of Representatives in 1863. His attention seems to have been at once attracted to the conditions of the civil service; and finally, as member of the retrenchment committee, he made the subject peculiarly his own. He spared no effort in making a thorough study of the problem, and entered into correspondence with Sir Charles E. Trevelyan and Sir Stafford H. Northcote, who had played an important part in the English reform movement. On December 20, 1865, he introduced his first bill. It shared the fate of Sumner's; its novelty was too great to allow of speedy acceptance, and many other things demanded attention.

The matter was not dropped, however; and in July, 1866, a concurrent resolution charged the joint select committee on retrenchment to examine into the "expediency of so amending the laws under which appointments to the public service are now made as to provide for the selection of subordinate officers after due examination by proper boards; their continuance in office during specified terms, unless dismissed upon charges preferred and sustained before tribunals designated for that purpose; and for withdrawing the public service from being used as an instrument of political or party patronage." The committee was enlarged in 1867; and on May 25, 1868, Mr. Jenckes, for the subcommittee on civil service, presented an elaborate report, which may be considered as the effective starting-point of reform in this country.[1] It contained a thorough discussion of the existing service, careful summaries of the systems employed in China, Prussia, France, and especially England, and to it there was appended a bill intended to adapt the best points in these systems to American conditions.

In general, Jenckes's suggestions were not very different from those of Sumner, but the plan was more elaborately worked out.

---

[1] *House Reports*, 40 Cong. 2 sess. ii. No. 47. Also printed separately. The committee consisted of Edmunds, Williams, Patterson, and Buckalew from the Senate; and Van Wyck, Randall, Walker, Halsey, Jenckes, Benjamin, and Benton from the House.

The most strikingly novel feature was the proposal to furnish employment for the vice-president by making him the head of a new department — that of the civil service. More pertinent suggestions were that there be periods of probation and regular promotions, and that the commissioners be authorized to hold examinations, not only for the inferior officers, but even for those of the presidential class if so requested by the Senate. Mr. Jenckes urged that his bill would throw the service open to every citizen, and that it was needed to relieve the president and heads of departments from pressure for office. It received some attention from Congress and some from the public; but it must be acknowledged that its novelty and the sweeping nature of the change suggested made defeat inevitable. It is rather surprising that the leading vote on the subject was as close as 72 to 66.[1]

Although Congress refused to act on the subject, agitation was persistent, and, while not perhaps very widespread, was powerful in the unselfish devotion of such men as George William Curtis and Carl Schurz. The report of 1868 made a good basis for argument; and occasional words of approval, from the few officials who made the pass-examinations count for something, freshly furnished the arsenal of the reformer.[2] Still victory was afar off, and it would have been long before the proposal received a trial had it not found an advocate in General Grant.

Between November, 1868, and March, 1869, the attitude of the president elect on this, as on other subjects, was eagerly canvassed, and before his inauguration he had expressed himself in favor of the suggested reform.[3] He not only favored it, but in his second annual message pressed upon Congress the advisability of a law which would "govern, not the tenure, but the manner of making all appointments." Thus adjured, Congress devoted itself assiduously to the civil service; in fact,

---

[1] This vote was on Jenckes's earlier bill, February 6, 1867. *Congressional Globe,* 39 Cong. 2 sess. 1036; 40 Cong. 3 sess. 266, 269.

[2] Jenckes, *Report,* 19, and Appendix L; Secretary of the Interior, *Annual Reports,* 1870; *Senate Reports,* 47 Cong. 1 sess. iii. No. 576; *Nation,* December 10, 1868.

[3] *Nation,* December 3, 1868, February 16, 1869.

from that time on, only the session of 1878–1879 has passed without formal discussion of the question. Suggestions were numerous. Senator Trumbull proposed that any member of Congress or territorial delegate who recommended any one for office without having received a written request from the executive should be fined one thousand dollars, while Senators Wilson and Schurz introduced bills; but the majority seemed disinclined to take action. It was only by a rider, attached at the last moment to the appropriation bill, that provision was made for carrying out the president's wishes.[1]

The effect of this legislation was to leave everything to the president's discretion. He was " to prescribe such rules and regulations for the admission of persons into the civil service of the United States as will best promote the efficiency thereof, and . . . to employ suitable persons to conduct said inquiries "; twenty-five thousand dollars were appropriated to pay for the services required. Grant prepared to make the most of the opportunity : he appointed an advisory board of seven, with George William Curtis as chairman, to report on the measures to be adopted.[2] Its first report, presented December 18, 1871, was based largely on that of Mr. Jenckes ; but it omitted the suggestion of employing the vice-president, and made one important advance by advising that no attempt be made to control the president's power of removal, thus completely separating the reform movement from the Senate's struggle for supremacy. On April 16, 1872, the rules thus formulated were applied to the departments at Washington and to the federal offices in New York, and a sincere attempt was made to give the new system a fair trial. President Grant, however, found it impossible to live up to the standard set for him by his new advisers, and an offensive appointment which he made in New York led to the resignation of Curtis.[3]

Meantime Congress vacillated in its attitude towards the

---

[1] *Congressional Globe*, 41 Cong. 2 sess. 17 ; 3 sess. 59, 594–595, 1935–1936.

[2] Cary, *Curtis*, 216. The other members were A. G. Cattell, J. Medill, D. A. Walker, E. B. Elliott, J. H. Blackfan, and D. C. Cox.

[3] *Congressional Globe*, 41 Cong. 3 sess. 217, 225 ; Lucy M. Salmon, *Appointing Power of the President*, 96–97.

new plan. It is probable that the provision for the advisory board owed its passage solely to the fact that it was attached to the general appropriation bill so late in the session that the effort to eliminate it would endanger the whole measure. At any rate, after two years the absolutely essential appropriation was cut off. President Grant continued his efforts, and constantly presented the matter to Congress, at last announcing on December 7, 1874: " If Congress adjourns without positive legislation on the subject of ' civil service reform ' I will regard such action as a disapproval of the system, and will abandon it, except so far as to require examinations for certain appointees, to determine their fitness. Competitive examinations will be abandoned." Congress paid no heed to this appeal. Yet in the same year it recognized the rules by placing under them certain clerks in the office of the secretary of war, and the passage of a law prohibiting the assessment of the salaries of government employees for political purposes showed the persistence of a desire to withdraw the service, in some measure at least, from politics.[1]

No one unfamiliar with the Washington atmosphere can realize how difficult it is for the president to administer the civil service with an eye single to merit, or how innocent are some acts which appear blameworthy on the surface ; reformers, moreover, are always peculiarly suspicious, and Grant was lamentably unfortunate in appointing some unworthy men to office.[2] It is not surprising, therefore, that many of the most active supporters of civil service reform were found in the ranks of the Liberal Republicans, through whom the principle found its first expression in a national party platform in the following plank: " The civil service of the government has become a mere instrument of partisan tyranny and personal ambition, and an object of selfish greed. It is a scandal and reproach upon free institutions, and breeds a demoralization dangerous

---

[1] *Congressional Globe,* 40 Cong. 3 sess. 262 ; 42 Cong. 2 sess. 453 ; 42 Cong. 3 sess. 195 ; *Senate Reports,* 47 Cong. 1 sess. iii. No. 576, p. v ; Richardson, *Messages,* gives the rules promulgated from time to time ; *Statutes at Large,* xix. 143, and 43 Cong. 1 sess. ch. 328 ; Eaton, *Civil Service in Great Britain,* Appendix C.

[2] John Jay, *North American Review,* cxxvii. 273-287, gives a reformer's view of Grant.

to the perpetuity of republican government. We therefore regard a thorough reform of the civil service as one of the most pressing necessities of the hour; that honesty, capacity, and fidelity constitute the only valid claims to public employment; that the offices of the government cease to be a matter of arbitrary favoritism and patronage and that public station shall become again a post of honor. To this end it is imperatively required that no President shall be a candidate for re-election." The regular Republican convention of 1872 adopted a somewhat similar plank, but disclaimed any idea of "creating a life-tenure of office."[1] The merit system may therefore be said to have been formally introduced into practical politics in 1872.

Again, in 1876, the programme of the leading parties included this reform. The Democrats called vaguely for reform in general; the Prohibitionists proposed to effect it by the election "of all civil officers, so far as practicable, by the direct vote of the people"; but the Republican candidate, Hayes, who in his letter of acceptance spoke of it as of "paramount necessity," was the special favorite of the reformers. So important did William Cullen Bryant regard the issue that he refused the nomination of elector on the Tilden ticket because Tilden had not definitely pledged himself to forego a general sweep should he be elected.[2]

President Hayes devoted two paragraphs of his inaugural to the civil service, and in his first annual message called attention to the fact that the commission appointed by Grant still existed, but was paralyzed because of lack of money. He said that he had already done something in the way of reform, but could accomplish nothing really noteworthy without the active support of Congress. The new Republican administration was therefore fully committed to reform, and the president exerted himself to fulfil this pledge. The appointment of Carl Schurz as secretary of the interior, the commissioning of Dorman B. Eaton to write a history of the civil service reform movement

---

[1] Stanwood, *History of the Presidency*, 343, 347; Blaine, *Twenty Years of Congress*, ii. 522.

[2] Bigelow, *Tilden*, i. 301–303; Stanwood, *History of the Presidency*, 365, 375.

in Great Britain, and the strict enforcement of the law against assessments [1] — all showed his favorable attitude.

It was in New York, however, that reform was most earnestly demanded, and there also the most vigorous resistance was to be expected, for it was the home alike of the most active of the innovators and of the most odious of the bosses. As a preliminary to action, the president appointed a committee, headed by John Jay, to investigate the custom-house. This committee recommended that one-fifth of the employees be dismissed, whereby three hundred thousand dollars a year would be saved; but in order to carry out the proposed reforms it was felt necessary to remove also the incumbent collector, Chester A. Arthur, and the naval officer, Alonzo B. Cornell. These men were supporters of Roscoe Conkling; and their removal enraged him beyond measure, and confirmed his opposition to the plans of the reformers. In the New York state convention he fell upon George William Curtis with the full force of his vituperative eloquence, and in the United States Senate he delayed the new nominations for the posts thus vacated. Confirmation came at last; and in 1879 competitive examinations were made the basis for appointments in the New York custom-house, under the rules drawn up by the new naval officer, the well-known reformer, Silas W. Burt. In 1880 the system was applied to the New York post-office, and the administration could congratulate itself on having taken some definite steps in advance.[2]

Congress was not disposed to do its share in the work. Although the president continually called attention to the matter, and gave assurance that such short, unsatisfactory trials as the new system had had proved its value, he was unable to secure any legislation to enable him to extend it or make it permanent. The House of Representatives made General Butler chairman of the committee on civil service

[1] Richardson, *Messages*, vii. 444–445, 466, 561–567; *Executive Journal*, xxi. 4, 450; Lambert, *Progress of Civil Service Reform in the United States*, 14.

[2] United States Civil Service Commission, 15th *Report* (1897–1898), 464; Richardson, *Messages*, vii. 450; *Executive Journal*, xxi. 171, 455, 488, 502–503; Cary, *Curtis*, 257; Lambert, *Progress of Civil Service Reform in the United States*, 9; Eaton, *Civil Service in Great Britain*, pp. x, 447.

reform, and in the Senate the president's nominations were frequently opposed.[1] President Hayes was held partly responsible for this inaction: his nominations were not all satisfactory to the reformers, and he ended his administration unpopular with many politicians of his party because of what he had done, and with the reformers because of what he had failed to do.[2]

Meantime, outside of Congress and government circles, the agitation for reform was active and was gaining the public ear. The first volume of *Poole's Index*, brought out in 1882, mentions about one hundred articles discussing some phase of the civil service problem. In May, 1877, the New York Civil Service Reform Association was formed, and in 1880 it claimed 583 members representing 33 states and territories. Other societies sprang up in Boston, Philadelphia, Milwaukee, San Francisco, and elsewhere; and in August, 1881, a "National League" was formed at Newport, with George William Curtis as president. This was followed by the organization of state societies,[3] and the movement was brought to the fighting stage. It is not by any means probable that the number of active reformers was so great as the number of their publications would lead one to think; but many of them were men highly educated and of literary tastes, and one such man wrote for ten. Nevertheless there was a widespread feeling of tolerant approval, and hopes rose high when James A. Garfield, known since 1870 as a friend of reform, was elected president on a platform which called for a change "thorough, radical, and complete."

Garfield, however, found Congress still unwilling to commit itself to the measures he desired, and he died without having been able to bring about any change in the legal condition of the service. His successor, Chester Alan Arthur, was reputed to be a thorough spoilsman; he owed his nomination for the vice-presidency solely to the influence of Conkling, and the reformers felt that all was lost. It is evident, however, that

[1] Richardson, *Messages*, vii. 603–605; Massachusetts Reform Club, *Report*, 1888; John Jay, *North American Review*, cxxvii. 273.

[2] E. Cary, *The Administration and Civil Service Reform* (*International Review*, vi. 227–233); *Congressional Record*, 47 Cong. 2 sess. 246.

[3] Lambert, *Progress of Civil Service Reform in the United States*, 10.

Arthur's reputation was worse than facts would justify; moreover, President Arthur proved to be a very much stronger man than Collector Arthur. He did not, indeed, fully recommend the system of competitive examinations; he pointed out that there were, and must always be, some differences between the English conditions and our own, and that these might make differences of system necessary. He expressed, however, his willingness to execute whatever law Congress should see fit to pass.[1]

With the executive less favorable to the competitive system than it had been for thirteen years, its supporters pressed it with more vigor than ever before in the second session of the forty-seventh Congress. The tragic incident of the death of Garfield at the hands of a disappointed office-seeker deeply affected public sentiment; and the fall elections of 1882 frightened the Republican leaders, particularly as in several cases the determining factor seemed to be the question of civil service reform.[2] Therefore the bill drawn up by Dorman B. Eaton and presented by George H. Pendleton, chairman of the Senate committee on civil service reform, was urged with good hope of success.

The debate on this measure was entirely unworthy of the occasion, hardly touching any of the serious considerations involved; and in this fact as well as in its subject-matter it was characteristic of nearly all congressional discussions of the civil service. The larger part of the time was taken up in making predictions as to the effect of the bill on the two parties, and in arguments based thereon. Senator Vest said that what was needed was not legislation, but a change of administration. Senator Miller pointed out that, whatever was true of the Republicans, the Democratic party would survive without patronage.[3] Throughout the debate Jefferson was paraded, now on one side, now on the other, as the founder of the spoils system,

[1] December 6, 1881, Richardson, *Messages*, viii. 11, 60.

[2] *Debate on Civil Service Reform before the Seventh Congress of the Protestant Episcopal Church*, 11–12, 19 ; Lambert, *Progress of Civil Service Reform in the United States*, 16–18 ; *Letters to Candidates* (New York, 1882) ; *Congressional Record*, 47 Cong. 2 sess. 204, 280–281.

[3] *Congressional Record*, 47 Cong. 2 sess. 283, 463–464.

and as demanding of applicants only honesty, capacity, and faithfulness to the constitution.

Senator Pendleton said that arguments in favor of his bill need not be presented, that the question was fully before the country. He confined his speech mainly to showing that there were good American facts to support the plan; that it was no longer an experiment; that within the last fifteen years it had become very common for congressmen to select their appointees for West Point and Annapolis by competition, and that the results were good; that since the introduction of the system into the New York post-office the volume of business had increased several times over, while the cost had grown but two per cent.

The best speech in favor of the bill was that of Senator Warner Miller of New York. He illustrated existing conditions by the case of the railroad mail service, in which men secured appointment through political influence. They were obliged to serve a six months' term of probation, and at the end of it from a third to a half of them were dropped, only those who were efficient being retained. The result, he said, was a good service, but the loss in trying inefficient men made it an extremely expensive one. He further urged the necessity of reducing the pressure for office upon the president and members of Congress. This point seemed to influence many, and Senator Hawley described how difficult it was, for men who had the power to aid, to refuse worthy but inefficient persons. The advocates of reform had to devote some attention to the question of the necessity of a bill at all. Did not the president have all-sufficient power to reform the service without the aid of Congress? In the previous session of this same Congress a bill had actually passed the House, appropriating fifteen thousand dollars to enable the president to enforce the clause adopted in 1871. Would not such action suffice? It was, however, very generally felt that this was a matter in which the legislature was in duty bound to guide the executive;[1] and it was evident to all that, without the support of Congress, no president could successfully make so bold an innovation.

[1] *Congressional Record*, 47 Cong. 1 sess. 5704, 6016; 2 sess. 204–208, 241, 284, 316, 318; *Congressional Globe*, 41 Cong. 3 sess. 1936.

The general attitude of the opposition was scoffing, as it usually is in such debates. "Sunset" Cox, in 1878, delivered the best comic speech on the subject, with allusions to the Chinese origin of the system; but the supposedly unsophisticated character of the reformers is always amusing, and the examination questions can always be so dovetailed together as to bring a laugh. Mr. Horr said that they were all humbug, and that he would prefer draw-poker or tossing coppers. Equally numerous were the objections to the new system on the ground that it was not an American product — was monarchical. Senator Brown expected that the officers of government would become a " prætorian guard," and Senator Carpenter that they would become a fixed aristocratic class.[1]

Many counter suggestions were made : that what was needed was the weeding-out of incompetents; that preference in appointments should be given to candidates belonging to the party having the smallest number of members in government service (the plan, of course, of a Democrat); that entrance by examination should not be confined to the lowest grades; that examinations should be strictly confined to matters directly relating to the duties of the offices to be filled; that under the new rules those in office should be forced to compete on equal terms with other citizens.[2]   The whole system was criticised as cumbrous; it was argued that the commissioners had too great power; some members found the whole bill unconstitutional, and could quote an opinion of Attorney-general Akerman to that effect; while Senator Ingalls was angry because it had not been devised by Congress, but had been forced upon it by a body of men " exceedingly holy and wise."[3]

The most serious discussion was over the power of removal : many who favored the proposed bill as a whole did not believe that it would prove sufficient simply to regulate appointments. John Sherman said that if removals were not mentioned, Hamlet

[1] *Senate Documents,* 55 Cong. 2 sess. i. No. 24 ; *Congressional Globe,* 42 Cong. 2 sess. 453 ff. ; 42 Cong. 3 sess. 195 ; *Congressional Record,* 47 Cong. 1 sess. 6014; 2 sess. 207, 277.

[2] *Congressional Record,* 47 Cong. 2 sess. 465, 600, 471, 247–248.

[3] *Congressional Globe,* 42 Cong. 2 sess. 453–456 ; *Congressional Record,* 47 Cong. 2 sess. 354, 357–360, 463.

would be left out; Senator Ingalls desired fixed terms during which removal should be made only for cause; and an elaborate list of legal causes was drawn up and a method of procedure arranged. In the end, however, this executive function was left untouched.[1]

In the Senate the bill passed 38 to 5, 33 being absent; in the House, where there was practically no debate, there were 155 for it and 47 against it, 87 not voting. The president approved, and the measure became a law, January 16, 1883. It provided for three commissioners to be appointed by and with the advice and consent of the Senate, for a chief examiner, state boards of examiners, and minor officers. The commissioners were to aid the president in preparing rules to carry out the provisions of the law, which called for the classification of clerks and for open competitive examinations of a practical nature; if there were no competition, the commission should arrange for a non-competitive examination. The rules were to exclude drunkards from the service, and were not to admit more than two members of a single family; they were to give veterans the preference accorded them by previous laws, to provide for a fair apportionment of the positions at Washington between citizens of the various states and the District of Columbia. They were not to apply to laborers. Applicants were to bring no recommendation except as to character and residence; those selected were to serve a six months' period of probation, and were to be under no obligation to contribute to any political fund; while all officers were forbidden, under heavy penalty, to solicit or receive any such contributions. These rules were to apply to the departments at Washington, and to custom-houses and post-offices with more than fifty employees. The commission was to keep records, to investigate cases in which the rules were supposed to be violated, and to make an annual report to the president, which was to be submitted to Congress.[2] The president could extend these rules to other parts of the service at his discretion, and could provide for exemption from them.

[1] *Congressional Record*, 210, 354, 227. The Tenure-of-Office Act, which was still in force, applied only to presidential officers.

[2] *Statutes at Large*, xxii. 403–407.

President Arthur appointed an efficient commission, with Dorman B. Eaton as president; good rules were drawn up; and February 11, 1885, the president, who had doubted the expediency of the innovation, reported that it was a success,[1] while he was himself commended for his administration of a law which was not of his choice.

In the campaign of 1884 the Republican, Democratic, and Prohibitionist parties all declared themselves in favor of the new law. The Republican party claimed the credit for its enactment; and their candidate for president, James G. Blaine, in his letter of acceptance, expressed a desire to see its provisions extended.[2]   Grover Cleveland, the Democratic candidate, was regarded as the most thorough reformer, however; and his election was largely due to the support of those enthusiastic young Mugwumps who cared more for good government than for party allegiance, and who left the party of their fathers because they doubted the good faith of its leader.   After tariff revision, the reform of the civil service was the chief issue of the campaign.

The position of the new president was undoubtedly a difficult one.   For twenty-four years the opposing party had been in power; and even the reformers acknowledged that it would be proper to bring about some approximation of equality between the parties, and were willing to agree with Cleveland that some men in office had "forfeited all just claim to retention." [3]   Yet when ninety per cent of the presidential officers were removed within sixteen months, and sixty-eight per cent of the unclassified employees of the interior department, besides the almost complete sweeping away of the fourth-class postmasters, many of the president's independent supporters began to cry out and to accuse him of breaking pledges.   The civil service rules were very well observed, only six and a half per cent of the department officials being removed in sixteen months;[4] but the

---

[1] Richardson, *Messages*, viii. 276.

[2] Stanwood, *History of the Presidency*, 430–444; *Civil Service Record*, June, 1884.

[3] *Civil Service Reformer*, April, 1887; Cleveland to Curtis, *Ibid.* August, 1885.

[4] H. C. Lea, *Mr. Cleveland and Civil Service Reform. Independent*, October 8, 1888; Wood, in National Civil Service Reform League, *Proceedings*, 1888, p. 66.

restrictions as yet applied to but a small proportion of the service, and the remainder was large enough to give rise to many old-fashioned squabbles over the patronage, which still further estranged the reforming element.[1] Yet the fact that the president, whether willing or unwilling, yielded to the pressure for a general sweep, did not mean that he had lost interest in the work of the Civil Service Commission. He was in constant communication with its members, made suggestions for the strengthening of the rules, and from time to time considerably extended the number of offices to which they should apply, finally including within them, at the end of his term, the railroad mail service.

President Harrison was inaugurated before this new order went into effect, and one of the greatest political weaknesses of the new system at once became apparent. The fact that, when the civil service rules are extended to a new class of offices, the incumbents are included within their protection without having to undergo the trial of an examination, has made it easier for presidents — has perhaps even tempted those who were retiring — to extend the classification and protect their party friends. When, however, the opposite party comes to power and finds its opponents securely lodged in offices which but just now were patronage and from which its own members may have been but recently expelled, a severe strain is put upon the belief in the morality of civil service reform; it seems like saying that to the vanquished belong the spoils. It is not surprising, therefore, that the order for enforcing the railway mail extension was postponed from time to time until, in fact, more removals had been made in this branch of the service than throughout President Cleveland's term,[2] and few, if any, Democrats remained to be protected.

In general there was a loud cry from Republicans for offices. One newspaper appeared with the headlines, " Hundreds of Offices," " Places to Suit all Classes," " Take your Choice." In both Senate and House a committee was appointed to investigate

---

[1] *Civil Service Reformer*, April, 1886, April, 1887.

[2] Richardson, *Messages*, ix. 53; *Congressional Record*, 51 Cong. 1 sess. House Bill No. 3722; *Civil Service Reformer*, April, 1890.

the Civil Service Commission; and, though it found nothing to discredit that body, it did find enough instances of removals to furnish a good *tu quoque* argument for the spoilsmen. Clarkson as patronage officer of the post-office revived the old argument of rotation in office, dismissing 201 postmasters "upon expiration of four years' service, and second commission not yet expired." By April, 1890, 35,800 removals had been made, about 15,000 more than in the previous administration; while the reformers had been alienated by the displacement of Silas Burt from the position in the New York custom-house which he had so long and honorably filled, and by the president's refusal to extend the rules to the census bureau of 1890.[1]

Although this broad sweep seemed a step backward in the progress of reform, President Harrison announced that he would firmly maintain the rules within their limits; and the appointment of Theodore Roosevelt as civil service commissioner, and soon as chairman of the commission, was a guarantee of his good faith. The annual reports at once revealed the presence of a new vigor and administrative power, and of a mind appreciative at once of ideal ends and practical possibilities.

The president himself was responsible for an important innovation in the rules, — that of providing for the keeping of efficiency records to be used in making promotions. It had been felt for some time that it was not well to rely entirely upon examinations in raising men from one class to another; the difficulty was to get a judgment and exclude favoritism. In his first annual message, President Harrison expressed his belief that some record of efficiency could be devised, and in 1891 announced that such a system had been established. As this was finally arranged, each officer was to receive a separate mark for attendance, industry, thoroughness, and general ability.[2]

In addition to this contribution to the system itself, the Harrison administration saw the extension of the rules over

[1] *Civil Service Reformer*, 1888 to 1891, *passim ; House Reports*, 51 Cong. 1 sess. vii. No. 2445.

[2] Richardson, *Messages*, ix. 52–54, 179–180, 207, 513; *Good Government*, July 15, 1893, November 15, 1895.

the Indian service, in which, perhaps, reform was more needed than anywhere else. Important also was the action of Secretary Tracy in applying to the navy yards rules for the registration of laborers, which had been devised in Massachusetts and had there proved satisfactory in improving the lower branches of the service and keeping them out of politics. So successful did this plan prove that it was extended by President Cleveland, in his second term, to many other departments, and became an established part of the system. Another order of Secretary Tracy, which forbade the employment of extra men in the navy yards during the sixty days before elections, put a stop to a long-established and convenient method of vote-buying.[1]

The second administration of Grover Cleveland brought mingled gall and sweetness to the believers in the non-political civil service. Congress was more eager for spoils than the government was to give them; and an investigation into the legislative, executive, and judicial appropriations resulted in a reduction of force which gave opportunity for partisan manipulation. Throughout the term, however, order followed order, extending the service by providing for the classification of light-house keepers, for the clerical force in the pension agency, and culminating in the regulation of May 6, 1896, which simplified and improved the whole system, and added 29,399 officers to the list of those under the commission, making a total of 85,000 out of a service of about 205,000.[2] Each of these extensions was hailed by most of the reformers with an enthusiasm tempered solely by a desire for more; but they might well have been disturbed by the fear that the Republicans, finding so many Democrats protected by the civil service fence, would attack the system itself. President Cleveland must, indeed, be accused of a grievous lack of tact, if not of a distinct discourtesy, when, as late as January 12, 1897, he placed under the rules the employees of the president's office. Jeffer-

---

[1] Richardson, *Messages*, ix. 176–178; C. T. Russell, Address to the National Civil Service Reform League, 16–20; *Good Government*, 1896–1897, *passim*.

[2] Richardson, *Messages*, ix. 614; *House Reports*, 52 Cong. 2 sess. ii. No. 2359; Massachusetts Reform Club, *Report*, 1898; *Good Government*, July 15, 1894, August 15, 1895.

son's doctrine in 1801, that the president should make no appointments after the election of his successor, is, of course, frivolous; but definitely to bind upon the incoming executive a corps of clerks, with whom he must come into personal contact, is to invite rebuff.

When William McKinley became president of the United State, as a band of the faithful declared, "by the grace of God and the efforts of the workers and zealous friends of the Republican party," an unusual number of the latter accompanied him to Washington in the hope of office. It would seem that never before, since the establishment of the new system in 1883, had it been subjected to such a strain; never before, indeed, had it kept so many choice places from the grasp of the politician. One Republican member of the House, in his eagerness, moved that all orders of the president between March 4, 1893, and March 4, 1897, be revoked; but the administration controlled the situation for the moment, and was not to be hurried. The unclassified service afforded some vent; and a rule promulgated by President Harrison, to the effect that a veteran dismissed from the classified service could be at any time reinstated without examination, afforded ground for a considerable number of changes.[1]

President McKinley, in his first annual message, affirmed that the system of competitive examination had been approved by the people, and that it would be his endeavor to "uphold and extend" it; that changes were needed, however, and that some places should be exempted. This led to a Senate investigation, and on May 9, 1898, a report was brought in which stated that the classification was too extensive, and recommended certain specific reductions, amounting in all to about 10,000; a minority reported in favor of about 3000 exceptions, and a second minority made no specific recommendations. Action was long delayed; the Spanish War served for a time to relieve the pressure for office by affording opportunity for temporary appointments, and itself absorbed the attention of the government. Its close, however, brought increased pressure. Effort

---

[1] *Congressional Record,* 55 Cong. 1 sess. House Resolution No. 46; *Good Government,* December 15, 1897, to July 15, 1899, *passim.*

was made to provide permanently for the men temporarily appointed; and finally, on April 29, 1899, the long-impending action was taken. A presidential order was issued by which 3693 places were removed from the classified service, 6414 transferred from the charge of the commissioners to that of the secretary of war, and 1000 temporary appointments made regular. It also removed some of the restrictions on transfers and reinstatements.[1]

As the first important retrograde step taken by any president since the inauguration of the system, it naturally was violently attacked. The best-informed assailant was Mr. McAnery, secretary of the National Civil Service Reform League, against whose attack Secretary of the Treasury Gage undertook to defend the administration in the columns of *Good Government*. The secretary of the League undoubtedly had the best of the controversy, as a controversy. President McKinley himself, in his second annual message, made a brief defence of his action. "The principal purpose of the order," said he, "was to exempt from competitive examination certain places involving fiduciary responsibilities or duties of a strictly confidential, scientific, or executive character which it was thought might better be filled either by non-competitive examination, or in the discretion of the appointing officer." This is doubtless true of many places; indeed, President Cleveland, at the time he made his blanket order of May 6, 1896, had stated to the commissioners that modifications would be necessary.[2]

It appears, however, that undue elasticity was allowed. Among the officers exempted were deputy collectors of customs, who could be appointed in great numbers, and many of whom were employed for mere clerical work.[3] The transfer to the regular list of those holding under temporary appointments was defended on the ground that the men had served long enough to demonstrate their fitness; and they have in fact proved

[1] *House Documents*, 55 Cong. 2 sess. i. No. 1, pp. xxxiii–xxxiv; *Senate Reports*, 55 Cong. 2 sess. No. 659; *Good Government*, December 15, 1898; July 15, 1899.

[2] *House Documents*, 56 Cong. 1 sess. i. No. 1, pp. lviii–lix; United States Civil Service Commission, *15th Report* (1897–1898), 77–83.

[3] Commission, *17th Report* (1899–1900), 17.

entirely satisfactory. Yet it is evident that such a precedent is dangerous to the competitive system as a system; and it appears that these appointments need never have been made in the first place, as the commission, even in the short time available, could have furnished all the clerks required, if it had been asked.[1] Another disappointment to the advocates of a mechanical system of selection was the fact that the census bureau for 1900 was not included within the rules, appointments being left to the director of the census, with the tacit understanding that he would leave them to the members of Congress.[2] On the whole, it would seem that, while some exemptions were advisable, the order of May 29, 1899, went farther than was required — farther than was best for the health of the system.

The administration did not pass, however, without signs of a better mind. A presidential order established the rule that removals should not be made from the classified service unless written charges were filed, and that the officer to be dismissed should have an opportunity to answer them. The Taft Commission, moreover, provided a merit system for the Philippines; and Porto Rico, although left unsupplied by Congress, was encouraged to establish one for herself.[3]

[1] F. A. Vanderlip, *Scribner's Magazine*, xxxiii. 400–410; *Good Government*, July 15, 1899.

[2] *Congressional Record*, 55 Cong. 3 sess. 419.

[3] United States Civil Service Commission, *18th Report* (1900–1901), 8, 28–29; J. H. Hollander, *Forum*, xxxiii. 77–84.

CHAPTER XI.

PRESENT STATUS OF THE CIVIL SERVICE
REFORM MOVEMENT.

ALTHOUGH the system of competitive examinations was begun so late in the nineteenth century, the beginning of the twentieth found it well established. The annual report of the Civil Service Commission for 1899–1900 showed 90,000 classified positions, and 100,000 unclassified, in the national service; but the salaries of the first amounted to about $75,000,000, while those of the latter amounted to only about $30,000,000. From 1883 to 1900, 78,791 officials had been appointed because of their standing in examinations. In the year 1900, 34,437 took the examinations offered, 22,985 received pass marks, and 9889 were appointed to some position. The appointing officers showed a growing tendency to select, from the three candidates certified to them by the commission as eligible, the one whose mark was highest; in about three-fourths of the cases this was done. That the extension of the system has not reached its limit is indicated by the inclusion of the rural delivery system within the rules in the year 1903.[1]

In the meantime, some states and cities followed the lead of the national government. New York, where the first reform association was formed, adopted, in 1883, a statute resembling that of the nation; Massachusetts, prolific of reform literature, followed in 1884; then, after an interval, the system received some degree of recognition from Illinois, Wisconsin, and Indiana in 1895, from Louisiana in 1896, and from Connecticut in 1897. Various cities forestalled the action of their state legislature — as Philadelphia in 1885 and Denver in 1896; while in many

[1] *Congressional Record*, 57 Cong. 1 sess. 1833.

other places the efforts, though unsuccessful as yet, have been persistent.[1]

The two most notable exceptions to the national classification at present are the fourth-class postmasters and the consular service. For fifteen years efforts have been continuous to apply the merit system to the first of these. March 3, 1890, Henry Cabot Lodge, then a member of the House of Representatives, introduced a bill to bring about this result; this was followed by one prepared by Sherman Hoar of Massachusetts; and the question was presented to Congress by President Cleveland in his message of December 7, 1896. No action has yet been taken, however, except that some minor post-offices have been consolidated with larger ones, and thereby brought within the civil service rules.[2]

The effort to provide for a trained consulate, as has been shown, dates farther back than the movement for competitive examinations. The small force of thirteen consular clerks has been long in existence, but has had no perceptible influence on the service. Nearly every Congress for fifteen years has had before it some measure intended to provide for a comprehensive reorganization; and in this movement, as in that to take the fourth-class postmasters out of politics, Senator Lodge has taken the lead. Unlike the interest in the latter agitation, however, that in the consular service has grown in the last few years, owing to our increased foreign trade and imperialistic proclivities. In 1900 the Cleveland chamber of commerce drew up a particularly good bill, which was presented to the House by Mr. Burton of that city. Action having been earnestly recommended by President Roosevelt, the matter was much debated in the first session of the fifty-seventh Congress; and, although nothing was decided, it may be said, in the congressional phraseology, to have been " passed over without prejudice." [3]

---

[1] United States Civil Service Commission, *15th Report* (1897–1898), 492.

[2] *Congressional Record*, 51 Cong. 1 sess. House Bill No. 7707; Cambridge Civil Service Reform Association, *Report*, 1891–1892; Richardson, *Messages*, ix. 740; *Good Government*, January 15, 1896.

[3] *Congressional Record*, 57 Cong. 1 sess. 75, 249, 415, 1991, 2496.

Meantime something had been done by the executive. President Cleveland issued rules classifying candidates, and providing for examinations, promotions, and the reinstatement of former consuls in preference to new appointments. In March, 1896, it was reported that since September 20, 1895, four had been promoted, four reinstated, four had passed examinations, and four had been rejected. President McKinley announced that this system would be continued. In July, 1899, it was stated that, of 112 candidates examined, 111 passed;[1] but who can say whether this indicates that the original selections were particularly excellent, or that the examinations had been devitalized?

Besides the attempts to extend the civil service rules, there have been efforts to make them more effective. July 8, 1886, the Civil Service Commission gave its opinion that, according to the laws and regulations governing the service, removals could legally be made for any reason except refusal to make political contributions, to do party service, or to submit to political dictation; but that as the reason for removal need not be stated, they could practically be made for any reason whatever. Now, in the beginning, the reformers were generally supporters of the prerogatives of the executive, and were disinclined to hamper the president's use of the removing power.[2] It was argued that if political appointments were impossible, there could no longer be any temptation to remove men without cause; and this view seemed justified to a great extent, when it was seen that in Cleveland's first administration the removals from the classified service amounted to only six and one-half per cent. Yet in the course of time, sentiment has grown to favor some regulation of the president's prerogative. Legislation has not yet been effective,[3] but the difficulty has been in great measure relieved by the above-mentioned order of President McKinley, requiring written charges to be filed, and giving

---

[1] Richardson, *Messages*, ix. 722; *Good Government*, March 15, 1896; March 15, 1899; July 15, 1899.

[2] *Civil Service Reformer*, April, 1886; Cary, *Curtis*, 199–203.

[3] *Good Government*, April 15, 1895; *Civil Service Reformer*, January, 1887; *Congressional Record*, 50 Cong. 1 sess. House Bill No. 1628.

the officer the right to answer. The executive itself has provided a definite rule for its own conduct.

Many suggestions for minor improvements have been made from time to time. The proceedings of the National League are filled with them; and every session of Congress sees bills introduced to prevent drunkenness, to prevent congressmen from making recommendations, to regulate applications for office in the unclassified service,[1] and for similar purposes, all indicating a healthy interest in the subject.

For thirty years the system of appointment by competitive examination has been on trial in America, and for twenty years it has been recognized by Congress and operated by an executive on the whole favorable. It is time, then, to form some idea of its success, and to say something definite as to the changes it has wrought. In making such an estimate, it should be borne in mind that the advocates of the system had two objects in view: while they differed from previous reformers in earnestly desiring to improve the service, — making that, in fact, their first object, — they were as anxious as their predecessors of 1836 to purify political conditions, and believed that the competitive system was admirably fitted to that end also.

Of the effect of the system on the service, details and statistics may be found in abundance in the Civil Service Commission reports, of which the fifteenth is particularly valuable, as it contains a general summary of results. In this summary it is estimated that two million dollars a year is saved in the collection of the customs by the merit system, and that the saving through the whole service is ten per cent of the salaries. Such definite statements, however, lack a firm basis. Efficiency cannot be reckoned in figures; and it is certainly improper to attribute to competitive examinations or to the Civil Service Commission all the improvements made since 1883. It is altogether likely that, under any circumstances, the service would have improved in the last twenty years. Much more convincing, therefore, than statistical expositions of benefits is the general testimony of the most trusted executive officers as

[1] Massachusetts Reform Club, *Report,* 1895; and *Congressional Record Index, Civil Service.*

to the change for the better; and the more efficient work that these men have been able to do, because relieved in large measure of importunities for office, must be counted among the most important of the gains.

There are other facts which statistics do not show. One is that, under the new conditions, an entirely different class of men is attracted into the service. Under the old lack of system, any position might lead anywhere, and that quickly; removal was constantly impending; government service was speculative, and because of the opportunities it afforded attracted clever, sometimes brilliant, men. Now it offers, in the main, the advantage of steady, light employment at a moderate remuneration and attracts the steady-going and unimaginative. Government service, moreover, in this country, is not held to be a badge of honor, as it is in Germany and France, and, to a degree, in England; it will never form the basis of a bourgeois aristocracy, and hence will attract of the steady-going only those who have no better financial opportunities. The question as to which of these two classes it is most desirable to secure is one of time and circumstances. During the middle of the century, when the American rotated in other professions, it was natural that he should rotate in office, and rotation and the spoils system probably secured, in most parts of the country, a better corps of civil servants than the present system would have done. To-day our general mode of life is more stable, and it is therefore natural that the government service should become more so; the class that is willing to settle down permanently to the prospect of a small but steady income, and a respectable but not distinguished station, is increasing. It must be acknowledged, however, that as yet the ordinary positions of the civil service — those offering no special inducements for research or travel — do not tempt as able young men as business opportunities of equal grade. It seems, also, that the examinations are so managed, doubtless partly in deference to public sentiment, that men of higher education are not encouraged to enter. In 1891, $62\frac{9}{10}$ per cent of those who took the examinations on the basis of a common-school education passed, $77\frac{3}{10}$ per cent of those who had been through high school, and only $67\frac{1}{10}$ per cent of the college men.[1] Of course many of the college men took more difficult technical examinations, yet the figures seem to indicate that many of the college-bred men who applied were of inferior capacity. Certainly an infusion of college men would benefit the service.

Until men of more ability are attracted by the examinations that give entrance to the civil service, the system of mechanical promotion cannot be extended up through the service to positions requiring executive power and independent judgment; though if such positions were included within the system, that fact of itself would of course afford an inducement to enter the lower grades which does not now exist. We may well doubt, however, whether, while business continues to hold out such opportunities as at present, the permanent civil service will be able to draw in many men fitted for the highest posts.[2]

When we turn to the political results of the competitive selection of candidates, it is necessary to keep in mind the *causa eundi* of the spoils system — the fact that it came into being to supply a means of supporting political organization, that its essence lies in making the offices the campaign fund of the different parties. The first point to be considered is whether it has taken the offices out of this category — whether promises of office count less in party warfare, and whether officers are less active party workers, than previously. The mere fact that appointment to so many offices has been taken from the discretion of the executive means that so many the fewer friends can be rewarded. The successive reports of the Civil Service Commission show that, although every campaign brings to light new methods of circumventing the law, assessments are really becoming much less common;[3] and also that

---

[1] *Good Government*, November 15, 1892; *Civil Service Reformer*, February, 1891.

[2] H. T. Newcomb, *Forum*, xx. 120–128; Benjamin Kidd, *Nineteenth Century*, xx. 491–502; F. A. Vanderlip, *Scribner's Magazine*, xxxiii. 404.

[3] An act of June 30, 1868, forbade any officer of the government to pay money for political purposes to a workman in the navy yards. A law of August 15, 1876, forbade any officer or employee of the United States, not appointed with the advice and consent of the Senate, to give to, or receive from, any other such officer or employee any money for political purposes. In 1886 the commission recommended that every one be forbidden to solicit such contributions.

other forms of political activity diminish, in spite of an evident itching on the part of public officers to take the lead in party management. It is noticed, however, that as the number of places disposable has become smaller, the pressure for them has increased; that the desire for this particular method of pay- ment for political service has not diminished as rapidly as civil service reform has advanced; and the tremendous stress brought upon the McKinley administration indicates that civil service reform will not find its further advancement along a pleasant path.

Whether a further withdrawal of the offices from politics will prove to be possible, depends upon circumstances. Practically we may omit the supposition that a modern democracy could exist without parties; it may be possible, but it is a condition which lies far in the future. Under existing conditions the possibility of a complete civil service reform, as generally under- stood, depends upon whether our parties can be convinced that they can exist without their present elaborate organizations, or can maintain these organizations without the cohesive power of the public offices.[1] If the organizations are maintained, reform is impossible, unless a substitute is found for the spoils system. If the substitute be money, the change is a bad one; if it be ar- gument and the devotion of earnest men, it is good; if it be the drawing of rich men into politics and an approximation of the English aristocratic system, there may be two opinions as to its value; or there might be a simplification of political machinery, as by the introduction of primary elections. All these tenden- cies are observable, and civil service reform is to be studied in connection with them and with all other political reform move- ments. Eternal vigilance, and not merely the mechanical selec- tion of public officers, is the price of liberty.

A troublesome minor question in this connection is how far the servants of the state may be allowed to indulge in politics. As has been pointed out, and as every man in middle life knows, the activity of office-holders is much less than it once was; but what are the proper limits? Present public sentiment in America would

---

[1] Gamaliel Bradford discusses this question in an interesting article on "The Progress of Civil Service Reform" in the *International Review* for September, 1882.

not countenance any effort to gag the civil service ; and we certainly do not wish the public employees to constitute a separate political body as they come very near doing in Australia. Some reformers have of late been taking very advanced ground ; Postmaster-general Heath has been criticised for allowing participation in caucuses and conventions,[1] and Commissioner Foulke for his circular of 1902, which argued that it was not a violation of the spirit of the law for members of the cabinet to take part in a political campaign.

Such extreme criticisms injure a good cause. The ideal condition, doubtless, is that all citizens should participate alike in politics ; but it is also true that, in order to discourage officials from taking that undue interest in politics to which they have been accustomed in times past, special repression will be long necessary. It should, however, be recognized that the influence which a collector of customs exerts over his subordinates and that by which a manufacturer controls his employees, are closely akin. Here again it is a broad, general problem that is to be solved.

One interesting result of the law of 1883 has been the more equal sharing of positions between the different states and parties. As a result of the long Republican dominance, the Southern states had a comparatively small number of citizens in the departments at Washington, and an undue proportion of these consisted of negroes, because of the political proclivities of the latter. At present there are no glaring inequalities ; and white Democrats from the South are more numerous, while the negroes from the North have increased.[2] Thus a result always aimed at, and especially desirable in a federal republic, has been brought about. It is a very valuble thing to have at the capital a large number of representatives of the different sections ; it creates a national atmosphere, and probably exerts an unconscious influence of a most beneficial character on Congress. The reflex influence on the states is, of course, not so great as in the days of rotation. Then the great numbers of men with four years of Washington experience and fresh from

---

[1] Massachusetts Reform Club, *Report*, 1898, p. 11.

[2] United States Civil Service Commission, *17th Report*, 1899–1900, pp. 405–465; T. Roosevelt, *Atlantic Monthly*, lxvii. 252–257 ; *Civil Service Record*, April, 1891.

contact with their fellow-citizens from far away, who scattered broadcast over the land, must have carried with them much information that was useful to their friends, and that probably strengthened the bonds of union, which in those days so much needed strengthening. With our present facilities of travel and our strong national spirit, this function may well be dispensed with; but it can never cease to be important to have at Washington a population drawn in proper proportion from all the states, centring there ties of family interest, and prepared to furnish knowledge of local conditions.

Having examined the advantages and disadvantages of the existing civil service system, we must briefly consider its elements of stability, and first the points of attack, internal and external. It is not the purpose of this study to detail minutely the workings of the system, — the reports of the Civil Service Commission are too candid and too easily available to make that necessary, — but certain plausible methods of evading restrictions must be mentioned. One of the most dangerous is reinstatement. It seems just that, if a man be dismissed without just cause or because of a reduction in force, he should be readmitted without having to run the gantlet as a novice. When, however, one recalls the conditions in the forties and fifties, it becomes obvious that, if this practice were freely allowed, rotation would be again introduced, each party turning out its opponents and reinstating the martyrs of its own faith. There would be two sets of men, — one in office, and the other working to obtain it by a party success. The civil service rules formerly allowed reinstatement within one year of dismissal, but not thereafter. President Harrison, as has been shown, provided that veterans might be taken back without regard to time. President McKinley, in his order of April 26, 1899, extended this provision to all officers in the classified service, with the restriction that those separated from the government for more than twelve months should take a pass-examination. The Civil Service Commission, in its seventeenth report, earnestly recommends that the former rule be reëstablished.[1]

[1] *House Miscellaneous Documents*, 52 Cong. 2 sess. i. No. 93; *Congressional Record*, 55 Cong. 1 sess. 721, 747, 793.

Transfers form another vexing problem. Constant attempts are made to obtain permission for men to be transferred from the unclassified service to positions included under the rules. The commission has recently recommended stricter regulations,[1] and has thus far been able to prevent any serious encroachments. Another method of evasion is illustrated by the abolition of the office of superintendent of the binding division, carrying a salary of nineteen hundred dollars, and the establishment of a chief of the division at the same salary. A new man was of course appointed.[2] Thus far the enforcement of the law has been practically always in the hands of friends. If it fell into those of its enemies, it could probably be much relaxed without any great surface changes; in fact, the conditions in some of our states and cities show that the working of the law depends almost entirely upon the animus of the controlling political forces.

A well-known American statesman once said, — of course in private, apropos of a pension bill, that the fact was that the grand army of the republic saved the country, and now it wanted it. It has been shown, from time to time, that military service has been thought to entitle a man to civil office. This sentiment was naturally strengthened by the Civil War; Lincoln felt it, and in 1865 it was provided by law that soldiers discharged "by reason of disability resulting from wounds or sickness incurred in the line of duty" should "be preferred for appointments to civil offices, provided they are found to possess the business capacity necessary." In 1876 they were given preference when reductions in force were to be made.[3] There is a certain justice in such provisions, and civil service reformers have been somewhat chary of opposing them; but since 1883 there has been a constant effort to extend their scope, and an equally steady effort to prevent this extension. The division has tended to lie between those favorable and those unfavorable to civil service reform.

---

[1] *17th Report*, 16 ; *Congressional Record*, 54 Cong. 1 sess. Senate Bill No. 2563.

[2] *Good Government*, September 15, 1894.

[3] *Senate Reports*, 38 Cong. 2 sess. i. No. 122 ; *Revised Statutes*, § 1754 ; *Statutes at Large*, xix. 143.

Congress has been flooded with bills to make the road to office easy for the soldier: in one session four such bills were presented to the Senate and thirteen to the House. Reports have been called for, chiefly by the Senate, to show how far the preference already provided for is observed. Bills have passed the Senate to extend the preference to all soldiers honorably discharged; bills have been introduced to extend it to Confederates.[1] Just when such measures were becoming less dangerous because of the age of the veterans of the great conflict, the Spanish War brought new candidates for recognition, and renewed interest in war and warriors, and since then new floods of measures have been presented. President Mc-Kinley, without waiting for legislation, properly extended to our new veterans the privileges of the old; but preference is still restricted to the wounded and sick, and in the classified service of course applies only to those who receive a pass mark.[2] The inclusion of all those honorably discharged would be most unwise, at a time when three hundred thousand young veterans have just come into existence; but the agitation will undoubtedly continue while there are men in Congress whose sympathy for the soldier, and appreciation of the soldier vote, is stronger than their desire for civil service reform.[3] In the past the South has on obvious grounds consistently opposed such legislation; but her position can no longer be predicted, as she now has Spanish War veterans of her own who might profit by the privileges to be granted. The problem is thus an open one.

Not all the dangers of the present system are internal: from the very first direct attack has not been lacking. The session of Congress next after the passage of the law of 1883 saw two

---

[1] *Senate Reports*, 47 Cong. 1 sess. iv. No. 780 ; *House Reports*, 52 Cong. 1 sess. vii. No. 1925 ; *Congressional Record*, 50 Cong. 1 sess. Senate Bill 2443 ; 51 Cong. 1 sess. ; 55 Cong. 2 sess. 718, 4275 ; 56 Cong. 1 sess. 5612.

[2] United States Civil Service Commission, *15th Report* (1897–1898), 34 ; *Civil Service Record*, November, 1885.

[3] The same movement has been going on in the states, notably in Massachusetts. See *Civil Service Record*, July, 1887, March, 1888, February, 1889 ; *Good Government*, December 15, 1895 ; May 15, 1896 ; New York Civil Service Reform Association, *Reports*, 1886, 1887.

bills to repeal it, and three or four such bills have been introduced in every succeeding Congress. These bills for repeal are seldom debated, being reported adversely by the civil service reform committee of the House, or the civil service and retrenchment committee of the Senate; but every Congress witnesses a debate over the appropriation for the expenses of the commission. It was the intention of the framers of the law that these expenses should be made a permanent charge; but precedent was lacking for such a course, and thus the entire system is in constant danger of being impaired, if not destroyed, by a hostile vote. Nevertheless, supplies have not failed, and have grown increasingly liberal.

The debates on these appropriations are not usually very edifying. Epithets are freely hurled: the Civil Service Commission has been called a " Republican, Pecksniffian, political machine "; the reformers, " eunuchs and sissiri of American politics, canting prelates and Pharisees "; while the system has been described as " conceived in iniquity and born of hypocrisy . . ., administered infamously, and sustained by cowardice and demagogy." Mr. Eaton was attacked because in a bill of expenses were included thirty cents for lemonade and a dollar for supper, gin, and ale; another commissioner for expending forty cents for "porter," but apprehension was relieved when it proved to be a Pullman car porter. By saner critics the system is said to disregard a man's moral character, or to allow no chance to size a man up.[1]

Mr. Bailey of Texas touched a politically weak point when he said, " If the civil service law continues on the statute books of the United States for twenty years it will be followed by a civil pension list, and that itself is objection enough to the system." General Grosvenor also, prompt to see the unpopularity of civil pensions, has insisted that under present conditions humanity demands them. This, indeed, seems to be one of the rocks threatening the progress of the movement. Now, as before 1830, the tendency is for clerks to remain in

[1] *Good Government,* June 15, 1894; Massachusetts Reform Club, *Report,* 1893; *Civil Service Reformer,* August, 1885, June, 1890 ; *Congressional Record,* 55 Cong. 3 sess. 459.

office to extreme old age; and the question arises as to how long they can be retained without detriment to the service, and whether it is just to dismiss them without providing for their last days. Of late this problem has been attracting much attention. Bills have been introduced fixing an age limit for retirement, providing for insurance systems, for civil pensions, and for the payment of a lump sum on retirement. Secretary Gage formulated a plan for an " honor roll," in which the names of clerks who had passed seventy were to be included; they were to be retained in the service, but their salaries were to be reduced to a nine-hundred-dollar basis. The scheme was not popular and has never been put completely into operation. Among the clerks themselves there have been attempts to form insurance arrangements;[1] but as yet none of these schemes have seemed to offer inducements superior to those of the regular companies.

It may seem inconsistent that a government so profuse with its military pensions should not grant them to the civil service. It is probably true, moreover, that in the long run a civil service pension system properly related to salaries would not cost the government one cent; for, when pensions are not given, pay must be high enough to allow of individual saving. Still, it cannot be denied that such a provision would be unpopular, and would indeed denote a change in the spirit of American institutions, which have been so strongly individualistic and so insistent that each man should take care of himself.[2] On the other hand, American individualism is being modified; and if many private corporations follow the example of the Pennsylvania Railroad, of Harvard University, and of other employers, the idea of pensions for the servants of the government will become less strange, and therefore less unpopular.

Many attempts, more or less avowed, have been made to

---

[1] National Civil Service Reform League, *Proceedings*, 1895, pp. 76–80; G. B. Raum, in *North American Review*, cxxxvi. 492–493; F. A. Vanderlip, in *Scribner's Magazine*, xxxiii. 403; *Civil Service Record*, June, 1891.

[2] The argument that a pension system would reduce the number of removals has ceased to be of significance, owing to the recent orders forbidding removal except on written charges. Australian experience would seem to prove that the system would not be efficacious for this object under any circumstances.

cripple the merit system before destroying it; for instance, bills have been introduced to allow the appointing officers to choose any applicant who has passed the examination, "to improve the civil service by affording advancement to those in the classified service who have been denied advancement through circumstances beyond their control," to suspend the law during the first year of every presidential term. Perhaps the most notable effort of this kind was that to place the employees of the bureau of the twelfth census, who had been appointed on pass-examinations, within the pale of the classified service. Senator Lodge pointed out that this would carry over, and place ahead of the highest eligibles, a thousand or twelve hundred names. An amendment was of course offered, giving a preference to those of them who had been soldiers in any of our wars, or who were the widows of soldiers. After a long debate it was arranged by a conference committee that the employees of the bureau should be admitted to the classified service, but should be eligible only to appointment in the new permanent census bureau; the preference for soldiers was retained.[1]

It is not to be supposed that the assailants of the present system are without a programme of their own. For a long time they seemed to be so, but of late a clearer idea may be obtained of what they desire beyond a return to the old lack of system. One idea that crops out continually is that of the New York constitution of 1820 — to extend the elective system to the minor offices. This is generally urged in regard to postmasters; but one bill has also been introduced providing that the various states and territories elect definite quotas and send them to Washington to work in the departments. More representative, however, is the plan which General Grosvenor of Ohio, who has made himself the leader in attacks on the merit system, set forth in an elaborate speech printed in the appendix to the *Congressional Record* for the first session of the fifty-fifth Congress. This is a careful and deliberate assault on existing methods, supplemented by suggestions as to what he thinks would prove better. He would divide the service into three

---

[1] *Congressional Record*, 50 Cong. 2 sess. Senate Bill No. 3927 ; 52 Cong. 2 sess. House Bill No. 1024 ; 54 Cong. 1 sess. 445 ; 57 Cong. 1 sess. 1770, 1839, 2395.

classes, — the executive, advising, and administrative class, the executing or clerical class, and the workman class. He would have a limited term and a strict pass-examination, would have each appointee recommended by his representative as a friend of the government, and would have congressional districts equally represented. He considers that congressmen shirk their duties at present. In other words, he would turn the appointing power over to legislators. At bottom, the present attack on the merit system is, in large part, a reappearance of the old jealousy of the executive so many times illustrated in the history of the patronage.[1]

What has enabled civil service reform to progress, unpopular as it has been because of its foreign origin, and interfering, as it has done, with our established political institutions? Why have not the congressmen, who have been deprived of the means of sustaining their political machines, and more than half of whom are probably hostile to the system, risen in successful revolt? These questions seem more difficult of answer if we consider the character of its advocates. In list after list of the members of civil service reform associations, not a name can be found that does not suggest to one acquainted with the nomenclature of the various localities, education, wealth, or social position; the very list of such societies existing in 1892 shows that centres of learning and wealth, and not of population, are represented. Addresses are occasionally made to workmen, pointing out the value of the reform to them; but the platforms of labor parties do not testify to their interest in it. In the main, it has been an agitation carried on by a comparatively small, educated class.

One great source of success has been the non-partisan character of the movement, at the same time that it has not been unpartisan. The bill was introduced by a Democratic senator, and passed by a Republican Congress; its supporters have come from both parties, and in the commission both parties

---

[1] *Congressional Record*, 47 Cong. 1 sess. 5707 ; 49 Cong. 2 sess. House Bill No. 10,209 ; 53 Cong. 1 sess. House Bill No. 246, and Appendix, 419–445 ; *Good Government*, April 15, 1893 ; Interview with Senator Wellington, *Boston Herald*, August 1, 1902.

have been represented by stalwart supporters, by men like Theodore Roosevelt and Governor Thompson of South Carolina, whose honest partisanship could not be mistrusted. This fortunate condition was seriously threatened when, in 1896 and 1900, the national platform of the Democratic party condemned the movement. Many advocates of reform were still in the Democratic ranks however, and the platform of 1904 once more pledged the party to the support of the reform measures undertaken by the government, and has thus prevented them from becoming an issue between the parties. As a result of this appeal to both parties, the progress of reform has received no serious check through the mutations of party fortunes. It has had constantly that support from the several presidents and from most of the heads of departments, which is a necessary condition of its success. This has given an unusual opportunity to test its value and demonstrate its merits to the public.

Another element of strength has been the publicity and candor which has characterized the movement from its initiation. The reformers have proceeded straightforwardly in the belief that, if the people saw what the system they proposed was, and how it worked, they would support it. By that truly democratic method they have taken the sting out of the gibes directed at the system as aristocratic, and have demonstrated that what the people can see and touch and find good they will have.

Not, however, to the members of civil service reform associations can we attribute the whole or the greater influence in bringing about the result, any more than we can attribute to the abolitionists the abolition of slavery. The civil service will ever assimilate itself to surrounding conditions. Before 1828 it tended to be staid and aristocratic. At that date tendencies which had long been gaining strength obtained the mastery; and the civil service shared in the blatant democracy, the dazzling confidence in results to be obtained, the lofty carelessness as to the methods of obtaining them, and all the other characteristics of the ruling class in the United States between 1830 and 1870. Since that time there has been a growing civic consciousness, an appreciation of the serious duties of citizenship, which has furnished the energy to start numerous reforms on the road to ultimate adoption. Most significant, however, are the two facts that the balance of power has for some time been held by the business class, and that business methods have, since the crisis of 1873, become more careful and systematic. To call competitive examinations businesslike in 1850 would have been absurd; yet that has been constantly and increasingly the most effective argument in favor of the system. As long as the controlling element in the country manage their private affairs in a careful, systematic manner, we may expect the government to conduct its business on approximately the same principles.

APPENDICES.

———

APPENDIX A.

TRANSFER OF OFFICERS (1789-1791).

TABLE I.

OFFICERS OF THE CONFEDERATION.

Old Position.		New Position.
Superintendent of Foreign Affairs	John Jay	Chief Justice.
Minister to France	Thomas Jefferson	Secretary of State.
Commissioner of Treasury Board	Samuel Osgood	Postmaster-general.
Secretary at War	Henry Knox	Secretary of War.
Governor of Northwest Territory	Arthur St. Clair	Governor of Northwest Territory.
Secretary of Northwest Territory	Winthrop Sargent	Secretary of Northwest Territory.
Judge of Northwest Territory	Samuel Holden Parsons	Judge of Northwest Territory.
Judge of Northwest Territory	John Cleves Symmes	Judge of Northwest Territory.
Continental Loan Officer in Virginia	John H. Hopkins	Commissioner of Loans for Virginia.
Assistant Secretary of Congress	Roger Alden	Place in State Department.

TABLE II.

STATE CUSTOMS OFFICES (1789-1791).

COLLECTORS.

Number of national offices	67
State collectors or equivalents made federal collectors	27

State collectors appointed to lower offices 4
State collectors not appointed to any customs office 8
New offices, or no data 28

NAVAL OFFICERS.

Number of national offices 13
State naval officers made federal naval officers 3
State collectors appointed 2
State naval officer not appointed to any customs office 1
New offices, or no data . . . . 7 (or 9)

SURVEYORS.

Number of national offices 56
State surveyors or searchers made federal surveyors 12
State collectors appointed 2
State surveyors not appointed to any customs office 6
New offices, or no data . . . . 36 (or 38)

TOTAL.

Whole number of offices at beginning of federal government . . . 136
State officers appointed to corresponding federal positions . . . 42
State officers appointed to some other customs place 46
State officers not appointed to any customs place 15
New offices, or no data 75

APPENDIX B.

NUMBERS OF HOLD-OVER OFFICIALS (1801-1897).

It is obvious that very little indication of the actual tenure of office can be given by tables of the number of removals only ; for frequent removals from a few offices make the same totals as removals distributed over the whole service at rarer intervals. These tables illustrate the fact that rotation was never complete, and that there was in the service a constant residuum of trained men.

The total number of employees in a given office, at a specified date, has been taken. This total is indicated in heavy type and the date is at the head of the column. The history of each of these corps is given in a separate line, the number of officers remaining at the several dates being given in the column at the head of which the date appears.

I. Subordinates of the First Auditor of the Treasury.

This table and table II. indicate the movement of officials in the departments at Washington.

1817	1828	1830	1839	1841	1849	1861	1867	1879	1889	1893	1897
15	9	9	5	4							
		13	8	5	1						
						30	12	4	4	3	1

II. Subordinates of Secretary of War.

1817	1828	1830	1839	1841	1849	1859	1861	1867	1879	1889	1897
20	6[1]	5	4[2]	4	1						
		17	7		4	2	1[3]				
						11	5	2	1		
									65	25	6[4]

III. District Attorneys.

This table and tables IV., V., and VI. illustrate the tenure of officers of the presidential class.

1801	1817	1828	1830	1839	1841	1849	1857	1861	1867	1871	1881	1887
22	4	2	1									
	26	4	2									
			37	7[5]	2							
					41	6						
								39	8	1		
											66	2

[1] In addition, there are apparently three cases in which a son or some other relative succeeded to the position.

[2] All of the four had been promoted, one being made commissioner of pensions, which office he retained until 1849.

[3] Apparently this survivor was succeeded by his son.

[4] Of the six five had been promoted, one degraded.

[5] In addition, a son apparently succeeded his father.

IV. District Marshals.

1801	1817	1828	1830	1839	1841	1849	1857	1861	1867	1871	1881	1887	1893
23	2												
	23	9	7	I									
			36	8									
					42	3	2						
								57	8	o			
											68	4	I

V. Collectors of Customs in New York State.

This table and table VI. afford a comparison of the relative permanency of office in North and South.

1817	1828	1830	1839	1841	1859	1861	1867	1879	1887
10	I[1]	2							
		10	4	o					
					11	o			
						11	2		
								14	o

VI. Collectors of Customs in Virginia.

1817	1828	1830	1839	1841	1849	1859	1861
12	2[1]	2	2	I			
	8	8	2	I			
				10	I		
						9	I[2]

[1] In addition, a son apparently succeeded his father.
[2] Only office filled (Alexandria).

VII. Consular Service.

	1801	1817[1]	1826	1830	1839	1841	1845	1853	1857	1859	1861	1867	1879	1881	1887	1889	1893	1897
		9	4	3	2	1[2]	6	5	4	1	1	1[3]				4	3	2
											4	2						
				18	10	9					69[5]							
	58	56	22	131	48	35	24	15[4]		224	248	43 [Not followed out]	13	272	61		26	14

[1] From 1817-1841 no change of consul-general was made at London.

[2] T. W. Fox at Falmouth, England, who was succeeded by his son, and whose family still (1903) hold the position.

[3] Mr. Dabney, succeeded by his son; another son was at one time in the service.

[4] One consul, serving in 1830 but not in 1845, was again in office.

[5] In 1859 there were 49 consuls who had been appointed from the South, and 124 from the North; almost all those from the South had disappeared in 1861; all the 69 unchanged were small posts and consisted largely of whole sets of consuls not yet reached, as those of Spain, Brazil, Peru, and Argentine Republic.

NOTES, TABLE VIII.— [1] There are in addition seven cases in which relatives of an officer seem to have obtained positions.

[2] Not one of the three in office in 1841, but one of the four in office in 1841 who had been dropped and was now replaced. [3] Total number of officers reduced to 16.

[4] There is in addition one case of apparent family succession.

VIII. Custom-houses at Boston and Charleston.
(PRESIDENTIAL AND ALL OTHER OFFICIALS.)

	1823	1829	1839	1841	1849	1859	1861
Boston . . .	94	26[1]	4	3	1[2]		
Charleston . .	40	13[3]	8[4]	5	5	2	
Boston . . .		98	15	11	3		
Charleston . .		16	9	6	5	2	

APPENDIX C.

REMOVALS UNDER TYLER AFTER WEBSTER'S RESIGNATION.

	Removals mentioned.	Name of last occupant, but not cause of vacancy.	Failure to reappoint.	Appointment vice non-acting appointee.	Total.
Ministers	I				I
Chargés d'affaires . . .	3				3
Secretaries of legation . .	I				I
Consuls	17			I	18
Attorneys	5				5
Marshals	15				15
Collectors	28		I		29
Surveyors	18	I	I		20
Naval officers	2		I		3
Appraisers	3				3
General land officers . .	2				2
Surveyors of land . . .	I				I
Registers of land offices .	7		2		9
Receivers of public money	9		I		10
Governors of territories .			2		2
Secretaries of territories .	2				2
Indian agents	4	I			5
Mint officials	2				2
Postmasters	21				21
Special commissioners .	2				2
Total	144	2	8	I	155
Military and naval . . .	10				10
Grand total	154	2	8	I	165

APPENDIX D.

LIST OF AUTHORITIES.

Most books on United States history contain some reference to the patronage ; and during the last thirty years we have been so well supplied with indexes to periodical literature that it has seemed superfluous to reprint here the titles of the hundreds of articles which, while they have contributed to the general conclusions of this monograph, have not been cited or used in its contents. It has been thought best, therefore, to confine this bibliography to those works which contain special information or which show some special excellency of treatment.

The greater part of the research for this volume was made in the Harvard College Library, which, valuable for the whole field, contains a particularly important collection of pamphlets on civil service reform. The library of the Harvard Law School is extremely rich in early editions of state laws. The American Antiquarian Society, at Worcester, possesses a very valuable collection of early newspapers; and the Wisconsin Historical Society has many rare tracts on early politics and much unique material on western history. The Chase manuscripts, to which reference is made in the footnotes, were in the possession of Professor Albert Bushnell Hart when I made use of them; they are now in the Library of Congress, and portions of them have been published by the American Historical Society in its report for 1902. The Foster manuscripts, in the possession of the Rhode Island Historical Society, are very instructive, though they are seldom mentioned in the footnotes: a few of them have recently been published in volume viii. of the *Publications* of the Society, under the editorship of J. Franklin Jameson. The kindness of Mrs. John R. Bartlett secured access to certain papers of the Hon. Thomas A. Jenckes of Rhode Island; and through Dr. U. B. Phillips was secured the use of some significant letters of William H. Crawford of Georgia.

The letters of application and of recommendation to office under the national government are in the keeping of the bureaus of appointments in the several departments. In the treasury department there is an elaborate system of filing for all current appointments, but those which are obsolete are relegated to the cellar; all matter relating to appointments in this department previous to the twenties was destroyed by fire. The state department has preserved its records from the foundation of the government, and has them all on file for reference. Mr. Gaillard Hunt made use of this material in writing his articles on office-seeking, and he has also prepared a calendar of all the material for the administration of Washington. These letters, however, are regarded as confidential and are not open to general use.

While this monograph was going through the press there appeared the *Guide to the Archives of the Government of the United States in Washington,* by Van Tyne and Leland, for the Carnegie Institution, in which the records of appointments and removals receive due attention.

BIBLIOGRAPHIES.

BIBLIOGRAPHY for the students of Civil Service Reform, recommended by the Executive Committee of the Woman's Auxiliary to the Civil Service Reform Association, 1899.

BIBLIOGRAPHY of Civil Service Reform and Related Subjects. New York, 1900.

FOSTER, W. E. References to the History of Presidential Administrations. New York, 1885.

HART, ALBERT BUSHNELL. Handbook of the History, Diplomacy, and Government of the United States (§§ 21, 101, 108). Cambridge, 1901.

SALMON, LUCY M. Syllabus for the Study of the History of Civil Service Reform. Published for the Massachusetts State Federation of Women's Clubs, 1903.

GENERAL WORKS.

Every book covering the general history of the United States for any period subsequent to 1789 contains some reference to the history of the civil service. Those which contain the best accounts are Henry Adams's *History of the Administrations of Jefferson and Madison* ; J. F. Rhodes's *History of the United States from the Compromise of 1850*; and Herman Van Holst's *The Constitutional and Political History of the United States*.

SPECIAL WORKS ON THE HISTORY OF THE CIVIL SERVICE AND THE PATRONAGE.

BECKER, CARL. Nominations in Colonial New York. *American Historical Review*, vi. 260–275. New York, etc., January, 1901.

CATTERALL, R. C. H. The Second Bank of the United States. Chicago, 1903.

CHADSEY, C. E. The Struggle between President Johnson and Congress over Reconstruction. Columbia University, *Studies in History*, viii. No. 1, pp. 1–142. New York, 1896.

DE WITT, D. M. The Impeachment and Trial of Andrew Johnson. New York, 1903.

DUNNING, W. A. Essays on the Civil War and Reconstruction, and related topics. New York, etc., 1898.

EATON, D. B. Civil Service in Great Britain, a History of Abuses and Reforms and their Bearing upon American Politics. New York, 1880. The result of an investigation begun at the request of President Hayes, June 25, 1877.

FISH, C. R. Lincoln and the Patronage. *American Historical Review*, viii. 53–69. New York, etc., October, 1902.

FISH, C. R. Removal of Officials by the President of the United States. American Historical Association, *Report*, 1899, i. 67–86. Washington, 1900.

HUNT, GAILLARD. Calendar of Applications and Recommendations for Office during the Presidency of George Washington. Washington, 1901.

HUNT, GAILLARD. Office-seeking during Washington's Administration. *American Historical Review*, i. 270–283. New York, etc., January, 1896.

HUNT, GAILLARD. Office-seeking during the Administration of John Adams. *American Historical Review*, ii. 241–261. New York, etc., January, 1897.

HUNT, GAILLARD. Office-seeking during Jefferson's Administration. *American Historical Review*, iii. 270–291. New York, etc., January, 1898. —

The material for these three articles is drawn from the files of the state department at Washington, and many letters, heretofore unprinted and at present inaccessible to the student, are given in full.

HUNT, GAILLARD. Office-seeking during Washington's Administration. *American Historical Review*, i. 270–283. New York, etc., January, 1896.

JOHNSON, E. R. The Early History of the United States Consular Service, 1776–1792. *Political Science Quarterly*, xiii. 19–40. New York, etc., March, 1898.

LAWTON, G. W. The American Caucus System : its Origin, Purpose, and Utility. New York, etc., 1885.

LUETSCHER, G. D. Early Political Machinery in the United States. Philadelphia, 1903.

MERRIAM, J. M. Jefferson's Use of the Executive Patronage (abstract). American Historical Association, *Papers*, ii. No. 1, pp. 47–52. New York, etc., 1887. Contains valuable statistics.

SALMON, LUCY M. History of the Appointing Power of the President. American Historical Association, *Papers*, i. No. 5. New York, etc., 1886.

TYLER, L. G. Parties and Patronage in the United States. New York, etc., 1891. — An attempt to vindicate President Tyler's administration of the patronage.

WHITE, W. H. History of Civil Service Reform. Brookline, Massachusetts, 1883.

TECHNICAL WORKS ON THE CIVIL SERVICE.

AMERICAN CALENDAR (The), or United States Register. Philadelphia, 1794, 1796, 1798.

BOWKER, R. R. Civil Service Examinations, being Question Papers with Actual Answers of Successful and Unsuccessful Candidates. New York, 1886.

COMSTOCK, J. M. The Civil Service of the United States ; also a description of the Civil Service of the States of New York and Massachusetts, and their Municipalities. New York, 1885.

CRAWLEY, W. J. C. Handbook of Competitive Examinations for Admission to every Department of her Majesty's Service.

DE LAND, T. L. Tables showing the Number of Positions in the Executive Civil Service of the United States, classified and unclassified, on June 30, 1896. Washington, 1897.

EWALD, A. C. The Complete Guide to the Home Civil Service. 17th edition. London, 1881.

MÉTÉRIÉ-LARREY. Les Emplois Publics. Paris, 1881.

MOSHER, R. B. Executive Register of the United States, 1789–1902. Baltimore, 1903. — A complete list of the heads of the executive departments from the beginning of the government.

NATIONAL CALENDAR (The). Published by Peter Force annually. Washington, 1820–1836.

SAVILLE, STANLEY. The Civil Service Coach. The Civil Service Series. London, 1881.

BIOGRAPHIES AND WORKS OF STATESMEN WHICH CONTAIN SOURCE MATERIAL.

The works and reminiscences of almost all the statesmen and prominent men of the period contain some material. In the same way the lives of nearly all statesmen, and many of those of other men, discuss some one phase of the subject, some another; some at length, some slightly. Among the best are those in the Statesmen Series, especially those by A. B. Hart and H. C. Lodge.

ADAMS, HENRY. Life of Albert Gallatin. Philadelphia, 1879.

ADAMS, JOHN. Works, with a Life of the Author. Edited by C. F. Adams. 10 vols. Boston, 1854–1856.

ADAMS, JOHN QUINCY. Memoirs, comprising parts of his Diary from 1795 to 1848. 12 vols. Philadelphia, 1874–1877. — The Index does not adequately open up these volumes for this subject. At the times when Adams was secretary of state and president almost every page contains some material. At later periods there is less, but still enough to repay a page by page examination.

BENTON, T. H. Thirty Years' View; a History of the Working of the American Government for Thirty Years from 1820 to 1850. New York, 1854–1856. — Particularly valuable for the administrations of Jackson and Polk.

CALHOUN, J. C. Correspondence. Edited by J. F. Jameson. American Historical Association, *Report*, 1899, ii. Washington, 1900. — Somewhat scattered material, particularly valuable for the Tyler administration. Calhoun's works contain only his speech of 1855, which is chiefly constitutional. The most important Calhoun material is in Edwards's History of Illinois.

CARPENTER, F. B. Six Months at the White House with Abraham Lincoln. New York, 1865. (The 24th edition, 1867, is entitled "Inner Life of Abraham Lincoln.") — Contains the best anecdotes of Lincoln and the patronage.

CARY, EDWARD. George William Curtis. (American Men of Letters Series.) Boston, etc., 1894. — Contains a good account of the beginnings of the reform movement.

CLAY, HENRY. Private Correspondence. Edited by Calvin Colton. Boston, 1856. — Valuable for beginnings of the administrations from 1816 to 1850. Clay's *Works* contain nothing on this subject that is not in the congressional publications.

CURTIS, G. T. Life of James Buchanan. 2 vols. New York, 1883. — Invaluable for administrations of Polk and Buchanan; also on rotation.

CURTIS, G. W. Orations and Addresses. Edited by Charles Eliot Norton. 3 vols. New York, 1894.

DALLAS, G. M.   Life and Writings of Alexander James Dallas.   Philadelphia, 1871. — Intimate correspondence with Madison while Dallas was secretary of the treasury.

DAVIS, M. L.   Memoirs of Aaron Burr.   2 vols.   New York, 1836-1837. — Correspondence is valuable about 1801.

EDWARDS, NINIAN.   The Edwards Papers, being portions of a collection of the Letters, Papers, and Manuscripts of Ninian Edwards.   Edited by E. B. Washburne.   Chicago Historical Society, *Collections*, iii.   Chicago, 1884. — Illinois politics and Illinois relations of national statesmen, particularly valuable because of the letters of Duff Green.

EDWARDS, N. W.   History of Illinois from 1778 to 1833, and Life and Times of Ninian Edwards.   Springfield, 1870.

GALLATIN, ALBERT.   Writings.   Edited by Henry Adams.   3 vols.   Philadelphia, 1879. — Invaluable for the intimate and constant correspondence with Jefferson, 1800-1812.

GIBBS, GEORGE.   Memoirs of the Administrations of Washington and John Adams.   2 vols.   New York, 1846. — Intimate correspondence between Oliver Wolcott and officials and distinguished men, 1789-1800.

HAMILTON, J. A.   Reminiscences; or Men and Events at Home and Abroad.   New York, 1869. — The inaccurate and prejudiced memoirs of a man who was very well acquainted with the Jackson and Van Buren administrations.

HIGGINSON, STEPHEN.   Letters, 1783-1804.   American Historical Association, *Report*, 1896, i.   704-841.   Washington, 1897. — Valuable for the whole period of federalist control.

HUNT, C. H.   Life of Edwar' Livingston; with introduction by George Bancroft.   New York, 1864. — Interesting correspondence during the period for which he was secretary of state.

JEFFERSON, THOMAS.   The Jefferson Papers.   Massachusetts Historical Society, *Collections*, 7th series, i.   Boston, 1900. — Much on the patronage.

JEFFERSON, THOMAS.   Writings.   Edited by P. L. Ford.   10 vols. New York, 1892-1899. — Valuable from 1789 to 1826, particularly 1789-1795 and 1801-1809.

JEFFERSON, THOMAS.   Writings.   Edited by H. A. Washington.   9 vols. Washington, 1853-1854.

KENDALL, AMOS.   Autobiography.   Edited by William Stickney.   Boston, 1872. — Invaluable for Jackson's administrations.

KING, C. R.   The Life and Correspondence of Rufus King.   6 vols. New York, 1894-1900. — Valuable material from 1789 to 1825.

LINCOLN, ABRAHAM.   Complete Works.   Edited by J. G. Nicolay and John Hay.   2 vols.   New York, 1894. — Valuable about 1849 and very rich from 1858 to 1865.

MACKENZIE, W. L.   The Life and Times of Martin Van Buren, etc.   Boston, 1846.

MACKENZIE, W. L.   The Lives and Opinions of B. F. Butler and Jesse

Hoyt, etc. Boston, 1845. — Throws a lurid, though untrustworthy, light on New York and national politics under Jackson and Van Buren.

MADISON, JAMES. Letters and Other Writings. By order of Congress. 4 vols. New York, 1884.

MADISON, JAMES. Papers. Edited by Henry D. Gilpin. 3 vols. Washington, 1840.

MORRIS, GOUVERNEUR. Diary and Letters. Edited by Anne Cary Morris. 2 vols. New York, 1888. — Useful from 1789 to 1803.

PARTON, JAMES. Life of Andrew Jackson. 3 vols. New York, 1860. — Contains much source material of varying value.

QUINCY, EDMUND. Life of Josiah Quincy. Boston, 1867. — Valuable for reform efforts of 1811.

QUINCY, JOSIAH. Memoir of the Life of John Quincy Adams. Boston, 1858. — Special information on the opening of J. Q. Adams's administration.

RAVENEL, MRS. ST. JULIEN. Life and Times of William Lowndes of South Carolina, 1782-1822. Boston, etc., 1901. — Valuable about 1812.

SEATON, W. W. William Winston Seaton of the " National Intelligencer ": a Biographical Sketch [by his son]. Boston, 1871. — Valuable letters from 1809 to 1860, particularly for Adams's administration.

SEWARD, F. W. William H. Seward. 3 vols. (i. Autobiography, 1831–1846; ii.–iii. Seward at Washington, 1846–1872.) New York, 1890. — Particularly valuable for Taylor's administration.

SHEPARD, E. M. Martin Van Buren. (American Statesmen Series.) New York, 1888. — One of the best secondary accounts of the spoils system.

SUMNER, W. G. Andrew Jackson as a Public Man. (American Statesmen Series) Boston, etc., 1882. — A good account of the origin of the spoils system, but not so good as that in Shepard's Van Buren.

TARBELL, IDA M. Life of Abraham Lincoln. 2 vols. New York, 1900. — Contains invaluable source material for Lincoln's administration.

TYLER, L. G. The Letters and Times of the Tylers. 3 vols. Richmond, 1884-1896.

WASHINGTON, GEORGE. Writings. Edited by W. C. Ford. 14 vols. New York, 1889-1893. — Full of details of the patronage; notes valuable.

WASHINGTON, GEORGE. Writings. Edited by Jared Sparks. 12 vols. Boston, 1837.

WEBB, S. B. Correspondence and Journals, 1772-1806. Edited by W. C. Ford. 3 vols. New York, 1893-1894. —Valuable correspondence relating to Washington's administration and to Georgia and New York politics.

WEBSTER, DANIEL. Letters. Edited by C. H. Van Tyne. New York, 1902.

WEBSTER, DANIEL. Private Correspondence. Edited by Fletcher Webster. 2 vols. Boston, 1857. — Particularly valuable for Adams's administration.

WEED, THURLOW. Autobiography. Edited by Harriet A. Weed. Boston, 1884. — Very valuable for period 1848-1870.

WELLES, GIDEON, Lincoln and Seward. New York, 1874. — Very important account of a cabinet meeting in 1861.

PAMPHLETS AND OTHER CONTEMPORARY DISCUSSION.

ADAMS, CHARLES FRANCIS. An Appeal from the New to the Old Whigs in consequence of the Senate's course, and particularly Mr. Webster's Speech upon the Executive Patronage Bill. Boston, 1835.

ADAMS, JOHN, and CUNNINGHAM, WILLIAM. Correspondence between the Hon. John Adams, late President of the United States, and the late William Cunningham, Esq., beginning in 1803, and ending in 1812. Boston, 1823. — Chiefly important for the dismissal of Pickering.

ADDRESS of the State Committee of Republicans, appointed to correspond with the Committees of the Several Counties of the State of Pennsylvania on the Concerns of the Election of 1802. Printed by William Duane. [Philadelphia], 1802.

ADDRESS to the People of the American States who Choose Electors . . . to which is added a short sketch of the Biography of General George Clinton, and several Essays. Washington, 1808. — On rotation.

ANDREWS, C. C. Administration Reform as an Issue in the next Presidential Canvass. Cambridge, 1888.

AUSTIN, BENJAMIN, JR. Constitutional Republicanism in Opposition to Fallacious Federalism. Boston, 1803.

BERNARD, G. S. Civil Service Reform *versus* Spoils System. New York, 1885. — Contains a bibliography.

BONAPARTE, C. J. Civil Service Reform as a Moral Question. New York, 1889.

BROWN, WILLARD. Civil Service Reform in the New York Custom-House. New York, 1882.

CALLENDER, J. T. The Prospect before Us. Richmond, 1800.

CALLENDER, J. T. Sedgwick & Co., or a Key to the Six Per Cent Cabinet. Philadelphia, 1798.

CALLENDER, "TOM." Letters to Alexander Hamilton. New York, 1802.

CAMILLUS. A History of French Influence in the United States, to which is added an Exposition of the Congressional Caucus. Philadelphia, 1812.

CARPENTER, G. M. The Reform of the Civil Service considered from the Party Standpoint. Read before the Rhode Island Historical Society, March 25, 1890. No title-page.

[COLEMAN, WILLIAM.] An Examination of the President's Reply to the New Haven Remonstrance . . . together with a List of Removals and New Appointments made since the Fourth of March, 1801. New York, 1801.

CURTIS, G. W. The Situation. New York, 1886.

DAYTON, JONATHAN. Public Speculation Unfolded: in sixteen letters addressed to F. Childs and J. H. Lawrence of New York, by Jonathan Dayton of New Jersey, while Speaker of the House of Representatives of the United States. New York, 1800.

DERBY, J. B. Political Reminiscences. Boston, 1835. — Giving an account of the situation in Washington in 1829, with letters of recommendation, etc.

EARLE, A. L. Our Revenue System and the Civil Service: shall they be reformed? Economic Monographs, No. 5. New York, 1878.

ELLIOT, JONATHAN. The Debates in the Several State Conventions on the Adoption of the Federal Constitution. 4 vols. Washington, 1836.

FEDERALIST (The). Edited by P. L. Ford. New York, 1898.

FOOTE, EBENEZER. Cheetham's View of the Political Conduct of Aaron Burr, Esq., Vice-President of the United States. New York, 1802.

FORD, P. L., editor. Essays on the Constitution of the United States. Brooklyn, 1892.

FORD, P. L., editor. Pamphlets on the Constitution of the United States. Brooklyn, 1888.

FOSTER, W. E. The Situation of Civil Service Reform in the United States. Boston, 1881.

FRIEZE, JACOB. A Concise History of the Efforts to obtain an Extension Suffrage in Rhode Island from the Year 1811 to 1842. Providence, 1842.

FULLERTON, ALEXANDER. How you may aid Civil Service Reform. Civil Service Reform Association of Philadelphia, *Publications*, No. 8. Philadelphia [1882].

GREY, EARL. Reciprocity and Civil Service Reform, with comments by M. M. Trumbull. Chicago, 1893.

HOWLAND, C. G. Civil Service Reform. Address read before the Michigan Conference of the Unitarian Churches in Detroit, October 21, 1880.

LAMBERT, HENRY. The Progress of Civil Service Reform in the United States. Boston, 1885.

[LOWELL, JOHN.] The New-England Patriot, being a Candid Comparison of the Principles and Conduct of the Washington and Jefferson Administrations. Boston, 1810.

MAY, JOSEPH. Reform of the Civil Service a Moral Duty. Sermon preached in Philadelphia, November 28, 1889. Philadelphia, 1889.

NEW YORK CIVIL SERVICE REFORM ASSOCIATION. Letters addressed to the Various Candidates for the Governorship, and for Congress, the Assembly, and City Offices during the Campaign of 1882. New York, 1882.

OBSERVATIONS upon the Duties and Emoluments of Certain Public Offices. New York, 1822. Criticism of the New York courts.

PILLSBURY, A. E. Soldiers' Exemption Bill. Speech in the Massachusetts Senate. No title-page.

POLITICAL MIRROR, or Review of Jacksonism. New York, 1835. Newspaper extracts, etc.

PRINCETON REVIEW. History and Literature of Civil Service Reform. *Biblical Repertory and Princeton Review*, xlii. 1–21. New York, January, 1870.

REPORT of the Subcommittee of the Committee on the Judiciary, appointed to investigate the Administration of the Civil Service Laws of the State of New York. Albany, 1895.

RICHMOND, H. A. The Workingmen's Interest in Civil Service Reform: the Spoils System in the Public Schools. Address before the Central Labor Union of Buffalo, April 4, 1888. [Buffalo, 1888.]

RUSSELL, C. T. Address before the National League of the Civil Service Reform Association. Boston, 1892.

SCHURZ, CARL. The Spoils System. Address to the Civil Service Reform League at Washington, December 12, 1895. [Philadelphia, 1896.]

SHEPARD, E. M. The Competitive Test and the Civil Service of States and Cities. (Economic Tracts, No. 14.) New York, 1884.

STICKNEY, ALBERT. Government Machinery. New York, 1880.

TACITUS [THOMAS EVANS]. A Series of Letters addressed to Thomas Jefferson, Esq., President of the United States. Philadelphia, 1802.

THREE PATRIOTS (The) ; or the Cause and Cure of Present Evils. Addressed to the voters of Maryland. Baltimore, 1811.

TOCQUEVILLE, ALEXIS DE. Democracy in America. Translated by Henry Reeve, and revised by Henry Bowen. 2 vols. Boston, 1863.

VAN BUREN, MARTIN. [Pamphlets on Van Buren, 1832–1848, *passim*. Harvard College Library, shelf number 7393.23.] On the Post-Office Removals in 1820.

WARREN, J. C. An Antidote to John Wood's Poison. New York, 1802.

WATERS, E. F. The Great Struggle in England for Honest Government, . . . with a Letter on Reform in New York City by Thomas B. Musgrove. New York, 1881.

WEBSTER, PELATIAH. Political Essays on the Nature and Operation of Money, Public Finances, etc. Philadelphia, 1791.

WHIG Convention of Young Men in New York City. New York, 1834.

WHITRIDGE, F. W. The Four Years' Term, or Rotation in Office. New York, 1883.

WHITRIDGE, F. W. Rotation in Office. *Political Science Quarterly*, iv. 279–295. New York, etc., June, 1889.

WHO shall be Governor, Strong or Sullivan ? or the Sham-Patriot Unmasked. 1806.

WISE, H. A. Seven Decades of the Union. Philadelphia, 1876. Tyler administration.

WOOD, JOHN. The History of the Administration of John Adams. New York, 1802.

PERIODICALS AND NEWSPAPERS.

At the time of the first issue of Poole's Index the civil service was prominently before the public, and consequently all articles in the periodicals which the index includes have been made so easily accessible that it is unnecessary to recapitulate them here. The two most useful periodical publications are *Niles's Register*, which furnishes contemporary comment and episode throughout the period of the establishment of the spoils system, and the *Nation*, the date of whose foundation (1865) coincides with the beginning of the effective reform movement. A useful list is found in the Fifteenth Report of the U.S. Civil Service Commission, pp. 511–517.

NORTH, S. N. D. History and Present Condition of the Newspaper and Periodical Press of the United States. (Census Report, 1880.) Washington, 1881.

ALBANY ARGUS. Albany, 1813, etc. Edited by Jesse Buel, and afterward by Leake and Croswell. — Often had the state printing, and was for many years the chief regency organ.

BOSTON COURIER. Boston, 1824, etc. — Chiefly commercial; Whig in politics, but not violent; valuable during the forties.

CINCINNATI CHRONICLE. Cincinnati, 1836–1850. Whig.

CITY GAZETTE OR DAILY ADVERTISER. Charleston, South Carolina, 1788–1817. — Jeffersonian Republican.

CIVIL SERVICE CHRONICLE. Indianapolis, 1889–1896.

CIVIL SERVICE RECORD. Boston, 1881–1892. — Organ of the Boston and Cambridge Civil Service Reform Associations.

CIVIL SERVICE REFORMER. Baltimore, 1885–1892. — Organ of the Baltimore Civil Service Reform Association. In 1892 it was united with the Civil Service Record, under the title " Good Government."

CLAYPOOLE'S AMERICAN DAILY ADVERTISER. Philadelphia, 1791–1800.

COLUMBIAN CENTINEL. Boston, 1790–1840. — Published and edited by Benjamin Russell for about forty years, ending 1828. Advocated the adoption of the constitution; Federalist, anti-Jacksonian, strongly partisan; very progressive, and the source of news for many New England papers, until the retirement of Mr. Russell.

CONNECTICUT COURANT. Hartford, 1764, etc. — Representative of Connecticut Federalism in its successive forms; generally reliable and up to date.

COURIER AND ENQUIRER. New York, 1829–1861. — Edited by Mordecai M. Noah. Supported Jackson strongly in 1828.

DAILY NATIONAL JOURNAL. Washington, 1822, etc. — Published and edited by Peter Force. In 1825, Clay transferred the printing under his control from Gales and Seaton to Force, who continued to be very near the administration for the next four years. The paper was very ably conducted, though of course partisan.

GLOBE. Washington, 1830–1845. — Published and edited by Blair and Rives. The official Democratic paper from its inception to its end; extremely partisan and unreliable.

GOOD GOVERNMENT. New York, 1892, etc. — Organ of the National Civil Service Reform League.

JACKSON GAZETTE. Jackson, Tennessee, 1824–1830. — Valuable between 1825 and 1830.

LANCASTER JOURNAL. Lancaster, Pennsylvania, 1794–1839. — Strongly Federalist; used about 1800.

LEXINGTON REPORTER. Lexington, Kentucky, 1807–1873. — Supported Adams in 1828.

LOUISIANA ADVERTISER. New Orleans, 1825, etc. — Supported Jackson.

MADISONIAN. Washington, 1842, etc. — Published and edited by Thomas Allen. Violently partisan, and supported the spoils system; official Whig paper in 1841, but followed Tyler in his break with that party; important only during this administration. Mr. Allen later became editor of the *Union.*

MASSACHUSETTS CENTINEL. Boston, 1784–1790. — In 1790 the name was changed to *Columbian Centinel.*

MASSACHUSETTS SPY AND WORCESTER COUNTY ADVERTISER. Worcester, 1771–1904. — Federalist and anti-Jacksonian; contains many long and violent communications, but its editorial and news columns are not unfair.

NASHVILLE GAZETTE. Nashville. Jacksonian.

NATION. New York, 1865, etc.

NATIONAL INTELLIGENCER. Washington, 1800–1869. — Published and edited by Samuel H. Smith and Joseph Gales, and later by Joseph Gales, Jr., and William Seaton. The administrative organ until 1825, when Clay took his patronage from it; it still supported Adams, however, and had the printing of the House. In 1843 it became the mouthpiece of the Whigs. After this date its importance diminished.

NATIONAL REPUBLICAN AND OHIO POLITICAL REGISTER. Cincinnati, 1823, etc. — From 1799 to 1823 its name was *Western Spy and Hamilton Gazette.*

NEW YORK EVENING POST. New York, 1801, etc. — Established and edited by William Coleman under the direction of Alexander Hamilton. Strongly Federalist, but not scurrilous. In 1828, William Cullen Bryant became editor. The paper supported Jackson, and remained Democratic during the period for which it is used here.

NEW YORK HERALD. New York, 1802, etc. — Published in the century in the interest of the Federalists.

NEW YORK HERALD. New York, 1835, etc. — The *Herald*, edited by James Gordon Bennett, and the *Tribune* (see below), edited by Horace Greeley, tended, in the fifties, to supplant the official organs at Washington. They were enabled to do this by the introduction of the telegraph, and by the energy and alertness of their skilled Washington reporters.

NEW YORK OBSERVER. New York, 1820–1850. — Religious. Its political notes are generally fair.

NEW YORK TRIBUNE. New York, 1841, etc. — Invaluable for Washington correspondence during the fifties and sixties. Independent and Republican.

NILES'S REGISTER. Baltimore, 1811–1849. — Edited by Hezekiah Niles until 1846. On the whole non-partisan, but violent on particular issues.

ORACLE OF DAUPHIN AND HARRISBURGH ADVERTISER. Harrisburgh, 1791, etc. — Jeffersonian Republican.

PENNSYLVANIA EAGLE. Huntington, Pennsylvania. Republican.

PHILADELPHIA GAZETTE AND UNIVERSAL DAILY ADVERTISER. Philadelphia, 1794–1840. — Strongly Federalist.

POULSON'S AMERICAN DAILY ADVERTISER. Philadelphia, 1800–1839. Federalist. — A continuation of Claypoole's *American Daily Advertiser*.

REPUBLIC. Washington, 1848–. Official Whig journal.

RICHMOND ENQUIRER. Richmond, 1804, etc. — Published and edited by Thomas Ritchie. From early in the century until 1845, when Ritchie was transferred to the *Union*, the exponent of Virginian principles. The best newspaper in the South; well gotten out, quoting many other papers, and fairly reliable.

SPRINGFIELD GAZETTE. Springfield, 1879, etc. — Whig.

TRUTH'S ADVOCATE AND MONTHLY ANTI-JACKSON EXPOSITOR. Cincinnati, January to October, 1828.

UNION. Washington, 1845, etc. —Established, with Thomas Ritchie as editor, to supplant the *Globe* as the official organ of the Democratic administration, because of the attitude of Blair on Texas and slavery. It continued to be the organ of the party until 1857, when the practice of having such a mouthpiece practically died out, although the *Union* continued to the close of the Buchanan administration.

UNITED STATES TELEGRAPH. Washington, 1826, etc. — Published and edited by General Duff Green. Strongly partisan, and supporter of the spoils system; official Democratic paper from 1828 to 1833, when the *Globe* was established to take its place because of Green's strenuous support of Calhoun.

WORCESTER PALLADIUM. Worcester. — Democratic.

PUBLICATIONS OF SOCIETIES.

So scattered is the material on this subject that it would be difficult to name a learned society whose publications could not furnish some little information. Only those specially useful will be mentioned here.

BOSTON CIVIL SERVICE REFORM ASSOCIATION. Publications.

CAMBRIDGE CIVIL SERVICE REFORM ASSOCIATION. Prize Essays on Municipal Reform. Boston, 1884.

CAMBRIDGE CIVIL SERVICE REFORM ASSOCIATION. Purposes, with Constitution and Officers. Cambridge, 1881.

CINCINNATI CIVIL SERVICE REFORM ASSOCIATION. Publication.

CLEVELAND MUNICIPAL ASSOCIATION. Bulletins.

MASSACHUSETTS REFORM CLUB. Publications, 1888–1900. Boston.

MISSOURI CIVIL SERVICE REFORM ASSOCIATION. Reports, 1883–1891. St. Louis.

NATIONAL CIVIL SERVICE REFORM LEAGUE. *Proceedings*, 1882–1903. New York.

NATIONAL CIVIL SERVICE REFORM LEAGUE. Six Reports of the Special Investigating Committee. Boston, 1891.

NATIONAL MUNICIPAL LEAGUE. Publications, 1894–1895. Philadelphia.

NEW YORK CIVIL SERVICE REFORM ASSOCIATION. Publications and Annual Reports, 1883–1901. New York.

Of the societies not specially devoted to this subject, the American Historical Society has published the most valuable material. Several collections of sources and several special articles are especially referred to elsewhere.

UNITED STATES DOCUMENTS.

Good Government, Vol. xvi. No. 4, p. 48, gives a list of public documents on the subject. The most important is the Executive Journal of the Senate, which contains all nominations sent by the president to the Senate with the action upon them. In addition it gives all the rules proposed and adopted in the Senate for the regulation of its relations with the president. The portion recently published, including the period from 1869 to 1892, is particularly rich in this latter kind of material.

The annual reports of the United States Civil Service Commission are very satisfactory, as they are exhaustive and well arranged.

The Blue Book or Official Register containing a complete biennial list of officials is indispensable.

The reports to the Senate on the patronage in 1826 and 1835, with Mr. Jenckes's report to the House in 1868, are the only special reports of much definite value, but there is hardly a report on an administrative question which does not yield some material.

MATERIAL VALUABLE FOR THE STUDY OF STATE CONDITIONS.

Few state histories contain material on the patronage, and the works and lives of statesmen contain little on state conditions. The most useful sources are found in the newspapers, the laws, and the following works.

MASSACHUSETTS.

AMORY, T. C. Life and Writings of James Sullivan. 2 vols. Boston, 1859.
AUSTIN, J. T. Life of Elbridge Gerry. 2 vols. Boston, 1828–1829.
LARNED, ELLEN D. History of Windham County, Connecticut. 2 vols. Worcester, 1874–1880.

NEW YORK.

CLINTON, GEORGE. Military Papers. 5 vols. New York, etc., 1899–1902.
GONTERMAN, J. T. New York Council of Appointment.
HAMMOND, J. D. The History of Political Parties in the State of New York. 2 vols. Cooperstown, 1846.
HAMMOND, J. D. The Life and Times of Silas Wright. Syracuse, 1848.
LEAKE, I. Q. Memoir of the Life and Times of General John Lamb. Albany, 1857.
MYERS, GUSTAVUS. The History of Tammany Hall. New York, 1901.

NEW YORK COUNCIL OF APPOINTMENT. Military Minutes, 1783-1821. Edited by Hugh Hastings. 4 vols. Albany, 1901.

SPEECHES of the Different Governors to the Legislature of New York, commencing with those of George Clinton. Albany, 1898.

TOMPKINS, D. D. Public Papers. Vol. i, Military. New York, etc., 1898.

PENNSYLVANIA.

ARMOR, WILLIAM. Lives of the Governors of Pennsylvania. Philadelphia, 1872. Correspondence of Governor McKean.

BIDDLE, CHARLES. Autobiography, 1745-1821. [Edited by J. S. Biddle.] Philadelphia, 1883.

BINNS, JOHN. Recollections of his Life, written by himself. Philadelphia, 1854.

BROWN, D. P. *The Forum.* Philadelphia, 1851.

BUCHANAN, ROBERDEAU. Life of the Hon. Thomas McKean. Lancaster, Pennsylvania, 1890.

GRAYDON, ALEXANDER. Memoirs of his Own Times, with Reminiscences of the Men and Events of the Revolution. Philadelphia, 1846.

HARDING, S. B. Party Struggles over the First Pennsylvania Constitution. American Historical Association, *Report*, 1894, pp. 371-402. Washington, 1895.

LINCOLN, C. H. The Revolutionary Movement in Pennsylvania, 1760-1776. University of Pennsylvania, *Series in History*, No. 1. Philadelphia, 1901.

MCMASTER, J. B., and STONE, F. D. Pennsylvania and the Federal Constitution, 1787-1788. [Philadelphia], 1888.

MARSHALL, CHRISTOPHER. Passages from his Diary, kept in Philadelphia and Lancaster during the American Revolution. Edited by William Duane. Philadelphia, 1839-1849.

MEIGS, W. M. Pennsylvania Politics early in this Century. *Pennsylvania Magazine*, xvii. 462-490. Philadelphia, January, 1894.

RHODE ISLAND AND GEORGIA.

[GILMER, G. R.] Sketches of Some of the First Settlers of Upper Georgia, of the Cherokees, and the author. New York, etc., 1855.

JERNEGAN, N. W. The Tammany Societies of Rhode Island. Brown University Historical Seminary, *Papers*, No. 8. Providence, 1897.

RHODE ISLAND. Report [to the General Assembly] of the Committee on the Subject of the Extension of Suffrage, June, 1829. [Providence, 1829.]

INDEX.